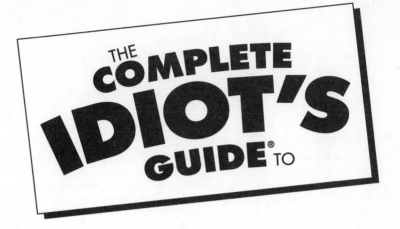

THE COMPLETE IDIOT'S GUIDE TO

French Verbs

by Gail Stein

ALPHA

A member of Penguin Group (USA) Inc.

This book is dedicated to:
My tremendously patient and supportive husband, Douglas
My incredibly loving and understanding sons, Eric and Michael
My proud parents, Jack and Sara Bernstein
My extremely artistically gifted sister, Susan J. Opperman
My superior consultant and advisor, Roger Herz

Copyright © 2004 by Gail Stein

THE COMPLETE IDIOT'S GUIDE TO and Design are registered trademarks of Penguin Group (USA) Inc.

International Standard Book Number: 1-59257-193-X
Library of Congress Catalog Card Number: 2003115289

06   05   04   8   7   6   5   4   3   2   1

Interpretation of the printing code: The rightmost number of the first series of numbers is the year of the book's printing; the rightmost number of the second series of numbers is the number of the book's printing. For example, a printing code of 04-1 shows that the first printing occurred in 2004.

Printed in the United States of America

Most Alpha books are available at special quantity discounts for bulk purchases for sales promotions, premiums, fund-raising, or educational use. Special books, or book excerpts, can also be created to fit specific needs.

For details, write: Special Markets, Alpha Books, 375 Hudson Street, New York, NY 10014.

Publisher: *Marie Butler-Knight*
Product Manager: *Phil Kitchel*
Senior Managing Editor: *Jennifer Chisholm*
Senior Acquisitions Editor: *Renee Wilmeth*
Development Editor: *Michael Koch*
Copy Editor: *Keith Cline*
Illustrator: *Chris Eliopoulos*
Cover/Book Designer: *Trina Wurst*
Indexer: *Tonya Heard*
Layout/Proofreading: *John Etchison, Rebecca Harmon, Ayanna Lacey*

Contents at a Glance

Part 1:   **Tenses and Moods**   1

    1   All About Verbs   3
         Shows the difference between a tense and a mood and how to form simple and compound tenses.

    2   Regularities and Irregularities   25
         Explains the difference between regular, spelling-change, and irregular verbs.

Part 2:   **Comparing Tenses**   37

    3   The Present Tense and the *Passé Composé*   39
         How to form and use the present, the imperative, and the passé composé of all verbs.

    4   The Imperfect and the Pluperfect   61
         How to form and use the imperfect and the pluperfect of all verbs.

    5   The *Passé Simple* and the *Passé Antérieur*   77
         How to form and use the passé simple and the passé antérieur of all verbs.

    6   The Future and the Future Perfect   85
         How to form and use the future and the future perfect of all verbs.

    7   The Conditional and the Conditional Perfect   95
         How to form and use the conditional, the past conditional, and conditional sentences.

    8   The Subjunctive and the Past Subjunctive   107
         How to form, use, and avoid the subjunctive and the past subjunctive of all verbs.

Part 3:   **Verbal Distinctions and Expressions**   133

    9   Common Verbal Distinctions   135
         Shows how certain verbs may have different meanings and connotations depending upon their usage.

    10   Common Verbal Expressions and Usages   153
         Teaches you how to express yourself like a native speaker of French.

Appendixes

A Answer Key   173

B Verb Charts   191

C Compound Verbs   275

D Regular -er Verbs   285

E Regular -ir and -oir Verbs   315

F Regular -re Verbs   319

G Common Reflexive Verbs   321

H Irregular Past Participles   325

   Index   327

Contents

Part 1: Tenses and Moods   **1**

1 All About Verbs   **3**

What Kind of Verb Is It?..4

What's the Subject? 4

What's the Right Mood? 5

What's the Right Time? 6

Forming Past Participles of Regular Verbs..........................8

Using *avoir* to Form Compound Tenses............................11

Using *être* to Form Compound Tenses.............................12

Using the Correct Helping Verb 13

Agreement of Past Participles 16

Using Past Participles in Other Ways 18

Forming Present Participles 19

Using Present Participles 20

Forming and Using Perfect Participles 21

Récapitulation 22

B Regularities and Irregularities   **25**

Regular Verbs...26

Verbs with Spelling Changes..26

   -cer *Verbs* 27

   -ger *Verbs* 28

   -yer *Verbs* 29

   -e + *Consonant* + er *Verbs That Add an Accent* 31

   -e + *Consonant* + er *Verbs That Double the Final Consonant* 32

-*é* + Consonant(s) + *er* Verbs 33

Irregular Verbs 34

Récapitulation 35

Part 2: Comparing Tenses   **37**

3 The Present Tense and the *Passé Composé*   **39**

The Present Tense of Regular Verbs 40

   The Present Tense of -er Verbs 40

   The Present Tense of -ir Verbs...............................41

   The Present Tense of -re Verbs 42

The Present Tense of Verbs with Spelling Changes 44

The Present Tense of -oir *or* -evoir *Verbs* *45*

Impersonal Verbs *46*

The Present Tense of Reflexive Verbs 46

Using Reflexive Pronouns *47*

The Present Tense of Irregular Verbs..............................49

Using the Present Tense 51

Forming and Using the Imperative..................................53

The Imperative of Reflexive Verbs 54

Forming and Using the *Passé Composé* 55

Agreement of Past Participles 56

Récapitulation 58

4 The Imperfect and the Pluperfect   61

The Imperfect of Regular, Irregular, and Reflexive Verbs..........62

Forming the Imperfect of Regular Verbs *62*

Forming the Imperfect of Irregular Verbs 63

Forming the Imperfect of Reflexive Verbs *64*

The Imperfect of Verbs with Spelling Changes 65

Verbs Ending in -cer *65*

Verbs Ending in -ger *65*

Using the *Passé Composé* and the Imperfect 66

Forming and Using the Pluperfect...................................73

Récapitulation 74

5 The *Passé Simple* and the *Passé Antérieur*   77

The *Passé Simple* of Regular and Reflexive Verbs..........78

The *Passé Simple* of Verbs with Spelling Changes 78

Verbs Ending in -cer *78*

Verbs Ending in -ger *79*

The *Passé Simple* of Irregular Verbs 79

Forming and Using the *Passé Antérieur* 82

Récapitulation 83

6 The Future and the Future Perfect   85

Using the Present to Express the Future 86

Using *aller* + Infinitive to Express the Future 86

The Future of Regular and Reflexive Verbs....................87

Forming the Future of Regular Verbs 87

The Future of Verbs with Spelling Changes 88
    Verbs Ending in -yer *88*
    Verbs ending in e + *Consonant* + er *88*
The Future of Irregular Verbs 89
Using the Future 91
Forming and Using the Future Perfect 92
Récapitulation 94

7 The Conditional and the Conditional Perfect   **95**

The Conditional of Regular and Reflexive Verbs 96
Forming the Conditional of Regular Verbs 96
The Conditional of Verbs with Spelling Changes 97
    Verbs Ending in -yer *97*
    Verbs Ending in -e + Consonant + er *97*
The Conditional of Irregular Verbs 98
Using the Conditional...100
Forming and Using the Past Conditional...............101
Conditional Sentences...102
    Real Conditions *103*
    Contrary-to-Fact Conditions...............................*103*
Récapitulation 104

8 The Subjunctive and the Past Subjunctive   **107**

The Present Subjunctive of Regular and Reflexive Verbs 108
    The Subjunctive of Verbs with Two Stems...............................*109*
The Subjunctive of Irregular Verbs 111
Using the Subjunctive 113
    The Subjunctive After Impersonal Expressions *113*
    Using the Subjunctive After Certain Verbs *116*
    When There's No Doubt About It...............................*117*
    Using the Subjunctive After Certain Adjectives...............................*119*
    The Subjunctive After Conjunctions *121*
    The Subjunctive in Relative Clauses *124*
    The Subjunctive in Third Person Commands *124*
    The Subjunctive After Superlative Expressions *124*
Forming and Using the Past Subjunctive 125
Avoiding the Subjunctive...126
Recognizing the Imperfect and Pluperfect Subjunctive...............129
Récapitulation 130

Part 3:   Verbal Distinctions and Expressions   133

9   Common Verbal Distinctions   135

Special Uses of Verbs 136
    devoir *136*
    faire *137*
    falloir *138*
    pouvoir *139*
    savoir *140*
    vouloir *141*
Verbs with Special Reflexive Meanings 142
Different Verbs with Different Connotations 145
    connaître and savoir *145*
    désirer and souhaiter *146*
    dépenser and passer *146*
    partir, sortir, quitter, and laisser *146*
    rendre, retourner, revenir, and rentrer *147*
    porter and mener *148*
    pouvoir and savoir *148*
    penser à and penser de *149*
    jouer à and jouer de *149*
    habiter (demeurer) and vivre *150*
Récapitulation 151

10   Common Verbal Expressions and Usages   153

What Is an Idiom? 154
    Idioms with Regular Verbs *155*
    Idioms with Irregular Verbs *158*
Common Verbal Expressions 161
    Expressions with avoir *161*
    Expressions with faire *163*
Other Verbal Expressions 165
The Passive Voice 167
    Substitute Constructions for the Passive *168*
Récapitulation 170

Appendixes

A   Answer Key   173

B   Verb Charts   191

C   Compound Verbs   275

D   Regular *-er* Verbs   285

E   Regular *-ir* and *-oir* Verbs   315

F   Regular *-re* Verbs   319

G   Common Reflexive Verbs   321

H   Irregular Past Participles   325

    Index   327

Introduction

The Complete Idiot's Guide to French Verbs will prove extremely practical and functional for anyone—students, travelers, business people—who wants a richer, more eloquent command of the French language. It is the book you want if you are no longer satisfied with speaking in infinitives or quickly slurring over verbs in the hopes that no one will notice that no differentiation was made between the past, present, or future, and if you are serious about learning, understanding, and mastering French verbs in all their tenses and moods. There are those who opt for the easy way out and purchase books that spoon-feed every verb form imaginable, even those that are rarely used, without any explanations that would help the reader develop mastery on his own. The truth is, if you want to speak a foreign language like a native, you need to fine-tune your conjugation skills. *The Complete Idiot's Guide to French Verbs* not only encourages, but also helps you to do just that.

This book provides you with all the tools you need for success: There are verb charts showing everything from simple regular verbs, to verbs with spelling changes, to every imaginable irregular verb; there are formulas that enable you to apply what you've learned to any verb you may encounter; and there are clear, simple, concise, yet detailed explanations that will enable you to express events, actions, and situations in their proper time frame. An abundance of examples are included to facilitate your understanding of rules and concepts. Finally, you are provided ample opportunity to practice what you've learned through a series of exercises intended to hone your skills at manipulating French verbs. The more committed you are to using the knowledge you've acquired, the faster you'll find yourself able to communicate on a more advanced level.

The *Complete Idiot's Guide to French Verbs* is an educational tool and an instructional instrument designed to guide you to a more thorough understanding of French verbs so that you can use them at will. This user-friendly book will make verb conjugation a snap: a pleasant, satisfying, and rewarding experience. The simple, clear-cut, straightforward approach will give you the expertise you need to use French verbs with ease and confidence.

How This Book Is Organized

This book is organized into three parts that provide you with the basic information you need to become proficient in conversing with others, reading newspapers and literary works, and using writing skills in a variety of situations in French.

Part 1, "Tenses and Moods," defines and explains the differences, and oftentimes subtle nuances, between verb tenses and moods. The appropriate use of simple and compound tenses in conversational situations, as well as in written tasks, is made clear and simple for your thorough understanding. This section presents you with the ins and outs of French regular verbs, verbs with spelling changes, and completely irregular verbs. It is meant to introduce you and to prepare you for the explanations and exercises that follow in ensuing chapters.

Part 2, "Comparing Tenses," provides very detailed specifics about each verb tense or mood and provides concrete explanations and examples. Step by step you will learn to unravel the mysteries of verb conjugations and how to add proper endings that will allow you to proficiently express exactly what's on your mind. The complexities of the enigmatic subjunctive, as well as the rules governing other tenses and moods, will be presented with clarity and ease. Sufficient opportunity is provided to study, to think about, and to practice all the material that has been presented through a wide variety of challenging exercises that promote mastery.

Part 3, "Verbal Distinctions and Expressions," lists and explains the verbal idioms and expressions that will not only afford you practice with the verbs you've learned, but will also give you the idiomatic, conversational vocabulary that is essential to proficiency in the language. If your goal is to speak French like a native, this section will certainly allow you to achieve that goal by making available to you the necessary explanations and tools.

Also take note of the appendixes, which provide detailed lists of regular, irregular, compound, and conjugated verbs, as well as the answer key to the practice exercises in this book. Appendix B provides a substantial list of verb charts with examples of each type of verb with every possible change or irregularity. Appendix C lists compound irregular verbs and verbs that have related conjugations due to similar endings. Appendixes D, E, and F list the regular -er, -ir, and -re verbs along with the -er verbs that require a spelling change. For the proper conjugation of the verbs listed in these appendixes, refer to Appendix B. Appendix G lists reflexive verbs, including examples of how these verbs are conjugated in each tense. Lastly, Appendix H lists the irregular past participles you'll need to form or recognize any of the seven compound tenses.

Extras

To enliven a seemingly dry topic and to make this book more fun and informative for you, the reader, I've added these boxes:

Définitions

This box provides you with definitions of terms that you may not know or may have forgotten. These sidebars serve as a quick refresher course.

Attention!

Take heed of these warnings to avoid making needless, inadvertent, or embarrassing mistakes.

Regarde!

This box points out those pesky little rules that tend to elude us or that we may occasionally forget. It tells you how to use verbs more easily and more efficiently so that your results are as correct and native sounding as possible.

Acknowledgments

I would like to acknowledge the contributions, input, support, and interest of the following people: Raymond C. Elias, Gary Goldstein, Martin S. Hyman, Michael Koch, Christina Levy, Renée Wilmeth, Christy Wagner, and the Alpha production department.

Special Thanks to the Technical Reviewer

The Complete Idiot's Guide to French Verbs was reviewed by an expert who double-checked the accuracy of what you'll learn here, to help us ensure that this book gives you everything you need to know about French. Special thanks are extended to Dr. Larry Riggs, head of the Modern Languages Department and Professor of French at Butler University.

Trademarks

All terms mentioned in this book that are known to be or are suspected of being trademarks or service marks have been appropriately capitalized. Alpha Books and Penguin Group (USA) Inc. cannot attest to the accuracy of this information. Use of a term in this book should not be regarded as affecting the validity of any trademark or service mark.

Part 1

Tenses and Moods

When we speak our native language, rarely, if ever, do we think about or agonize over which tense or mood to use—they just seem to flow from us automatically. When we speak a foreign language, however, it is essential that we make a conscious effort and every possible attempt to properly express what we want to say.

Part 1 familiarizes you with the world of French tenses and moods. You will learn how to form both simple and compound tenses and when to use each. You will also be taught about present and past participles so that you'll be able to use any verb listed in the appendixes of the book with great facility. Lastly, you'll get all the practice you'll need before proceeding to Part 2.

All About Verbs

In This Chapter

- ◆ French subject pronouns
- ◆ Forming and using the past participle
- ◆ Agreement of past participles
- ◆ Forming compound tenses
- ◆ Forming and using present and perfect participles

Are you looking for action? Then look at a verb! Verbs show motion, movement, or a state of being or thinking: speak, walk, jump, be, wish, want. You can't form a sentence without a verb, yet you can create the shortest sentence with one small verb: Go! No matter what language you are speaking, if you choose the verbs that best express your ideas, you will be able to communicate and make yourself understood.

The order of language acquisition, whether it is your native language or a second language is: listening, speaking, reading, and then writing. As children, we learn our first language automatically without thinking about how we are constructing our sentences. We listen carefully and internalize language patterns that enable us to use moods and put verbs in tenses correctly. Assuming that we are not thus immersed in a second, or foreign, language we must then follow, learn, and memorize certain guidelines and rules that will enable us to communicate in a proper, educated fashion. In this chapter, you'll learn what you need to know to master the art of French verbs.

What Kind of Verb Is It?

French verbs are regular, irregular, or defective and end in *-er*, *-ir*, *-oir*, or *-re*. A regular verb follows the model conjugation of a verb with the same particular ending. An irregular verb deviates in some tenses or persons from the model conjugation. A defective verb is one that is lacking in some of the moods, tenses, or persons.

French has three families of regular verbs, those whose infinitives end in *-er* (the largest group), *-ir*, and *-re*. The same rules for conjugation (the change that must be made to the verb—so that it agrees with its subject) apply to all verbs within each of the families. When you've learned the endings for each respective family of verbs, you can easily and confidently conjugate any regular verb in that family.

There is a very small fourth group of verbs, generally considered irregular, whose infinitives end in *-oir*. Some of these verbs are very high-frequency verbs and their forms and tenses require memorization. Some verbs within this group follow a conjugation pattern, which will make the task of learning them easier.

French also contains many irregular verbs that follow no pattern whatsoever. Because you will use them frequently in daily conversation, you should memorize them. If you need a quick reminder, you can look them up in the Appendix B.

What's the Subject?

Subject pronouns in French are given a person (first, second, or third), a gender, and a number (singular or plural) as shown in Table 1.1.

Table 1.1   French Subject Pronouns

	Singular		Plural	
1st person	je	I	nous	we
2nd person	tu	you	vous	you
3rd person	il	he	ils	they
	elle	she	elles	they
	on	one, you, we, they		

Note the following about French subject pronouns:

◆ *Je* is only capitalized at the beginning of a sentence.

◆ *Je* requires elision and becomes *j'* before a vowel or vowel sound (*h, y*).

◆ *Tu* is used when speaking to one friend, relative, pet, child, or person with whom one is very familiar. The letter *u* for *tu* is never dropped for elision: *Tu adores le français*. (You admire the French man.)

◆ *Vous* is used in the singular to show respect to an older person or when speaking to someone you don't know well or who is unfamiliar to you. *Vous* is referred to as the polite form.

◆ The subject pronoun *ils* refers to more than one male or to a combined group of males and females.

◆ *On* means one or someone and may also refer to an indefinite you, we, they, or people in general. *On* is often used in place of *nous* and requires the third person singular form of the verb: *On part*. (We're leaving.)

Regarde!

These days, students and others wanting to emphasize common membership in a group or class use the familiar form even with those they don't know personally.

What's the Right Mood?

Chances are that none of your language arts teachers has ever spent a class period introducing you to and explaining the concept of mood (also referred to as mode). It's just one of those topics that is easily bypassed because traditional, formal grammatical explanations tend to occupy an increasingly minor role in English classes today. To help you understand what is meant by this term, let's take a closer look at verb moods.

Mood shows the manner in which the action or state of being is conceived, or the way in which the subject looks at the action or state of being that is expressed. In English there are three moods: the indicative, the imperative, and the subjunctive. In French there are two additional moods: the conditional and the infinitive.

Définitions

A mood indicates the way a person looks at the action or state of being that he or she wants to express.

◆ The indicative mood is, by far, the most commonly used mood in both English and French. The indicative mood states a fact or asks a question: *Can I help you? No, I can do this by myself.*

◆ The imperative mood expresses a command: *Please help me figure this out.*

◆ The subjunctive mood indicates a subjective response or attitude—wishing, emotion, doubt, need, fear, and supposition, among other things—in sentences generally consisting of more than one clause, each with a different subject: *I would like you to help me with this grammar.* The subjunctive is used more frequently in French than in English and will require a bit of patience and a good deal of study.

◆ The conditional mood shows what the subject *would do* or *would have done* under certain circumstances or situations: *If I could take my vacation now, I would go to France.*

◆ The infinitive mood is the verb in its "to" form: *to speak, to walk, to jump, to be, to wish, to want.* The phrase "To be or not to be, that is the question" is the perfect example of a verb being used in its infinitive mood.

What's the Right Time?

We refer to the tense of a verb to express the time period in which the action or state of being occurs. Tenses are either simple (consisting of one verb form) or compound (consisting of two parts). English has three simple tenses: past, present, and future, and three compound tenses: past perfect, present perfect, and future perfect. In French, however, there are seven simple tenses that have corresponding compound tenses. Although this may seem overwhelming, it is really quite simple, once you get the hang of it. Table 1.2 shows the relationship between simple and compound tenses and their respective English equivalent meanings. A careful look reveals that you need not worry that this concept is too difficult to understand.

Table 1.2   Corresponding Simple and Compound Tenses

Simple Tense	Compound Tense
Present	Past Definite (Compound Past)
le présent	*le passé composé*
do/does; am/are/is	have, did
Imperfect	Pluperfect
l'imparfait	*le plus-que-parfait*
was; used to	had

Simple Tense	Compound Tense
Past Definite (Simple Past) *le passé simple* have, did	Past Anterior *le passé antérieur* had
Future *le futur* will	Future Perfect (Future Anterior) *le futur antérieur* will have
Conditional *le conditionnel* would	Conditional Perfect *le conditionnel passé* would have
Present Subjunctive *le présent du subjonctif* do/does; am/are/is; will	Past Subjunctive *le passé du subjonctif* have/did
Imperfect Subjunctive *l'imparfait du subjonctif* have, did	Pluperfect Subjunctive *le plus-que-parfait du subjonctif* had

Very specific endings identify each simple tense. These endings are invariable whether the verb is regular, irregular, or defective, or if it has an interior spelling change. As soon you become proficient at recognizing and using the various endings, you will be able to communicate in any mood or any tense. Each simple tense will be presented separately with its corresponding compound form in the chapters that follow, giving you the maximum opportunity to familiarize yourself with and to practice all verb forms.

Although compound tenses are made up of two parts, a simple explanation will explain how they are formed and help dispel any fears that this is a complicated matter. A careful look at Table 1.2 reveals the word "perfect" in one form or another in the title of each compound tense. You can form any compound tense by taking the corresponding simple tense of the helping verb *avoir* (to have) or the helping verb *être* (to be) and adding the past participle of the action performed.

Attention!

The imperfect subjunctive and pluperfect subjunctive exist in French but have virtually disappeared from use in conversation and informal letter writing. In current formal or literary writing, the pluperfect subjunctive and, to a lesser degree, the imperfect subjunctive are still used sporadically.

Regarde!

Conjugate the verb *avoir* (to have) or *être* (to be for certain verbs only) in any simple tense, add a past participle, and you have the corresponding compound tense. If the conditional tells you what the subject *would* do, then the conditional perfect tells you what the subject *would have* done.

You have to memorize two verbs, *avoir* and *être*, in all of their simple forms. This will enable you to form any compound tense or to recognize one when reading. Because the past participle of any verb remains the same, no matter which compound tense is formed, and because the number of irregular past participles is limited, to a certain degree, forming compound tenses is easier than forming simple tenses! Follow this easy formula to form a compound tense:

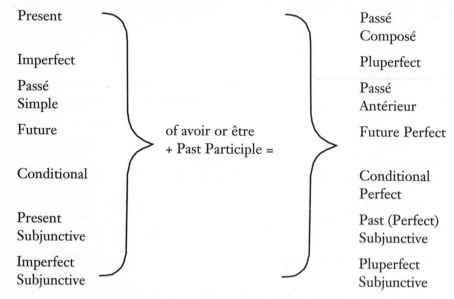

Present		Passé Composé
Imperfect		Pluperfect
Passé Simple	of avoir or être + Past Participle =	Passé Antérieur
Future		Future Perfect
Conditional		Conditional Perfect
Present Subjunctive		Past (Perfect) Subjunctive
Imperfect Subjunctive		Pluperfect Subjunctive

Forming Past Participles of Regular Verbs

To form the past participle of an *-er* verb, drop the *-er* infinitive ending and add *-é*. To form the past participle of an *-ir* verb, drop the *-ir* infinitive ending and add *-i*. To form the past participle of an *-re* verb, drop the *-re* infinitive ending and add *-u* as shown in Table 1.3.

Table 1.3   Forming the Past Participle of Regular Verbs

Ending	Verb	Meaning	Past Participle	Meaning
-er	*parler*	to speak	*parlé*	spoken
-ir	*finir*	to finish	*fini*	finished
-re	*perdre*	to lose	*perdu*	lost

Verbs ending in *-oir* have irregular past participles that drop the *-oir* ending and add *-u*. If the infinitive ends in *voir* preceded by an unaccented vowel or vowels (*a, e, eu,* or *ou*), drop the vowel(s) + *voir* and simply add *-u*, except for *avoir* and *asseoir*, which are totally irregular, as shown in Table 1.4.

Regarde!

The past participles of the seven regular verbs ending in *-evoir* (see Chapter 3) are formed by dropping the *-evoir* ending and adding *-u*.

Table 1.4　Past Participles of *-oir* Verbs

Verb	Meaning	Past Participle	Meaning
avoir	to have	eu	had
asseoir	to seat	assis	seated
devoir	to owe, have to	dû	owed, had to
falloir	to be necessary	fallu	was necessary
mouvoir	to move	mû	moved
pleuvoir	to rain	plu	rained
pourvoir	to provide	pourvu	provided
pouvoir	to be able to	pu	was able to
prévoir	to foresee	prévu	foreseen
recevoir	to receive	reçu	received
savoir	to know	su	knew
valoir	to be worth	valu	was worth
voir	to see	vu	saw
vouloir	to want, wish	voulu	wanted, wished

The verbs in Table 1.5, their compounds (a prefix is added to the main verb), or other verbs that follow the same rules of conjugation are irregular and must be memorized. Verbs marked with an asterisk (*) use *être* as their helping verb.

Attention!

Verb compounds are made by adding a prefix to a verb that already exists. For example: *mettre* (to put) and *permettre* (to permit). You can look up these compounds in Appendix C.

= etre

Table 1.5   Irregular Past Participles

Verb	Meaning	Past Participle	Meaning
acquérir	to acquire	acquis	acquired
boire	to drink	bu	drank
conduire	to drive	conduit	drove
connaître	to know	connu	knew
coudre	to sew	cousu	sewed
courir	to run	couru	ran
craindre	to fear	craint	feared
croire	to believe	cru	believed
croître	to grow	crû	grew
dire	to say, tell	dit	said, told
distraire	to distract	distrait	distracted
écrire	to write	écrit	wrote, written
être	to be	été	was
faire	to make, do	fait	made, did
joindre	to join	joint	joined
lire	to read	lu	read
mettre	to put	mis	put
mourir*	to die	mort	died
naître*	to be born	né	was born
nuire	to harm	nui	harmed
offrir	to offer	offert	offered
ouvrir	to open	ouvert	opened
paraître	to seem	paru	seemed
peindre	to paint	peint	painted
plaire	to please	plu	pleased
prendre	to take	pris	took
résoudre	to resolve	résolu	resolved
	to result	résous	resulted
rire	to laugh	ri	laughed
suffire	to be enough	suffi	was enough
suivre	to follow	suivi	followed
taire	to conceal	tu	concealed
venir*	to come	venu	came
vêtir	to dress	vêtu	dressed
vivre	to live	vécu	lived

Note the following exceptions to the rules:

◆ The past participles of *absoudre* (to absolve) and *dissoudre* (to dissolve) are *absout* (or *absous*) and *dissout* (or *dissous*).

◆ The past participles of *accroître* (to increase) and *décroître* (to decrease) are un-accented: *accru* and *décru*. *Recroître* (to grow again) is accented only in the masculine singular form: *recrû*.

◆ The past participles of *exclure* (to exclude) and *conclure* (to conclude) are regular, *exclu* and *conclu*; whereas the past participle of *inclure* (to include) is irregular, *inclus*.

Exercice 1

Try your hand at forming the past participles of the following French verbs.
Pay attention to any irregular verbs or their compounds.

1. travailler (*to work*) _____

2. regarder (*to look at*) _____

3. choisir (*to choose*) _____

4. agir (*to act*) _____

5. répondre (*to answer*) _____

6. vendre (*to sell*) _____

7. comprendre (*to understand*) _____

8. décrire (*to describe*) _____

9. découvrir (*to discover*) _____

10. sourire (*to smile*) _____

Using *avoir* to Form Compound Tenses

Let's take a closer look at the simple forms of the verb *avoir* to see how we can use it in our formula for compound tense formation.

	Present	Imperfect	Passé Simple	Future	Conditional	Subjunctive	Imperfect Subjunctive
j'	ai	avais	eus	aurai	aurais	aie	eusse
tu	as	avais	eus	auras	aurais	aies	eusses
il	a	avait	eut	aura	aurait	ait	eût
nous	avons	avions	eûmes	aurons	auraient	ayons	eussions
vous	avez	aviez	eûtes	aurez	auriez	ayez	eussiez
ils	ont	avaient	eurent	auront	auraient	aient	eussent

(handwritten annotations above columns: "had" over Imperfect, "–ed" over Passé Simple, "will have" over Future, "could have" over Conditional, "that –ed" over Imperfect Subjunctive)

Now you can form the compound tenses that take *avoir* as their helping verb as follows.

Name of Compound Tense	French Form	English Equivalent
Passé Composé	J'ai travaillé.	I worked.
Pluperfect *Imparfait*	J'avais travaillé.	I had worked.
Passé Antérieur *Simple*	J'eus travaillé.	I worked.
Future Perfect	J'aurai travaillé.	I will have worked.
Conditional Perfect	J'aurais travaillé.	I would have worked.
Past Subjuntive	… que j'aie travaillé	… that I worked.
~~Imperfect Subjunctive~~	… ~~que j'eusse travaillé~~	… ~~that I had worked.~~

Using *être* to Form Compound Tenses

Let's take a closer look at the simple forms of the verb *être*, to see how we can use it in our formula for compound tense formation.

	Present	Imperfect	Passé Simple	Future	Conditional	Subjunctive	Imperfect Subjunctive
je (j')	suis	étais	fus	serai	serais	sois	fusse
tu	es	étais	fus	seras	serais	sois	fusses
il	est	étais	fut	sera	serait	soit	fût
nous	sommes	étions	fûmes	serons	serions	soyons	fussions
vous	êtes	étiez	fûtes	serez	seriez	soyez	fussiez
ils	sont	étaient	furent	seront	seraient	soient	fussent

(handwritten annotation: "plus" over Future column)

Now you can form the compound tenses that take *être* as their helping verb as follows.

Name of Compound Tense	French Form	English Equivalent
Passé Composé	Je suis allé(e).	I went.
Pluperfect	J'étais allé(e).	I had gone.
Passé Antérieur	Je fus allé(e).	I went.
Future Perfect	Je serai allé(e).	I will have gone.
Conditional Perfect	Je serais allé(e).	I would have gone.
Past Subjunctive	… que je sois allé(e)	… that I went.
Imperfect Subjunctive	… que je fusse allé(e)	… that I had gone.

Regarde!

To form the negative of any compound tense, put *ne* before the conjugated helping verb and put the negative word (*pas, plus, jamais, rien,* and so on) after the conjugated helping verb.

Je ne suis pas allé(e) en ville hier.
I didn't go to the city yesterday.

Il n'avait jamais fait de la planche à voile.
He had never gone windsurfing.

Using the Correct Helping Verb

Use the following guide to select *avoir* or *être* as the helping verb when forming a compound tense:

- Most verbs form their compound tenses using the verb *avoir*.

- Reflexive verbs, identified by the reflexive pronoun *se* that precedes the infinitive, only use *être* as their helping verb.

- The most common intransitive verbs (those without a direct object) also use *être* as their helping verb.

Table 1.6 lists the most common intransitive verbs that require *être* as the helping verb. These verbs tend to show motion or change of place, state, or condition.

Table 1.6 Verbs Requiring *être*   18

Infinitive		Past Participle
aller	*to go*	allé
arriver	*to arrive*	arrivé
descendre*	*to go down*	descendu
devenir	*to become*	devenu
entrer	*to enter*	entré
monter*	*to go up, come up*	monté
mourir	*to die*	mort
naître	*to be born*	né
partir	*to leave, go away*	parti
parvenir	*to reach, succeed*	parvenu
passer*	*to pass by*	passé
rentrer*	*to go in again, return*	rentré
rester	*to remain, stay*	resté
retourner*	*to go back, return*	retourné
revenir	*to come back*	revenu
sortir*	*to go out, leave*	sorti
tomber	*to fall*	tombé
venir	*to come*	venu

Handwritten margin notes (left): Auntie, Anna, Decided, Dogs, Each, Munch, mostly, Noodles, Pretty, Pansy, Parker, Rents, Rowboats, Roger, Roberts, Says, Trust, Verily

Handwritten note (right): amuser

The verbs marked with an asterisk (*) are conjugated with *avoir* instead of *être* when they have a direct object. Note the differences in meanings:

Ils ont descendu l'escalier.
They went downstairs.

Ils ont descendu leurs bagages.
They took down their bags.

Ils sont descendus du train.
They got off the plane.

Elle a monté l'escalier.
She went upstairs.

Elle a monté son livre.
She brought her book upstairs.

Elle est montée.
She went up to study.

As-tu passé un mois en France?
Did you spend a month in France?

Es-tu passé(e) par sa maison?
Did you pass by his house?

Il a rentré son chien.
He brought in his dog.

Il est rentré à minuit.
He came home at midnight.

Il a retourné son papier.
He turned over his paper.

Il est retourné au Canada.
He returned to Canada.

J'ai sorti mon portefeuille.
I took out my wallet.

Je suis sortie.
I went out.

Exercice 2   Avoir   Être

See if you can select the correct helping verb in the present tense to complete each sentence describing what each person did on Saturday afternoon. You'll see that you'll get the hang of it in no time flat.

1. Nous _____ allés au cinéma.

2. Janine _____ regardé la télévision.

3. Vous _____ fait vos devoirs.

4. Je (J') _____ resté à la maison.

5. Tu _____ joué aux cartes.

6. Luc et Roger _____ passés par le centre commercial.

7. Gisèle _____ sortie avec son amie.

8. Robert s'_____ amusé au parc.

Agreement of Past Participles

Past participles of verbs conjugated with *avoir* agree in gender (add *-e* to the end of the past participle to get the feminine form) and number (add *-s* to the end of the past participle to get the plural form, unless it already ends in *-s*) with a preceding direct object (noun, pronoun, or antecedent).

> Je les ai cru(e)s.
> *I believed them.*

> Les livres? Il les a pris.
> *The books? He took them.*

> As-tu lu la lettre qu'il a écrite?
> *Did you read the letter he wrote?*

Past participles of verbs conjugated with *être* agree in gender and number with the subject.

> Elle est tombée.
> *She fell.*

> Ils sont allés au parc.
> *They went to the park.*

> Elles sont arrivées en retard.
> *They arrived late.*

With reflexive verbs, the past participle only agrees with the reflexive pronoun when that pronoun serves as a direct object. When the reflexive pronoun serves as an in-direct object (the direct object follows the verb), then there is no agreement.

> Elle s'est lavée.
> *She washed herself.*
> (The direct object, herself, precedes the verb and agreement is required.)

> Elle s'est lavé la figure.
> *She washed her face.*
> (The direct object, her face, follows the verb and no agreement is necessary.)

Attention! _____

The past participle of a verb conjugated with *avoir* remains unchanged before an infinitive with its own direct object because the direct object belongs to the infinitive and not to the conjugated verb. Note that *les filles* is a direct object noun of the verb *chanter*. When replaced with the direct object pronoun, *les*, there is no agreement of the past participle, *entendu*, because *les* is linked to chanter.

J'ai entendu chanter les filles.   Je les ai entendu chanter.
I heard the girls singing.   *I heard them singing.*

Past participles of verbs conjugated with *être* agree in gender (add an *-e* for the feminine) and number (add an *-s* for the plural) with the subject.

Masculine Subjects	Feminine Subjects	Meaning
je suis arrivé	je suis arrivée	I arrived
tu es arrivé	tu es arrivée	you arrived
il est arrivé	elle est arrivée	he/she arrived
nous sommes arrivés	nous sommes arrivées	we arrived
vous êtes arrivé(s)	vous êtes arrivée(s)	you arrived
ils sont arrivés	elles sont arrivées	they arrived

Past participles of reflexive verbs are conjugated with *être* as follows:

Masculine Subjects	Feminine Subjects	Meaning
je me suis lavé	je me suis lavée	I washed myself
tu t'es lavé	tu t'es lavée	you washed yourself
il s' est lavé	elle s'est lavée	he/she washed him/herself
nous nous sommes lavés	nous nous sommes lavées	we washed ourselves
vous vous êtes lavé(s)	vous vous êtes lavée(s)	you washed yourself/selves
ils se sont lavés	elles se sont lavées	they washed themselves

Exercice 3

Now try forming the compound tenses by using the correct helping verb and by using agreement, where necessary. You'll see that you'll get the hang of it in no time flat.

Express in French what everyone did and then give the English meaning.

1. chanter (*to sing*); passé composé

   Nous _____ en choeur. _____.

2. finir (*to finish*); pluperfect

   Tu _____ ton travail tôt. _____.

3. défendre (*to defend*); passé antérieur

   Le soldat _____ son patrie. _____.

4. partir (*to leave*); future perfect

   Je _____ avant son retour. _____.

5. aider (*to help*); conditional perfect

   Les filles? Vous les _____, n'est-ce pas? _____.

6. devenir (*to become*); past subjunctive

   Il est possible que ces garçons _____ chefs. _____.

7. faire (*to do*); pluperfect subjunctive

   Il était bon qu'il _____ ce travail. _____.

Using Past Participles in Other Ways

Past participles may also be used in the following ways:

♦ With *être* as adjectives that agree in number and gender with the nouns they modify:

Cet homme est respecté.   Les portes sont ouvertes.
This man is respected.   *The doors are open.*

♦ With *être* to express the passive voice:

La voiture a été lavée par les enfants.
The car was washed by the children.

◆ In rare cases, to form a noun from a verb:

Ne parle pas à des inconnus.
Don't speak to strangers.

Forming Present Participles

In English both present participles and gerunds end in *-ing*. In English, unlike in French, there is a difference between the present participle (While *driving*, I listened to the radio) and a gerund (*Swimming* is fun). In the second example, *swimming*, the subject of *is*, is a gerund. In French, however, the present participle may not be used as a noun subject and an infinitive is used: *La natation est amusante* (Swimming is fun).

The present participle of almost all French verbs is formed by replacing the *-ons* ending from the *nous* form of the present tense with *-ant* as shown in Table 1.7.

Table 1.7   Forming the Gerund of Regular Verbs

Ending	Verb	Nous Form	Present Participle	Meaning
-er	parler	parl~~ons~~	parlant	speaking
-ir	finir	finiss~~ons~~	finissant	finishing
-re	répondre	répond~~ons~~	répondant	receiving
-oir	voir	voy~~ons~~	voyant	seeing

The three irregular present participles are

◆ avoir   ayant   having

◆ être   étant   being

◆ savoir   sachant   knowing

CAUTION

Attention!

Verbs ending in *-ger* add an *-e* before the *-ons nous* ending of the present tense: *nous nageons, nageant*. Verbs ending in *-cer* change *-c* to *-ç* before the *-ons nous* ending of the present tense: *nous prononçons, prononçant*. No other verbs have interior spelling changes for the present participle.

Exercice 4

Try forming the present participles of the following French verbs.

1. chercher (*to look for*) _____

2. réfléchir (*to think*) _____

3. attendre (*to wait*) _____

4. voyager (*to travel*) _____

5. avancer (*to advance*) _____

6. appeler (*to call*) _____

7. acheter (*to buy*) _____

8. célébrer (*to celebrate*) _____

Using Present Participles

Present participles have the following uses:

◆ Some present participles may be used as adjectives that follow the nouns they describe and agree with them in number and gender.

Il a raconté des histoires amusantes.
He told funny stories.

◆ The present participle may follow the preposition *en* to express while, by, in, or upon.

Elle regarde la télévision en cuisinant.
She watches television while cooking.

En rentrant à la maison elles se sont reposées.
Upon returning home they rested.

◆ The present participle has a verbal function and may be used without *en*. When used this way there is no agreement with the subject.

Elle est sortie riant.
She left laughing.

Exercice 5

Express what each person did while doing something else by using the present participle.

1. (jouer) En _____ au football, il s'est cassé la jambe.

2. (prononcer) Janine a rougi en _____ le mot de vocabulaire.

3. (manger) Georges s'est brûlé la langue en _____ de la soupe.

4. (applaudir) Les gens parlaient en _____.

5. (tondre) M. Lamont parlait à son voisin en _____ la pelouse.

6. (promener) Lise chantait en _____ son chien.

Forming and Using Perfect Participles

The perfect participle expresses *having done something*. It is formed by combining the present participle of *avoir* or *être* with the past participle of the verb showing the action:

Ayant fini mon travail, je suis sorti.
Having finished my work, I went out.

Étant né au Sénégal, il parlait français couramment.
Having been born in Senegal, he spoke French fluently.

Exercice 6

Express what everyone did by using the perfect participle. Give the English meaning.

1. (rentrer) _____ tard, Lisette s'est couchée immédiatement.

2. (avoir) _____ un mal de tête pendant toute la journée, Martin a quitté le bureau tôt.

3. (faire) _____ tous ses devoirs, Lucien a allumé la télévision.

4. (arriver) _____ au cinéma trop tard, les filles sont allées à un café.

5. (vouloir) _____ plaire à ses enfants, Mme Ricard a fait un grand gâteau au chocolat.

6. (tomber) _____ amoureuse de Robert, Charlotte lui a écrit une lettre d'amour.

Regarde! _____

A reflexive pronoun precedes both a present and perfect participle:

> Je suis tombée en me promenant.
> *I fell while going for a walk.*

> S'étant réveillé très tôt ce matin, il avait l'air fatigué.
> *Having awakened very early this morning, he looked tired.*

Récapitulation

◆ French regular verbs end in *-er*, *-ir*, and *-re*. All verbs with these infinitive endings follow the same rules of conjugation. French verbs ending in *-oir* are considered irregular.

◆ French also contains verbs with spelling changes and totally irregular verbs.

◆ The mood of a verb indicates the way in which the person looks at the action or state of being that is expressed.

◆ The tense of a verb indicates the time period in which the action occurred.

◆ Simple tenses consist of one verb form, whereas compound tenses require the helping verb *avoir* or *être* (conjugated in the appropriate simple tense) plus a past participle.

◆ *Avoir* is the helping verb for most verbs, whereas *être* is used for all reflexive verbs and for intransitive verbs showing motion or change of place, state, or condition.

◆ Past participles of verbs conjugated with *être* agree in number and gender with the subject pronoun. For reflexive verbs, the past participle agrees with a preceding direct object pronoun only.

◆ The present participle ends in *-ant* and is the equivalent of English verbs ending in *-ing*.

◆ The perfect participle is formed by using the present participle of *avoir* or *être* and by adding the past participle of the verb denoting the action.

The Least You Need to Know

◆ All French verbs end in -*er*, -*ir*, -*oir*, or -*re*.

◆ A mood indicates how a person views an action, whereas a tense indicates the time of the action.

◆ Tenses may be simple (one verb form) or compound (two verb forms: the helping verb *avoir* or *être* + a past participle).

◆ Present and perfect participles express what the subject was doing.

2

Regularities and Irregularities

In This Chapter

- ◆ All about regular verbs
- ◆ All about spelling-change verbs
- ◆ All about irregular verbs

Regular and irregular verbs exist in every language. A native language is acquired as children listen and repeat the models they hear. A formal explanation and knowledge of the rules governing verb conjugation is totally unnecessary for natives, as they learn to simply replicate and internalize the correct structure and forms of their role models. As time goes by, their command of the language improves as they read and develop a more extensive vocabulary. Communication is automatic and achieved with ease and with little forethought. In today's language arts classes, the once onerous task of diagramming sentences and labeling the parts of speech of various sentences is rather obsolete. Most native speakers would be hard pressed to identify regular and irregular verbs in their language or to explain why certain verbs are spelled in a certain way or have certain changes. We rely on our instincts: If a sentence sounds correct, then it must be correct, and the rules are unimportant as long as we can communicate and be understood. Many of us speak well, but not perfectly, and this rarely causes a problem.

For the non-native, however, an understanding of how verbs work is essential for good communication. In this chapter, you'll learn how to recognize regular verbs, verbs with spelling changes, and verbs that follow no rules at all: irregular verbs.

Regular Verbs

All French verbs, in the infinitive, end in -*er*, -*ir*, -*oir*, or -*re*. Fortunately, the vast majority of French verbs within each of these groups are regular: They follow simple, specific, invariable rules for conjugation in all simple and compound tenses. These verbs are completely predictable, and, if you follow the rules and know your endings, you will avoid mistakes. A large proportion of these verbs are cognates: They are easily recognizable because they closely resemble English verbs in spelling or pronunciation, or both.

Although there are comparatively few irregular verbs, they tend to be the ones that are most frequently used and that are the basis for idiomatic expressions in French. You must memorize these verbs, because there are no hard and fast rules to explain why they undergo the changes they do.

Exercice 1

Give the English meaning of these regular French verbs that are easily recognizable cognates:

1. adorer _adore_
2. accomplir _accomplis_
3. correspondre _correspond_
4. applaudir _applaud_
5. inviter _invite_
6. défendre _defend_
7. finir _finish_
8. descendre _go down_
9. organiser _organize_
10. garantir _garantee_
11. répondre _respond_ _answer_
12. téléphoner _phone_

Verbs with Spelling Changes

For certain regular French -*er* verbs, an internal spelling change is required to maintain correct pronunciation of certain forms. Verbs with spelling changes sound regular to the ear, but when written, they look different from the original infinitive. These verbs are often referred to as "shoe verbs" (and will be referred to as such throughout this book) because the subject pronouns that follow one set of rules can be placed inside the shoe, whereas the subject pronouns that follow a different set of rules remain outside the shoe.

-cer Verbs

Verbs ending in -cer (see Appendix D) change c to ç before a and o to maintain a soft c sound. This change occurs as follows:

♦ In the *nous* form of the present tense:

j'avance BUT: nous avançons

♦ In the *je*, *tu*, *il* (*elle*), and *ils* (*elles*) forms of the imperfect:

j'avançais BUT: nous avancions

♦ In all forms of the *passé simple* except *ils:*

j'avançai BUT: ils avancèrent

♦ In the imperative *nous* form:

Avançons!

♦ In all forms of the imperfect subjunctive

Attention!

Spelling changes only occur in certain tenses and only before certain letters to maintain correct sound and stress. These spelling changes require either the addition of a letter, the addition of an accent mark, or a change in an accent mark.

Exercice 2

A. Express what each person gives up doing by filling in the missing letters from the verb in the present:

(renoncer) Je renon___e à cuisiner, les garçons renon___ent à jouer aux échecs, Marie et moi renon___ons à étudier l'allemand, tu renon___es à jouer du piano, Sylvie renon___e à faire de la poterie, et vous renon___ez à vous entraîner.

B. Express what each person was beginning to do when a storm broke out by filling in the missing letters from the verb in the imperfect:

(commencer) Tu commen___ais à promener ton chien, vous commen___iez à faire du vélo, Richard commen___ait à faire de la planche à voile, nous commen___ions à jouer au tennis, je commen___ais à faire une randonnée, les filles commen___aient à faire les cent mètres.

C. Express what each person did during a strike by filling in the correct form of the verb in the *passé simple:*

1. (lancer) Tu lan___as quelque chose.

2. (menacer) Certains employés mena___èrent des autres.

3. (renoncer) Je renon___ai à travailler.

4. (anoncer) Le patron anon___a son chagrin.

5. (avancer) Nous avan___âmes vers un accord.

6. (influencer) Vous m'influen___âtes.

-ger Verbs

Verbs ending in -ger (Appendix D) add *e* after *g* before *a* and *o* to maintain a soft *g* sound. This change occurs as follows:

♦ In the *nous* form of the present tense:

je nage BUT: nous nageons

♦ In the *je, tu, il (elle),* and *ils (elles)* forms of the imperfect:

je nageais BUT: nous nagions

♦ In all forms of the *passé simple* except *ils:*

je nageai BUT: ils nagèrent

♦ In all forms of the imperfect subjunctive

Exercice 3

A. Express what each person is eating by filling in the missing letters from the verb in the present:

(manger) Vous man___ez du poulet, je man___e du bifteck, les filles man___ent du poisson, nous man___ons du veau, Luc man___e un hamburger, et tu man___es du rosbif.

B. Express what each person was putting in order before company came by filling in the missing letters from the verb in the imperfect:

(ranger) Mireille ran___ait le salon, je ran___ais le garage, les garçons ran___aient leurs chambres, Carine et moi nous ran___ions nos papiers, tu ran___ais tes vêtements, vous ran___iez le living.

C. Express what each person did yesterday by filling in the missing letters from the verb in the *passé simple:*

1. (démenager) Les Dupont déména___èrent.
2. (nager) Tu na___as dans une piscine couverte.
3. (corriger) Vous corri___âtes vos devoirs.
4. (diriger) Je diri___ai mon attention vers mes études.
5. (changer) Lucette chan___a les draps dans sa chambre.
6. (arranger) Nous arran___âmes nos affaires.

-yer Verbs

Verbs ending in *-yer* (Appendix D) change *y* to *i* before a silent *e*. This change occurs as follows:

♦ In the *je, tu, il (elle),* and *ils (elles)* forms of the present:

j'emploie BUT: nous employons

♦ In all forms of the future

♦ In all forms of the conditional

♦ In the *je, tu, il (elle),* and *ils (elles)* forms of the present subjunctive:

que j'emploie BUT: que nous employions

 Regarde! _____

Verbs ending in -ayer (see Appendix D) formerly preserved the *y* in all conjugations. Nowadays, however, the *y* is generally changed to *i* before mute *e*. Bear in mind that either verb form is correct and acceptable: *je paie* or *je paye.*

Exercice 4

A. Express what tool each person is using by filling in the missing letters from the verb in the present:

(employer) Tu emplo___es des ciseaux, Serge et moi nous emplo___ons un marteau, M. Henri emplo___e un tournevis, vous emplo___ez des pinces, j'emplo___e une clef anglaise, et les garçons emplo___ent une perceuse.

B. Express how much each person will pay for a shirt by filling in the missing letters from the verb in the future:

(payer) Nous pa___erons quinze dollars, vous pa___erez vingt dollars, les filles pa___eront dix dollars, Laurent pa___era dix-huit dollars, je pa___erai cinquante dollars, tu pa___eras trente dollars.

C. Express what each person would use to complete his work by filling in the missing letters from the verb in the conditional:

(employer) La fille emplo___erait un dictionnaire, nous emplo___erions un ordinateur, les hommes emplo___eraient une calculette, j'emplo___erais un programme de traitement de texte, tu emplo___erais une encyclopédie, vous emplo___erez une règle.

D. Express what it is important for each person to do by filling in the missing letters from the verb in the subjunctive:

1. (essuyer) Il est important que nous essu___ions les pieds avant d'entrer dans la maison.

2. (payer) Il est important que Mme Lelouche pa___e ses factures.

3. (envoyer) Il est important que j'envo___e un télégramme à ma famille.

4. (essayer) Il est important que tu essa___es de faire de ton mieux.

5. (nettoyer) Il est important que vous netto___iez la maison.

6. (employer) Il est important que Roger et Bernard emplo___ent un dictionnaire de synonymes pour faire leur travail.

-e + Consonant + er Verbs That Add an Accent

Many verbs ending in -e + consonant + er (Appendix D) change the silent e before the consonant to è when the next syllable contains another silent e. This change occurs as follows:

- In the *je*, *tu*, *il* (*elle*), and *ils* (*elles*) forms of the present:

  j'achète BUT: nous achetons

- In all forms of the future

- In all forms of the conditional

- In the *je*, *tu*, *il* (*elle*), and *ils* (*elles*) forms of the present subjunctive:

  que j'achète BUT: que nous achetions

Regarde! _____

Verbs ending in -ier have two i's in the nous and vous forms of the imperfect and the present subjunctive, because an ending beginning with -i is added to a stem ending in -i: (que) nous criions, (que) vous criiez.

Exercice 5

Express the thoughts of each person by filling in the missing letters from the verb in the tense indicated:

1. (acheter—present) Laure ach___te toujours de très jolis vêtements.

2. (amener—future) J'am___nerai mes parents au restaurant ce week-end.

3. (promener—subjunctive) Il est nécessaire que vous prom___niez le chien ce soir.

4. (achever—conditional) S'ils avaient le temps ils ach___veraient leur travail.

5. (peser—subjunctive) Il est essentiel que tu p___ses le pour et le contre avant d'agir.

6. (enlever—present) *take off* Charles et moi nous enl___vons toujours nos coudes de la *elbows* table.

7. (élever—future) *raise/rear* Les Caron él___veront leurs enfants selon des principes stricts.

8. (emmener—conditional) Nous emm___nerions nos amis au cinéma s'ils étaient libres.

-e + Consonant + er Verbs That Double the Final Consonant

Other verbs ending in -e + consonant + er (see Appendix D) double the final consonant instead of changing e to è. This change occurs as follows:

◆ In the *je, tu, il (elle)*, and *ils (elles)* forms of the present:

j'appelle BUT: nous appelons

◆ In all forms of the future

◆ In all forms of the conditional

◆ In the *je, tu, il (elle)*, and *ils (elles)* forms of the present subjunctive:

que j'appelle BUT: que nous appelions

Exercice 6

Express the facts about each person by filling in the missing letters from the verb in the tense indicated:

1. (appeler—future) M. et Mme Laforêt appe__eront leur enfant Christine.

2. (jeter—subjunctive) Mme Louche ne veut pas que sa fille je__e ses jouets par terre.

3. (rappeler—present) Quand mes amis me téléphonent, je les rappe__e toujours.

4. (feuilleter—conditional) Si tu avais envie de lire tu feuill__terais au moins ce livre.

5. (rejeter—present) Vous reje__ez toujours mes idées.

6. (épousseter—subjunctive) Est-il urgent que nous épousse__tions les meubles maintenant?

7. (renouveler—conditional) Janine renouve__erait sa connaissance avec Aimée si elle avait son numéro de téléphone.

8. (épeler—future) Les enfants épe__eront bien tous les mots de vocabulaire.

Regarde! _____

Verbs ending in *-éer* have two *e*'s (the first accented and the second, not) in the *je, tu, il,* and *ils* forms of the present and the present subjunctive, and in all forms of the future and the conditional. This occurs because an ending beginning with *-e* is added to a stem ending in *-é:*

Present: je crée BUT: nous créons

Subjunctive: que je crée BUT: que nous créions

Future: je créerai, nous créerons

Conditional: je créerais, nous créerions

-é + Consonant(s) + er Verbs

Verbs ending in *-é* + consonant + *er* (Appendix D) change *é* to *è* before *-e, -es,* and *-ent.* This change occurs as follows:

◆ In the *je, tu, il (elle),* and *ils (elles)* forms of the present:

je célèbre BUT: nous célébrons

◆ In the *je, tu, il (elle),* and *ils (elles)* forms of the present subjunctive:

que je célèbre BUT: que nous célébrions

Exercice 7

A. Express the types of movies each person prefers by filling in the missing letters from the verb in the present tense:

(préférer) Tu préf___res les films de science-fiction, Claire et moi nous préf___rons les comédies, Jacques et Henri préf___rent les westerns, Mariane préf___re les histoires d'amour, je préf___re les films policiers, vous préf___rez les films d'aventure.

B. Express what it is necessary for each person to do by filling in the missing letters from the verb in the subjunctive:

1. (tolérer) Il est nécessaire que tu tol___res les autres.

2. (coopérer) Il est nécessaire que tout le monde coop___re.

3. (révérer) Il est nécessaire que vous rév___riez les professeurs.

4. (révéler) Il est nécessaire que je rév___le mes projets d'avenir.

5. (compléter) Il est nécessaire que nous compl___tions notre travail ensemble.

6. (délibérer) Il est nécessaire que les politiques délib___rent sur cette question importante.

Attention!

Only a few verbs end in *-éger*. These verbs follow the rules for both *-ger* verbs and é + consonant + *-er* verbs.

Present: je protège, nous protégeons

Imperfect: je protégeais, nous protégions

Passé simple: je protégeai, nous protégeâmes

Present subjunctive: que je protège, que nous protégions

Irregular Verbs

Irregular verbs must be memorized because they do not generally follow any specific set of rules. These high-frequency verbs, so commonly used in everyday conversation and writing, will enable you to read, write, and speak French like a native. The most common irregular verbs, those you will use more or less on a daily basis, are illustrated in Appendix B. They include the following:

aller (to go)	paraître (to seem)
avoir (to have)	partir (to leave)
boire (to drink)	plaire (to please)
conduire (to drive)	pleuvoir (to rain)
courir (to run)	pouvoir (to be able to)
croire (to believe)	prendre (to take)
dire (to say, tell)	rire (to laugh)
dormir (to sleep)	savoir (to know)
écrire (to write)	sentir (to feel, smell)

être (to be)

faire (to make, do)

falloir (to be necessary)

lire (to read)

mettre (to put)

mourir (to die)

naître (to be born)

offrir (to offer)

ouvrir (to open)

servir (to servir)

suivre (to follow)

sortir (to go out)

valoir (to be worth)

venir (to come)

vivre (to live)

voir (to see)

vouloir (to wish, want)

Lesser-used irregular verbs include the following:

acquérir (to acquire)

assaillir (to assail)

asseoir (to seat)

battre (to beat)

bouillir (to boil)

conclure (to conclude)

coudre (to sew)

craindre (to fear)

croître (to grow)

cueillir (to pick)

distraire (to distract)

faillir (to almost)

fuir (to flee)

haïr (to hate)

joindre (to join)

mouvoir (to move)

pourvoir (to provide)

résoudre (to resolve)

suffire (to suffice)

taire (se) to be quiet

vaincre (to conquer)

vêtir (to dress)

These verbs are also included in Appendix B.

Récapitulation

- ◆ All French verbs end in -*er*, -*ir*, -*oir* or -*re*.
- ◆ All regular verbs with each infinitive ending are conjugated in the same manner in all tenses.

♦ Certain *-er* verbs have spelling changes as follows:

-cer verbs change *c* to *ç* before *a* or *o* to maintain a soft sound.

-ger verbs add *e* after *g* before *a* or *o* to maintain a soft sound.

-yer verbs change *y* to *i* before silent *e*.

Some verbs ending in *-e* + consonant + *er* change silent *e* to *è* when the next syllable contains another silent *e*.

Other verbs ending in *-e* + consonant + *er* double the final consonant.

Verbs ending in *-é* + consonant(s) + *er* change *é* to *è* before *-e*, *-es*, and *-ent*.

The Least You Need to Know

♦ Most French verbs are regular.

♦ Only certain *-er* verbs have spelling changes.

♦ Verbs with spelling changes require an internal change.

♦ Verbs with spelling changes do not change in every tense.

♦ Some French verbs are completely irregular and must be memorized.

Part 2

Comparing Tenses

Be completely honest with yourself! If you want to communicate effectively, creatively, and correctly, you have to know your verbs—you can't produce cohesive thoughts and ideas without understanding the meaning of verbs and without knowing how to conjugate them properly in all their tenses.

This part takes you into the world of French verbs. You'll progress on an even keel from tenses that are relatively easy to those that require more time, more patience, more skill, and more memorization. You'll get a clear and concise explanation of what the different tenses and moods are, how to form them, and when to use them properly. Finally, you will be provided with plenty of exercises, so that by the time you've finished this section, you'll be feeling like a pro.

Chapter 3

The Present Tense and the *Passé Composé*

In This Chapter

◆ Forming and using the present tense of regular verbs and irregular verbs

◆ Forming the present tense of verbs with spelling changes

◆ How to use reflexive verbs

◆ Forming and using the imperative

◆ Forming and using the *passé composé*

The present tense is a simple tense that expresses an action or state of being that occurs now: He practices; that does occur now: He does practice; or that is occurring now: He is practicing. The *passé composé*, on the other hand, is the compound equivalent of the present that describes an action or state of being that started and was completed at a particular time in the past: He practiced yesterday. In this chapter, you'll learn how to use both tenses in French.

The Present Tense of Regular Verbs

A verb expresses an action or state of being and is normally shown in its infinitive form, the "to" form: for example, to sing. In English, regular verbs and many irregular verbs have only two different forms:

I **sing**	We sing
You sing	You sing
He/She **sings**	They sing

In French, however, regular verbs have several different forms, which requires that you memorize several distinct endings. Let's take a look at the French verb *chanter* (to sing):

Je chant**e**	Nous chant**ons**
Tu chant**es**	Vous chant**ez**
Il, Elle, On chant**e**	Ils, Elles chant**ent**

All regular verbs within each infinitive group (*-er*, *-ir*, and *-re*) follow the same rules of conjugation: Each subject has its own ending that does not change. When you have learned the ending, you may then apply it to any regular verb with the corresponding infinitive ending.

Attention!

Verbs ending in *-éer*, *-ier*, and *-uer* are regular in the present tense.

The Present Tense of *-er* Verbs

The *-er* verb infinitives comprise, by far, the largest infinitive group in French. To form the present tense of these verbs, drop the *-er* infinitive ending and add the endings shown in Table 3.1.

Table 3.1   *-er* Verb Conjugation

Infinitive	Meaning	Subject	Ending	Conjugated Verb
danser	to dance	je	-e	dans**e**
parler	to speak	tu	-es	parl**es**
préparer	to prepare	il	-e	prépar**e**
étudier	to study	elle	-e	étudi**e**
continuer	to continue	on	-e	continu**e**
travailler	to work	nous	-ons	travaill**ons**
gagner	to win	vous	-ez	gagn**ez**

Infinitive	Meaning	Subject	Ending	Conjugated Verb
téléphoner	to phone	ils	-ent	téléphon**ent**
créer	to create	elles	-ent	cr**éent**

You should now feel comfortable working in the present tense with any of the *-er* verbs listed in Appendix D.

Exercice 1

Express what each person does by giving the correct form of the verb:

1. (marcher) ils _____
2. (donner) je _____
3. (expliquer) nous _____
4. (crier) vous _____
5. (regarder) tu _____
6. (traverser) vous _____
7. (dîner) elle _____
8. (demander) on _____
9. (dessiner) il _____
10. (remercier) elles _____

The Present Tense of *-ir* Verbs

The next group is that of *-ir* verbs. To form the present tense of these verbs, drop the *-ir* infinitive ending and add the endings shown in Table 3.2.

Table 3.2 *-ir* Verb Conjugation

Infinitive	Meaning	Subject	Ending	Conjugated Verb
finir	to finish	je	-is	fin**is**
agir	to act	tu	-is	ag**is**
choisir	to choose	il	-it	chois**it**

continues

Table 3.2 *-ir* Verb Conjugation (continued)

Infinitive	Meaning	Subject	Ending	Conjugated Verb
grandir	to grow	elle	-it	grand**it**
rougir	to blush	on	-it	roug**it**
avertir	to warn	nous	-issons	avert**issons**
réussir	to succeed	vous	-issez	réuss**issez**
punir	to punish	ils	-issent	pun**issent**
bâtir	to build	elles	-issent	bât**issent**

The regular *-ir* verbs in Appendix E should now be easy to conjugate in the present tense.

Exercice 2

Express what each person does by giving the correct form of the verb:

1. (maigrir) nous _____

2. (grossir) ils _____

3. (nourrir) vous _____

4. (trahir) tu _____

5. (saisir) elle _____

6. (accomplir) vous _____

7. (obéir) on _____

8. (garantir) il _____

9. (remplir) je _____

10. (réfléchir) elles _____

The Present Tense of *-re* Verbs

To form the present tense of *-re* verbs, drop the *-re* infinitive ending and add the endings shown in Table 3.3.

Table 3.3   *-re* Verb Conjugation

Infinitive	Meaning	Subject	Ending	Conjugated Verb
perdre	to lose	je	-s	perd**s**
entendre	to hear	tu	-s	attend**s**
attendre	to wait	il		attend
vendre	to sell	elle		vend
défendre	to defend	on		défend
rendre	to return	nous	-ons	rend**ons**
pendre	to hang	vous	-ez	pend**ez**
étendre	to stretch	ils	-ent	étend**ent**
confondre	to confuse	elles	-ent	confond**ent**

Use the verbs in Appendix F in conjunction with Table 3.3 to practice the *-re* verb present tense conjugation.

Attention!

The verbs *rompre* (to break), *interrompre* (to interrupt), and *corrompre* (to corrupt) are irregular only in the third person singular form of the present tense, where a final *-t* is added: *il rompt, il interrompt, il corrompt.*

Exercice 3

Express what each person does by giving the correct form of the verb:

1. (descendre) ils _____
2. (dépendre) vous _____
3. (répandre) nous _____ *spill*
4. (prétendre) il _____
5. (mordre) elles _____
6. (prétendre) tu _____
7. (répondre) on _____
8. (revendre) vous _____ *sell back*
9. (suspendre) je _____
10. (tond) elle _____ *mow*

The Present Tense of Verbs with Spelling Changes

In the present tense, all verbs ending in -*cer* and -*ger* have a spelling change to preserve the proper sound of the consonant in the *nous* form. All verbs ending in -*yer*, -*e* + consonant + *er*, and -*é* + consonant + *er* have a change within the shoe (see Chapter 2)—that is, in the *je*, *tu*, *il* (*elle*), and *ils* (*elles*) forms, as shown in Table 3.4.

Table 3.4   The Present Tense of -*cer*, -*ger*, -*yer*, -*e* + Consonant + *er*, and -*é* + Consonant + *er* Verbs

	je	tu	il	nous	vous	ils
-cer	berce	berces	berce	**berçons**	bercez	bercent
-ger	nage	nages	nage	**nageons**	nagez	nagent
-yer,	**essaie**	**essaies**	**essaie**	essayons	essayez	**essaient**
e+con.+er	**mène**	**mènes**	**mène**	menons	menez	**mènent**
	jette	**jettes**	**jette**	jetons	jetez	**jettent**
é+con.+er	**préfére**	**préféres**	**préfére**	préférons	préférez	**préférent**

Regarde!

Remember that for verbs ending in -*ayer*, you have the option of changing *y* to *i*, or retaining the *y*.

A small number of -*é* + consonant + *er* verbs end in -*ger* and require two changes:

abréger (to shorten)   piéger (to trap)

agréger (to aggregate)   protéger (to protect)

alléger (to lighten)   siéger (to be in session)

assiéger (to lay siege to)

Exercice 4

Following the rules given above, fill in the following table for the verbs listed. Consult the appendixes if you are unsure of the verb.

Verb	Meaning	Je	Nous	Ils
envoyer	to send	_____	_____	_____
ranger	to tidy	_____	_____	_____
acheter	to buy	_____	_____	_____
effacer	to erase	_____	_____	_____

Verb	Meaning	Je	Nous	Ils
célébrer	to celebrate	_____	_____	_____
rappeler	to recall	_____	_____	_____
partager	to share	_____	_____	_____
employer	to use	_____	_____	_____
achever	to complete	_____	_____	_____
rejeter	to reject	_____	_____	_____
protéger	to protect	_____	_____	_____
prononcer	to pronounce	_____	_____	_____

The Present Tense of *-oir* or *-evoir* Verbs

To form the present tense of the seven regular verbs with these endings, drop the *-oir* or *-evoir* infinitive ending and add the endings shown in Table 3.5. All other verbs ending in *-oir* (*avoir*, *voir*, and so on) are irregular and must be memorized. Note that in verbs ending in *-cevoir*, *c* changes to *ç* before *o* and *u* to preserve the soft *-s* sound.

Table 3.5   *-oir, -evoir* Verb Conjugation

Infinitive	Meaning	Subject	Ending	Conjugated Verb
apercevoir	to notice	je	-ois	aperçois
concevoir	to conceive	tu	-ois	conçois
décevoir	to deceive	il	-oit	déçoit
devoir	to owe, have to	elle	-oit	doit
percevoir	to perceive	on	-oit	perçoit
recevoir	to receive	nous	-evons	recevons
redevoir	to still owe	vous	-evez	redevez
apercevoir	to notice	ils	-oivent	aperçoivent
devoir	to owe, have to	elles	-oivent	doivent

Exercice 5

Express what each person receives for his birthday by giving the present tense of recevoir.

(recevoir) Je _____ une montre, Syvlie _____ du parfum, Tu _____ un magnétoscope, Richard et moi nous _____ des livres, Hervé et Paul _____ des CDs, vous _____ un bracelet.

Impersonal Verbs

Some verbs, because of their meanings, are only conjugated in the third person singular form:

advenir (to happen)	il advient
bruiner (to drizzle)	il bruine
convenir (to suit)	il convient
dégeler (to thaw)	il dégèle
falloir (to be necessary)	il faut
geler (to freeze)	il gèle
grêler (to hail)	il grêle
importer (to be of importance)	il importe
neiger (to snow)	il neige
pleuvoir (to rain)	il pleut
regeler (to freeze again)	il regèle
tonner (to thunder)	il tonne

The Present Tense of Reflexive Verbs

The pronoun *se* identifies a verb as being reflexive, which means it is a verb that shows that the subject is acting upon itself: for example, *s'appeler* (to call oneself). The subject and the reflexive pronoun, therefore, refer to the same person(s) or thing(s): *Je m'appelle Gail.* (I call myself Gail or My name is Gail.) The reflexive pronoun acts as a direct or indirect object.

In many instances, a verb can be reflexive or not depending upon whether the subject is acting upon itself or upon someone or something else.

Je m'appelle Gail.   J'appelle Raymond.
I call myself Gail.   *I call Raymond.*
(*My name is Gail.*)

Some verbs that are generally not used reflexively may be made reflexive by adding the reflexive pronoun:

Je prépare le repas.   Je me prépare.
I prepare the meal.   *I prepare myself.*

You can find a list of common reflexive verbs in Appendix G.

Take note of the following verbs that are always used reflexively in French but are not generally used that way in English. Verbs in boldface are irregular.

s'écrier	to exclaim, cry out
s'écrouler	to collapse
s'efforcer de	to strive to
s'empresser de	to hasten to
s'en **aller**	to leave, go away
s'**enfuir**	to flee
s'évanouir	to faint
se fier à	to trust
se lamenter de	to lament, grieve about
se méfier de	to distrust
se moquer de	to make fun of
se soucier de	to care about
se **souvenir** de	to remember

Using Reflexive Pronouns

Reflexive verbs, like all other verbs, are conjugated in all tenses according to their endings and according to any spelling changes or irregularities. Unlike other verbs, however, a reflexive verb must be accompanied by its appropriate reflexive pronoun.

Each subject has its own pronoun that is generally placed before the conjugated verb in the present tense, as shown in Table 3.6.

Table 3.6   The Present Tense of Reflexive Verbs

Subject	Reflexive Pronoun	Verb
je	me	lave
tu	te	couches
il, elle, on	se	lève
nous	nous	dépêchons
vous	vous	rasez
ils, elles	se	rappellent

Nous nous reposons.   Il s'inquiète.
We rest.   *He worries.*

Some passive constructions (where the subject is acted upon) may be replaced by a reflexive verb:

Le français se parle à Montréal.
French is spoken in Montreal.

Les billets se vendent ici.
Tickets are sold here.

Exercice 6

Express what each person does by using a reflexive pronoun and by conjugating the verb.

1. (se raser) Il _____ le matin.

2. (se disputer) Ils _____.

3. (s'inquiéter) Je _____ de tout.

4. (s'exprimer) Vous _____ bien.

5. (se peigner) Elles _____ souvent.

6. (se spécialiser) Nous _____ en français.

7. (s'appeller) Tu _____ comment?

8. (se lever) On _____ de bonne heure.

The Present Tense of Irregular Verbs

The endings of irregular verbs in the present tense follow the following general rules also shown in Table 3.7:

◆ The *je* form always ends in -*e* or -*s*. When the *je* form ends in -*e*, the *tu* form ends in -*es* and the *il/elle/on* form ends in -*e*. When the *je* form ends in -*s*, the *tu* form ends in -*s* and the *il/elle/on* form ends in -*t* or -*d* (only if -*d* also occurs in the other singular forms).

◆ The *nous* form always ends in -*ons*.

◆ The *vous* form always ends in -*ez*.

◆ The *ils/elles* form always ends in -*ent*.

Table 3.7   Irregular Present Tense Endings

je	tu	il/elle/on	nous	vous	ils/elles
-e	-es	-e	-ons	-ez	-ent
		or			
-s	-s	-t or -d	-ons	-ez	-ent

Some common, high-frequency irregular verbs that are exceptions to the preceding rules are listed in Table 3.8.

Table 3.8   Common Exceptions to the Rule

Verb	Meaning	Conjugation
aller	to go	**vais, vas, va**, allons, allez, **vont**
avoir	to have	**ai, as, a**, avons, avez, **ont**
dire	to say	dis, dis, dit, disons, **dites**, disent
être	to be	**suis, es, est, sommes, êtes, sont**
faire	to make, do	fais, fais, fait, faisons, **faites, font**
pouvoir	to be able	**peux, peux**, peut, pouvons, pouvez, peuvent
vaincre	to defeat	vaincs, vaincs, **vainc**, vainquons, vainquez, vainquent
valoir	to be worth	**vaux, vaux**, vaut, valons, valez, valent
vouloir	to wish, want	**veux, veux**, veut, voulons, voulez, veulent

The verbs listed in Table 3.9 are also commonly used verbs in French that are irregular in the present tense. A few have regular forms. All irregular forms are indicated in boldface.

Table 3.9   Irregular French Verbs

Verb	Meaning	je	tu	il	nous	vous	ils
battre	to beat	**bats**	**bats**	**bat**	battons	battez	battent
boire	to drink	bois	bois	**boit**	**buvons**	**buvez**	**boivent**
conduire	to drive	conduis	conduis	**conduit**	**conduisons**	**conduisez**	**conduisent**
courir	to run	**cours**	**cours**	**court**	courons	courez	**courent**
craindre	to fear	**crains**	**crains**	**craint**	**craigons**	**craignez**	**craignent**
croire	to believe	crois	crois	**croit**	**croyons**	**croyez**	croient
cueillir	to pick	**cueille**	**cueilles**	**cueille**	**cueillons**	**cueillez**	**cueillent**
distraire	to distract	distrais	distrais	**distrait**	**distrayons**	**distrayez**	distraient
dormir	to sleep	**dors**	**dors**	**dort**	dormons	dormez	dorment
écrire	to write	écris	écris	**écrit**	**écrivons**	**écrivez**	**écrivent**
fuir	to flee	fuis	fuis	**fuit**	**fuyons**	**fuyez**	**fuient**
joindre	to join	**joins**	**joins**	**joint**	**joignons**	**joignez**	**joignent**
lire	to read	lis	lis	**lit**	**lisons**	lisez	lisent
mettre	to put	**mets**	**mets**	**met**	mettons	mettez	mettent
offrir	to offer	**offre**	**offres**	**offre**	**offrons**	offrez	**offrent**
ouvrir	to open	**ouvre**	**ouvres**	**ouvre**	ouvrons	ouvrez	**ouvrent**
paraître	to seem	**parais**	**parais**	**paraît**	**paraissons**	**paraissez**	**paraissent**
partir	to leave	**pars**	**pars**	**part**	partons	partez	partent
prendre	to take	prends	prends	prend	**prenons**	**prenez**	**prennent**
savoir	to know	**sais**	**sais**	**sait**	savons	savez	savent
sentir	to feel	**sens**	**sens**	**sent**	**sentons**	**sentez**	**sentent**
servir	to serve	**sers**	**sers**	**sert**	**servons**	**servez**	**servent**
sortir	to go out	**sors**	**sors**	**sort**	**sortons**	**sortez**	**sortent**
suivre	to follow	**suis**	**suis**	**suit**	suivons	suivez	suivent
venir	to come	**viens**	**viens**	**vient**	venons	**venez**	**viennent**
vivre	to live	**vis**	**vis**	**vit**	vivons	vivez	vivent
voir	to see	**vois**	**vois**	**voit**	**voyons**	**voyez**	**voient**

The above verbs, and others, are irregular in other tenses and some have irregular present or past participles. They will be addressed in the sections that pertain to them in particular. Bear in mind that all compounds of these verbs, listed in Appendix C, follow the same rules of conjugation.

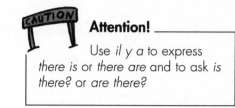

Attention! _____

Use *il y a* to express *there is* or *there are* and to ask *is there?* or *are there?*

Exercice 7

Complete each sentence using the correct form of the verb in parentheses to speak about each person at work:

1. (aller) On _____ travailler dur.

2. (être) Nous _____ diligents.

3. (pouvoir) Tu _____ résoudre tous les problèmes.

4. (avoir) Nous _____ de bonnes idées.

5. (venir) Elle _____ souvent en retard.

6. (prendre) Je _____ le bus pour aller au bureau.

7. (écrire) Ils _____ écrivent une longue lettre.

8. (faire) Vous _____ de votre mieux tout le temps.

Using the Present Tense

The present tense is used as follows:

◆ To ask for instructions or to discuss an action that will take place in the near future:

J'invite les Pierrot?
Shall I invite the Pierrots?

Je te rappelle dans une heure.
I'll call you back in an hour.

◆ To express an event or action that began in the past and is continuing in the present by using *depuis* + an expression of time:

Depuis quand étudies-tu le français?
Depuis combien de temps étudies-tu le français?
How long have you been studying French?

J'étudie le français depuis deux mois.
I've been studying for two months.

Other constructions that express a past action or event that continues in the present are:

◆ *il y a* + expression of time + *que* + present

Combien de temps y a-t-il que tu étudies le français?
How long have you been studying French?

◆ *voilà … que* and *cela (ça) fait … que* + present

Cela (Ça) fait combien de temps que tu étudies le français?
How long have you been studying French?

Cela (Ça) fait deux mois que j'étudie le français.

Voilà deux mois que j'étudie le français.
I've been studying French for two months.

Attention!

In the negative *passé composé*, the *ne* + negative word surround the conjugated helping verb.

Il n'est pas arrivé à l'heure.
He didn't arrive on time.

N'es-tu jamais allé(e) en France?
Haven't you ever gone to France?

Attention!

When one subject is followed by two verbs, the first verb is conjugated in the appropriate tense and the second verb remains in its infinitive form. A reflexive pronoun will remain before the infinitive:

Il sait bien danser.
He knows how to dance well.

Elle est allée faire des achats.
She went shopping.

Nous allons nous amuser à la fête.
We're going to have fun at the party.

Exercice 8

Express what each person no longer does by giving the correct form of the present tense.

1. (grossir) Ils ne _____ pas depuis un mois.

2. (fumer) Ça fait un an que tu ne _____ pas.

3. (conduire) Voilà trois mois que M. Richard ne _____ pas.

4. (vivre) Je ne _____ pas au Canada depuis cinq semaines.

5. (manger) Voilà deux ans que nous ne _____ pas de viande.

6. (aller) Ça fait trois jours que les filles ne _____ pas au club de français.

Forming and Using the Imperative

The imperative is the form of the verb used to give commands or make requests or suggestions. Because the subject of a command is understood to be you, the imperative is formed with the *tu* or *vous* form of the present tense of the verb with the omission of these subject pronouns.

Tu represents a familiar command and is used when speaking to one friend or family member. *Vous* represents a polite command and is used when speaking formally to someone you don't know well, or when speaking to more than one person, regardless of relationship.

To form the imperative, use the corresponding present tense and omit the subject pronoun. This is true for regular and irregular verbs alike, except for the three mentioned at the end of this section. Note that the *tu* command of *-er* verbs drops the final *-s* from its present tense form as shown in Table 3.10.

Regarde! _____

Verbs conjugated like *-er* verbs in the present (*cueillir, ouvrir, offrir,* and so on) and the verb *aller* drop the final *-s* in the familiar command form.

Ouvre les fenêtres!
Open the window!

Va tout droit!
Go straight ahead!

Table 3.10   The Imperative French Verbs

Familiar		Polite	
Écoute!	Listen!	Écoutez!	Listen!
Finis!	Finish!	Finissez!	Finish!
Attends!	Wait!	Attendez!	Wait!
Bois!	Drink!	Buvez!	Drink!
Fais ça!	Do that!	Faites ça!	Do that!
Viens!	Come!	Venez!	Come!

To offer a suggestion by expressing "Let's," use the *nous* form of the verb without the subject pronoun:

Allons au cinéma!
Let's go to the movies.

The three common verbs with irregular imperatives are as follows:

Regarde! _____
Affirmative familiar (tu) -er verb commands retain their final -s before the pronouns *y* (there) and *en* (some): *Vas-y!* (Go there!) *N'y va pas!* (Don't go there!) *Manges-en!* (Eat some!) *N'en mange pas!* (Don't eat any!)

avoir (to have)   aie, ayez, ayons

etre (to be)   sois, soyez, soyons

savoir (to know)   sache, sachons, sachez

All commands are negated by placing the negative expression around the conjugated verb:

Ne va plus au parc!   Ne travaillez jamais si dur.
Don't go to the park anymore! *Don't ever work so hard.*

Ne faisons pas de promenade.
Let's not go for a walk.

The Imperative of Reflexive Verbs

Note the following rules regarding the imperative of reflexive verbs:

◆ In negative commands, the reflexive pronoun precedes the verb:

Ne te dépêche pas! (Don't hurry!)
Ne vous inquiétez pas! (Don't worry!)
Ne nous disputons pas! (Let's not argue!)

◆ In affirmative commands, the reflexive pronoun follows the verb and is attached to it by a hyphen. The pronoun *te* becomes *toi* after the verb:

Lève-toi! (Get up!)
Peignez-vous! (Comb your hair!)
Préparons-nous! (Let's prepare ourselves!)

Exercice 9

Express what you tell a friend who is on a diet to do and not to do according to what is logical.

1. (avoir/être) _____ confiance. _____ pessimiste.

2. (consommer/boire) _____ beaucoup de chocolat. _____ beaucoup d'eau.

3. (suivre/manger) _____ un régime. _____ tout ce que tu veux.

4. (s'inquiéter/s'habituer) _____ de tes progrès. _____ à choisir des plats nourrissants.

5. (choisir/prendre) _____ des légumes. _____ de pommes frites.

Forming and Using the *Passé Composé*

The *passé composé* is a compound tense, which means that it is made up of more than one part. The two elements that are needed to form the *passé composé* are as follows:

1. The present tense of the helping verb *avoir* or *être* (see Chapter 1), which expresses that something has taken place. *Avoir* is the helping verb for most verbs. Reflexives verbs and those intransitive verbs showing motion or change of place, state, or condition use *être* as their helping verb (see Chapter 1).

2. The past participle of the verb, which expresses what the action was.

The following figure shows how the *passé composé* is formed:

Passé composé of verb =   when + what

/   \

Passé composé of verb = (what) has + happened

/   \

Passé composé of verb = helping verb + main verb

/   \

Passé composé of verb = avoir (to have) + past participle
        être

Formation of the passé composé.

The formula for the formation of the passé composé is as follows:

subject noun or pronoun + *avoir* (*être*) in present + past participle

I already explained the formation of past participles in Chapter 1. To review:

for *-er* verbs, drop *er* and add *-é*

for *-ir* verbs, drop *ir* and add *-i*

for *-re* verbs, drop *re* and add *-u*

Irregular past participles are listed in Table 1.4 and in Appendix F.

The *passé composé* is used to express the following:

◆ An action or event that was started and completed at a definite time in the past (even if the time isn't mentioned).

Il est rentré tard. (He came home late.)

◆ An action or event that occurred at a specific point of time in the past:

J'ai travaillé hier. (I worked yesterday.)

◆ An action or event that was repeated a stated number of times:

Ils sont allés deux fois en France. (They went to France two times.)

Agreement of Past Participles

As discussed in Chapter 1, past participles must agree in the following cases:

1. Past participles of verbs conjugated with *avoir* agree in number and gender with a preceding direct object noun, pronoun, or antecedent element:

A-t-il vu les photo que tu as prises?
Did he see the photos you took?

Nous les avons fini(e)s.
We finished them.

La robe? Elle l'a mise.
The dress? She put it on.

2. Past participles of verbs conjugated with être agree in number and gender with the subject:

Elle est partie.
She left.

Ils sont rentrés.
They came home.

Elles sont revenues.
They came back.

3. Past participles of reflexive verbs agree in number in gender with the preceding reflexive pronoun only if it acts as a direct object:

Elles se sont brûlées.
They burned themselves.

Elles se sont brûlé les mains.
They burned their hands.

Exercice 10

Use the *passé composé* to express what feat each person has accomplished:

1. (se maquiller) Lucie _____ en une minute.

2. (lire) Vous _____ trois romans en un jour.

3. (aller) Marie et Josette _____ en Afrique six fois en un an.

4. (passer) Serge et Jean _____ trois heures à s'entraîner.

5. (arriver) Janine et Étienne _____ à apprendre à conduire en deux heures.

6. (s'arrêter) Je _____ de fumer en cinq jours.

7. (sortir) Tu _____ chaque nuit pendant un mois.

8. (avoir) Nous _____ les meilleurs notes de la classe.

9. (devenir) Claude et Martin _____ experts en informatique en deux semaines.

10. (s'habiller) Renée _____ en trois minutes.

11. (peindre) Tu _____ ta chambre en une heure.

12. (se bronzer) Liliane _____ en trente minutes.

Récapitulation

1. To conjugate regular *-er* verbs, drop the *-er* infinitive ending and add *-e, -es, -e, -ons, -ez, -ent*.

2. To conjugate regular *-ir* verbs, drop the *-ir* infinitive ending and add *-is, -is, -it, -issons, -issez, -issent*.

3. To conjugate regular *-re* verbs, drop the *-re* infinitive ending and add *-s, -s, -, -ons, -ez, -ent*.

4. Spelling-change *-cer* and *-ger* verbs change *c* to *ç* and add *e* after *g* respectively in the *nous* form of the present tense.

5. Verbs ending in *-yer* change *y* to *i* in all forms of the present within the "shoe" (see Chapter 2) (the *je, tu, il,* and *ils* forms).

6. Verbs ending in *-e* + consonant + change *er* change *e* or *é* and those ending in *é* + consonant(s) + *er* change *é* to *è* in all forms of the present within the "shoe" (see Chapter 2) (the *je, tu, il,* and *ils* forms).

7. Reflexive verbs can be identified by the reflexive pronoun *se* that precedes the infinitive. Reflexive verbs show that the subject is acting upon itself and require the use of reflexive pronouns that agree with the subject.

8. Reflexive pronouns precede the conjugated verb. When there are two verbs, the reflexive pronoun precedes the infinitive.

9. The imperative is used to give a command or to make a request or a suggestion. The imperative is formed by using the *tu, vous,* or *nous* form of the present tense while omitting the subject pronouns. The final *-s* is dropped from the *tu* command of *-er* verbs when not followed by the pronouns *y* or *en*.

10. For the negative imperative of reflexive verbs, put the reflexive pronoun before the verb. For the affirmative command of reflexive verbs, put the pronoun after the verb and attach it to the verb with a hyphen. *Te* becomes *toi* in an affirmative command.

10. Irregular present tense endings are *-e, -es, -e, -ons, -ez, -ent* or *-s, -s, -t* (or *-d*), *-ons, -ez, -ent*. The stems of irregular verbs in French must be memorized.

11. The *passé composé* is the compound form of the present. It expresses an action or event that was started and completed at a definite time in the past (even if the time isn't mentioned), an action or event that occurred at a specific point of time in the past, or an action or event that was repeated a stated number of times.

12. Past participles of verbs that use *avoir* agree in number and gender with a preceding direct object. Past participles of verbs that use *être* agree in number and gender with the subject. Past participles of reflexive verbs agree with the preceding reflexive pronoun if that pronoun serves as a direct object.

The Least You Need to Know

◆ The endings for regular *-er* verbs are *-e, -es, -e, -ons, -ez, -ent.*

◆ The endings for regular *-ir* verbs are *-is, -is, -it, -issons, -issez, -issent.*

◆ The endings for regular *-re* verbs are *-s, -s, -, -ons, -ez, -ent.*

◆ Verbs with spelling changes require special changes.

◆ Irregular verbs must be memorized.

◆ The *passé composé* (the compound form of the present) is formed by taking the present of *avoir* or *être* and adding a past participle.

Chapter 4

The Imperfect and the Pluperfect

In This Chapter

- ◆ Forming the imperfect of French verbs
- ◆ Forming the imperfect of verbs with spelling changes
- ◆ When to use the *passé composé* and the imperfect
- ◆ Forming and using the pluperfect

The imperfect, which has no English equivalent, is a simple tense that expresses a continuing state or a continuous action (an action that was taking place or that used to happen repeatedly) in the past. It is unclear and unimportant when the action started and when it ended. An imperfect past action is considered incomplete. Whereas the *passé composé* relates specific actions that have occurred, the imperfect describes scenes, settings, situations, or states in the past.

The imperfect expresses what the subject was doing or used to do: She was driving ...; She used to drive .... The pluperfect is the imperfect's compound equivalent that shows what the subject had been doing before another action took place, whether that other action is stated or implied. In this chapter, you'll learn how to form and use the imperfect and how to differentiate when it is more appropriate to use the *passé composé* or the imperfect. You'll also become familiar with the formation and uses of the pluperfect.

The Imperfect of Regular, Irregular, and Reflexive Verbs

While the concept of the imperfect is totally unfamiliar to speakers of English, it proves to be a remarkably easy tense to master because there is only one verb that is formed in an irregular manner.

Forming the Imperfect of Regular Verbs

To form the imperfect of regular verbs, drop the *-ons* ending from the *nous* form of the present tense and add the imperfect endings shown in Table 4.1.

Table 4.1   The Imperfect of Regular Verbs

	-er verbs	*-ir* verbs	*-re* verbs
	parler (*to speak*)	choisir (*to choose*)	attendre (*to wait*)
	nous parl~~ons~~	nous choisiss~~ons~~	nous attend~~ons~~
Je	parl**ais**	choisiss**ais**	attend**ais**
Tu	parl**ais**	choisiss**ais**	attend**ais**
Il, Elle, On	parl**ait**	choisiss**ait**	attend**ait**
Nous	parl**ions**	choisiss**ions**	attend**ions**
Vous	parl**iez**	choisiss**iez**	attend**iez**
Ils, Elles	parl**aient**	choisiss**aient**	attend**aient**

CAUTION

Attention!

For infinitives ending in *-ier* end in *-ions* in the *nous* form of the present tense, only the *-ons* is dropped when forming the imperfect. These verbs, therefore, will have double *i* in the *nous* and *vous* forms of the imperfect, when *-ions* or *-iez* is added:

Present	Imperfect
nous crions	nous cri**i**ons
nous étudions	vous étudi**i**ez

Forming the Imperfect of Irregular Verbs

The only verb with a completely irregular stem is *être* (to be). The imperfect endings remain the same:

j'étais	nous étions
tu étais	vous étiez
il étatit	ils étaient

Because all other irregular verbs drop *-ons* from the *nous* form of the present before adding the imperfect ending, it is essential to memorize this form. Table 4.2 gives a quick refresher course on the most commonly used irregular verbs.

Attention!

Compound verbs (Appendix C) and verbs that follow the same conjugations as other verbs (Appendix C) form their respective imperfect forms accordingly.

Table 4.2   The Imperfect of Irregular Present Tense Verbs   *Imparfait*

aller (to go)	nous allons	allions
avoir (to have)	nous avons	avions
battre (to beat)	nous battons	battons
boire (to drink)	nous buvons	buvions
conduire (to drive)	nous conduisons	conduisions
connaître (to know)	nous connaissons	connaissions
courir (to run)	nous courons	courions
craindre (to fear)	nous craignons	craignions
croire (to believe)	nous croyons	croyions
cueillir (to pick)	nous cueillons	cueillions
devoir (to have to)	nous devons	devions
dire (to say, tell)	nous disons	disions
distraire (to distract)	nous distrayons	distrayions
dormir (to sleep)	nous dormons	dormions
écrire (to write)	nous écrivons	écrivions
faire (to make, do)	nous faisons	faisions
fuir (to flee)	nous fuyons	fuyions
joindre (to join)	nous joignons	joignions
lire (to read)	nous lisons	lisions
mettre (to put)	nous mettons	mettions

continues

Table 4.2   The Imperfect of Irregular Present Tense Verbs

offrir (to offer)	nous offrons	offrions
ouvrir (to open)	nous ouvrons	ouvrions
paraître (to seem)	nous paraissons	paraissions
partir (to leave)	nous partons	partions
pouvoir (to be able to)	nous pouvons	pouvions
plaindre (to pity)	nous plaignons	plaignions
plaire (to please)	nous plaisons	plaisions
prendre (to take)	nous prenons	prenions
recevoir (to receive)	nous recevons	recevions
résoudre (to resolve)	nous résolvons	résolvions
savoir (to know)	nous savons	savions
sentir (to feel)	nous sentons	sentions
servir (to serve)	nous servons	servions
sortir (to go out)	nous sortons	sortions
suivre (to follow)	nous suivons	suivions
taire (to conceal)	nous taisons	taisions
vaincre (to defeat)	nous vainquons	vainquions
valoir (to be worth)	nous valons	valions
venir (to come)	nous venons	venions
vivre (to live)	nous vivons	vivions
voir (to see)	nous voyons	voyions
vouloir (to wish, want)	nous voulons	voulions

Forming the Imperfect of Reflexive Verbs

The only difference in the formation of the imperfect of reflexive verbs is that the reflexive pronoun must be used before the verb:

Pendant l'été je me levais tard.
During the summer I would get up late.

Nous nous promenions dans le parc chaque soir.
We used to go for a walk in the park every night.

The Imperfect of Verbs with Spelling Changes

Verbs ending in *-cer* and *-ger* are the only verbs with spelling changes that require a change in the imperfect.

Verbs Ending in *-cer*

Verbs ending in *-cer* change *c* to *ç* before imperfect endings beginning with an *a* to maintain the soft *c* sound:

j'avançais	nous avancions
tu avançais	vous avanciez
il avançait	ils avançaient

Verbs Ending in *-ger*

Verbs ending in *-ger* add a silent *e* between *g* and imperfect endings beginning with an *a* to maintain the soft *g* sound:

je mangeais	nous mangions
tu mangeais	vous mangiez
il mangeait	ils mangeaient

Exercice 1

Describe the scene before a wedding by giving the correct form of the imperfect.

1. (s'amuser) Les enfants _____.

2. (être) Le marié _____ très nerveux.

3. (manger) Des filles _____ des hors-d'oeuvre.

4. (jouer) L'orchestre _____.

5. (danser) Tu _____.

6. (commencer) Tout le monde _____ à s'impatienter.

7. (garnir) Le chef _____ des plats.

8. (perdre) Le père de la mariée _____ patience.

9. (boire) Nous _____ de l'eau.

10. (vérifier) Vous _____ votre montre.

11. (se plaidre) Une petite fille _____ de rien.

12. (paraître) La mère du marié _____ heureuse.

Using the *Passé Composé* and the Imperfect

Determining whether to use the *passé composé* or the imperfect sometimes presents a challenge. In many instances, it's the intended meaning of the speaker that determines whether the action is viewed as completed in the past at a particular moment or if it was taking place for an indefinite period in the past with no determined beginning or end.

To eliminate any unnecessary confusion, visualize a camera. The *passé composé* represents an action that could be captured by a snapshot—the action happened and was completed and could be represented by a dot indicating a moment in time. The imperfect, on the other hand, represents an action that could be captured by a video camera—the action continued to flow and could be represented by a wavy line. From another point of view, the *passé composé* states an action that occurred, whereas the imperfect describes an action that was taking place.

The following lists provide a more detailed look at the differences between these two tenses.

The *passé composé* …

♦ Expresses specific actions or events that were started or completed at a definite time in the past (even if the time isn't mentioned):

Je suis sorti(e) hier soir.
I went out last night.

Elle a été contente de retourner en France.
She was happy to return to France.

♦ Expresses a specific action or event that occurred at a specific point in time:

Hier soir nous avons dîné dans un restaurant.
Last night we ate in a restaurant.

♦ Expresses a specific action or event that was repeated a stated number of time:

Il a vu ce film deux fois.
He saw that film two times.

♦ Expresses the beginning or end of a specific action:

Elles ont fini leurs devoirs à huit heures.
They finished their homework at eight o'clock.

♦ Expresses a series of completed events:

Je me suis levé, j'ai mangé, et je suis sorti.
I got up, I ate, and I went out.

The imperfect …

♦ Describes ongoing or continuous actions in the past (which might or might not have been completed):

Il travaillait avec son frère.
He was working with his brother.

Nous jouions au tennis.
We were playing tennis.

♦ Describes repeated or habitual actions that took place in the past:

Je me réveillais à six heures.
I used to wake up at six o'clock.

♦ Describes an action that continued for an unspecified period of time:

Elles voyageait souvent à l'étranger.
They often traveled abroad.

♦ Describes a person, place, thing, weather, time, day of the week, state of mind, and emotion:

Il faisait beau et les oiseaux chantaient.
The weather was nice and the birds were singing.

♦ The imperfect describes a situation that was going on in the past when another action or event, expressed by the *passé composé*, took place:

J'ouvrais la porte quand le téléphone a sonné.
I was opening the door when the phone rang.

♦ Describes simultaneous actions taking place at the same time:

Janine parlait pendant que Louis étudiait.
Janine was speaking while Louis was studying.

Attention!

Use the imperfect when "would" expresses "used to." When "would" states what the subject would do under certain conditions, use the conditional. (For details, see Chapter 7.)

Use the imperfect with the following verbs that express a state of mind in the past:

> aimer (to like, love)
>
> croire (to believe)
>
> désirer (to desire)
>
> espérer (to hope)
>
> être (to be)
>
> penser (to think)
>
> pouvoir (to be able to)
>
> préférer (to prefer)
>
> regretter (to regret, be sorry)
>
> savoir (to know [how])
>
> vouloir (to want)

Some words and expressions generally indicate a specific time period and require the use of the *passé composé*, whereas other words and expressions imply repetition or habitual action and require the use of the imperfect. Table 4.3 gives you valuable clues that will help you select the correct past tense to use.

Table 4.3   Clues for the Use of the *Passé Composé* and the Imperfect

Indicates the *Passé Composé*	Indicates the Imperfect
l'année passée (last year)	autrefois (formerly)
avant-hier (the day before yesterday)	chaque jour, semaine, mois, année (each [every] day, week, month, year)
d'abord (at first)	de temps à autre (from time to time)
enfin (finally, at last)	de temps en temps (from time to time)
ensuite (then, next)	d'habitude (usually)
l'été/l'hiver passé (last summer/winter)	d'ordinaire (usually, generally)
finalement (finally)	en ce temps-là (at that time)
une fois (one time)	en général (generally)
hier (yesterday)	fréquemment (frequently)
hier soir (last night)	généralement (generally)
l'autre jour (the other day)	habituellement (habitually)
ce jour-là (that day)	parfois (sometimes)
un jour (one day)	quelquefois (sometimes)

Indicates the *Passé Composé*	Indicates the Imperfect
le mois passé (dernier) (last month)	souvent (often)
la semaine passée (dernière) (last week)	toujours (always)
soudain (suddenly)	tous les jours (mois) (every day, month)
tout à (d'un) coup (suddenly)	tout le temps (all the time)

Exercice 2

Describe what the friends did by choosing the correct form of the verb in the *passé composé* or in the imperfect:

Ça (C') (a été, était) ___1___ une journée d'hiver et il (a fait, faisait) ___2___ très froid. Je (n'ai pas eu, n'avais pas) ___3___ grand'chose à faire. J' (ai été, étais) ___4___ en train de regarder un programme de télévision assez ennuyeux quand tout à coup j' (ai entendu, entendais) ___5___ sonner quelqu'un à la porte. Je (J') (ai couru, courais) ___6___ l'ouvrir. À ma grande surprise, je (j') (ai vu, voyais) ___7___ que ça (c') (a été, était) ___8___ mes amis Claire et Jean. Eux aussi, ils (se sont ennuyés, s'ennuyaient) ___9___ à la maison et ils (sont venus, venaient) ___10___ me demander si je (j') (ai voulu, voulais) ___11___ les accompagner au musée d'art moderne. Je (J') (ai trouvé, trouvais) ___12___ cette idée splendide car j' (ai eu, avais) ___13___ une composition à écrire pour ma classe d'art. Alors je (j') (ai éteint, éteignais) ___14___ la télévision, je (j') (ai mis, mettais) ___15___ mon manteau, et j' (ai écrit, écrivais) ___16___ une note à mes parents pour leur dire où je (j') (suis allé, allais) ___17___ et nous (sommes partis, partions) ___18___.

Exercice 3

Complete Jean's story by completing each sentence with the correct form of the *passé composé* or the imperfect:

Ça (c') (être) un ___1___ samedi du printemps et j' (avoir) ___2___ très envie de sortir. Malheureusement j' (être) ___3___ un peu enrhumé et ma mère m' (interdire) ___4___ de sortir. Je (j') (lire) ___5___ mes bandes dessinées quand tout d'un coup j' (entendre) ___6___ mes amis dans la rue. J' (ouvrir) ___7___ ma fenêre pour voir ce qui (se passer) ___8___. Tous les garçons (vouloir) ___9___ jouer au base-ball et ils (être) ___10___ en train de faire des équipes. Finalement, ils (se mettre) ___11___ à jouer. Richard (être) ___12___ le premier à frapper le ballon. Nicolas (essayer) ___13___ de l'attraper pendant que Richard (courir) ___14___ vers la premier base. Le soleil (briller) ____15____ très fort et Nicolas (ne pas pouvoir) ____16____ voir bien. Il (se cogner) ____17____ contre Richard qui (tomber) ____18____. Tout le monde (être) ____19____ très choqué, quand après deux minutes, Richard (ne pas se lever) ____20____ et il (commencer) ____21____ à pleurer. Qu'est-ce qui (arriver) ____22____? Apparemment Richard (se casser) ____23____ la jambe et ne (pouvoir) ____24____ pas se tenir droit. Tout le monde (crier) ____25____. Moi, je (j') (téléphoner) ____26____ à l'hôpital et une ambulance (arriver) ____27____ tout de suite après. Le pauvre Richard (ne plus aller) ____28____ jouer au base-ball ce printemps.

Exercice 4

Express what each person did by combining the two sentences and using the *passé composé* and the imperfect to replace the present.

Exemple:
Je reste chez moi. J'ai du travail à faire.
Je suis resté(e) chez moi parce que j'avais du travail à faire.

1. Nous tombons. Nous ne faisons pas attention.

   _____

2. Tu appelles Lise. Tu veux aller au cinéma.

   _____

3. Elle va chez le docteur. Elle a mal à la gorge.

   _____

4. Je sors mon parapluie. Il commence à pleuvoir.

   _____

5. Elles se réveillent tard. C'est dimanche.

   _____

6. Vous devenez nerveux. Vous changer de résidence.

   _____

Exercice 5

Describe the bad luck of these people by completing the sentences with the *passé composé* and the imperfect:

1. (conduire/avoir) Pierre _____ en ville quand il _____ un accident.

2. (se promener/piquer) Élise _____ dans le parc quand une abeille l' _____.

3. (tomber/courir) Mariane _____ quand elle _____ vers son ami.

4. (perdre/voyager) Les Chénier _____ leur passeport quand ils _____ en Europe.

5. (boire/voir) Je (j') _____ de l'eau quand je (j') _____ une mouche dans le verre.

6. (rester/ne pas pouvoir) Les filles _____ à la maison quand elles _____ trouver leurs clefs de la maison.

7. (prendre/aller) Vous _____ le mauvais bus quand vous _____ chez votre ami.

8. (être/s'éteindre) Nous _____ en train de travailler quand la lumière _____.

To express an event or action that began and continued in the past use *il y avait* + expression of time + *que* + the imperfect or *cela (ça) faisait* + expression of time + *que* + imperfect:

Combien de temps y avait-il que vous étudiiez?
Cela (Ça) faisait combien de temps que vous étudiiez?
How long had you been studying?

Il y avait deux heures que j'étudiais.
Cela (Ça) faisait deux heures que j'étudiais.
I'd been studying for two hours.

Exercice 6

Gisèle wants to know how long her friends had been doing certain things. Give her questions by using *Combien de temps y avait-il que …?* and the answers by using *Il y avait … que ….*

Exemple:
Georges/travailler/deux ans.
Combien de temps y avait-il que Georges travaillait?
Il y avait deux ans qu'il travaillait.

1. Hélène/aller à l'université/un an

   _____

   _____

2. François et Jacques/être amis/dix ans

   _____

   _____

3. Nous/jouer de la guitare/deux mois

   _____

   _____

4. Patrick/avoir sa propre voiture/une semaine

   _____

   _____

5. Tu/habiter aux États-Unis/cinq ans

   _____

   _____

6. Vous/suivre un régime/six jours

   _____

   _____

Forming and Using the Pluperfect

The pluperfect is a compound tense, which means that it is made up of more than one part. The following two elements are needed to form the pluperfect:

◆ The imperfect tense of the helping verb *avoir* (*avais, avais, avait, avions, aviez, avaient*), or *être* (*étais, étais, était, étions, étiez, étaient*), which expresses that something had already taken place

◆ The past participle of the verb, which expresses what the action was

The following figure shows how the pluperfect is formed.

Pluperfect of verb =   when + what   *Formation of the pluperfect.*
                        / \
Pluperfect of verb =   (what) had + happened
                        /   \
Pluperfect of verb =   helping verb + main verb
                      /   \
Pluperfect of verb = *avoir* (to have) + past participle
                    être (to be)

The formula for the formation of the pluperfect is as follows:

subject noun or pronoun + *avoir* (*être*) in imperfect + past participle

The formation of past participles is explained in Chapter 1. Irregular past participles are listed in Table 1.3 and in Appendix F.

Note the following about the use of the pluperfect:

◆ The pluperfect describes an action or event that was completed in the past before another action took place and is usually expressed by the English "had" + past participle.

Il y avait réfléchi avant de donner sa réponse.
He had thought about it before giving his response.

◆ Because the pluperfect is used in relation to another past action, that action is usually in the *passé composé* or the imperfect.

Quand le professeur est arrivé les élèves s'étaient déjà assis.
When the teacher arrived, the students had already sat down.

Quand il allait en France, sa famille avait déjà fait des projets pour lui.
When he would go to France, his family had already made plans for him.

◆ When using the pluperfect, it is not always necessary to have the other past action expressed:

Il avait trouvé son cahier dans son bureau.
He had found his notebook in his desk.

Exercice 7

Give reasons for the situations that ensued by using the pluperfect.

Exemple:
Charles était triste. (perdre son argent de poche)
Il avait perdu son argent de poche.

1. Nous pleurions. (recevoir de mauvaises notes)

   _____

2. Christine était fatiguée. (s'endormir tard hier soir)

   _____

3. Tu gagnais beaucoup d'argent. (devenir médecin)

   _____

4. Les filles se plaignaient. (avoir la mauvaise chance)

   _____

5. Tu t'ennuyais. (rester à la maison)

   _____

6. Vous suffriez. (se casser le bras)

   _____

Récapitulation

1. The imperfect of regular verbs is formed by dropping the *-ons* ending from the *nous* form of the present tense and adding *-ais, -ais, -ait, -ions, -iez, -aient.*

2. The imperfect of irregular verbs is formed in the same manner.

3. The only verb with an irregular imperfect stem is *être: ét-* + imperfect endings.

4. Reflexive verbs form the imperfect in the same manner but retain their reflexive pronoun before the conjugated verb.

5. Only two categories of verbs with spelling changes have irregularities in the imperfect: *-cer* verbs change *c* to *ç*, and *-ger* verbs add *e* before all imperfect endings beginning with *a* (*je, tu, il, ils* forms).

6. The *passé composé* expresses a completed past action.

7. The imperfect describes an incomplete or habitual past action. The imperfect also expresses time of day, weather, states of mind, and emotions in the past.

8. The imperfect describes a situation that was going on in the past when another action or event, expressed by the *passé composé*, took place.

9. To express an event or action that began in the past and continued in the past, use *il y avait* + time + *que* or *cela (ça) faisait* + time + *que*.

10. The pluperfect expresses what had occurred, and it is formed by conjugating *avoir* or *être* in the imperfect tense and adding a past participle (which remains the same for all subject pronouns).

The Least You Need to Know

◆ The imperfect endings for regular verbs are *-ais, -ais, -ait, -ions, -iez, -aient*.

◆ The only verb that has an irregular stem in the imperfect is *être*.

◆ The imperfect describes a continuous past action, whereas the *passé composé* expresses a completed past action.

◆ The pluperfect is formed by taking the imperfect of *avoir* or *être* and adding a past participle.

5

The *Passé Simple* and the *Passé Antérieur*

In This Chapter

- ◆ Forming the *passé simple* of regular and reflexive verbs
- ◆ Forming the *passé simple* of verbs with spelling changes
- ◆ Forming the *passé simple* of irregular verbs
- ◆ Forming and using the *passé antérieur*

In French, actions or events that took place in the past may be expressed using the *passé simple*, known as the simple past or the past definite. Like the *passé composé*, the *passé simple* is used to convey a completed past action. The difference between the two tenses is that the *passé composé* is used primarily in conversation and informal writing, whereas the *passé simple* is used mainly in formal, literary, and historical writings. Because the *passé simple* is not used when speaking, it should be learned only for purposes of recognition and identification in readings.

The *passé antérieur* is the compound equivalent of the *passé simple* and is used after conjunctions of time to denote that an action was completed before another action, expressed in the *passé simple*, took place. The *passé antérieur* is used in formal writings and narratives and should also only be learned for purposes of recognition.

The *Passé Simple* of Regular and Reflexive Verbs

The *passé simple* of regular verbs is formed by dropping the *-er, -ir,* or *-re* infinitive ending and by adding the endings shown in Table 5.1.

Table 5.1 The *Passé Simple* of Regular Verbs

	-er verbs	*-ir* verbs	*-re* verbs
	marcher (to walk)	bâtir (to build)	défendre (to defend)
Je	march**ai**	bât**is**	défend**is**
Tu	march**as**	bât**is**	défend**is**
Il, Elle, On	march**a**	bât**it**	défend**it**
Nous	march**âmes**	bât**îmes**	défend**îmes**
Vous	march**âtes**	bât**îtes**	defend**îtes**
Ils, Elles	march**èrent**	bât**irent**	défend**irent**

The only difference in the formation of the *passé simple* of reflexive verbs is that the reflexive pronoun must be used before the verb:

> En 1940 Charles de Gaulle se réfugia en Angleterre.
> *In 1940 Charles de Gaulle took refuge in England.*

You should now be able to recognize regular and reflexive verbs in the *passé simple* and understand their meaning when you see them.

The *Passé Simple* of Verbs with Spelling Changes

Verbs ending in *-cer* and *-ger* are the only verbs with spelling changes that require a change in the *passé simple*.

Verbs Ending in *-cer*

Verbs ending in *-cer* change *c* to *ç* before *passé simple* endings beginning with an *a* to maintain the soft *c* sound:

j'annonçai	nous annonçâmes
tu annonças	vous annonçâtes
il annonça	ils annoncèrent

Verbs Ending in -*ger*

Verbs ending in -*ger* add a silent *e* between *g* and *passé simple* endings beginning with an *a* to maintain the soft *g* sound:

je chang**e**ai	nous changeâmes
tu changeas	vous changeâtes
il changea	ils changèrent

Exercice 1

Give the meaning for each verb in the *passé simple* that provides a fact about French history.

1. La conquête romaine <u>donna</u> à la Gaule la paix et la sécurité.

2. Clovis, roi des Francs, <u>se convertit</u> au christianisme, la religion officielle du pays.

3. On <u>trahit</u> Jeanne d'Arc et la <u>brûla</u> vive à Rouen.

4. François I^e <u>encouragea</u> l'exploration.

5. Le Cardinal Richelieu <u>améliora</u> la vie économique de la France et <u>réforma</u> les finances et la législation.

6. Pendant le règne de Louis XV, la France <u>perdit</u> le Canada.

7. Napoléon Bonaparte <u>exerça</u> sur son temps une grande influence. Il <u>essaya</u> de conquérir l'Europe. Quand les ennemis de la France <u>envahirent</u> le pays, il <u>se retira</u> à Elbe.

8. La Grande Guerre entre la France et l'Allemagne <u>éclata</u> en 1914.

The *Passé Simple* of Irregular Verbs

All verbs that are irregular in the *passé simple* add the following endings to their stems.

je	-*s*	nous	-*̂mes*
tu	-*s*	vous	-*̂tes*
il, elle, on	-*t*	ils, elles	-*rent*

The stem of irregular verbs in the *passé simple* is generally easy to remember because it resembles or is exactly the same as the past participle used for the *passé composé*, as shown in Table 5.2.

CAUTION

Attention!

The circumflex accent (ˆ) is placed above the vowel of the stem: *i* or *u*. In rare cases, the vowel does not immediately precede the ending: *nous vînmes* (we came); *vous fîntes* (you held).

Table 5.2 The *Passé Simple* of Irregular Present Tense Verbs

Infinitive	Stem for *Passé Simple*
aller (to go)	all-
avoir (to have)	eu-
battre (to beat)	batti-
boire (to drink)	bu-
conduire (to drive)	conduisi-
connaître (to know)	connu-
courir (to run)	couru-
craindre (to fear)	craigni-
croire (to believe)	cru-
cueillir (to pick)	cueilli-
devoir (to have to)	du-
dire (to say, tell)	di-
distraire (to distract)	not applicable
dormir (to sleep)	dormi-
écrire (to write)	écrivi-
être (to be)	fu-
faire (to make, do)	fi-
falloir (to be necessary)	il fallut
fuir (to flee)	fui-
joindre (to join)	joigni-
lire (to read)	lu-
mettre (to put)	mi-
mourir (to die)	mouru-
naître (to be born)	naqui-

Infinitive	Stem for *Passé Simple*
offrir (to offer)	offri-
ouvrir (to open)	ouvri-
paraître (to seem)	paru-
partir (to leave)	parti-
pouvoir (to be able to)	pu-
plaindre (to pity)	plaigni-
plaire (to please)	plu-
pleuvoir (to rain)	il plut
prendre (to take)	pri-
recevoir (to receive)	reçu-
résoudre (to resolve)	résolu-
savoir (to know)	su-
sentir (to feel)	senti-
servir (to serve)	servi-
sortir (to go out)	sorti-
suivre (to follow)	suivi-
vaincre (to defeat)	vainqui-
valoir (to be worth)	valu-
venir (to come)	vin-
vivre (to live)	vécu-
voir (to see)	vi-
vouloir (to wish, want)	voulu-

Because you will not be using the *passé simple* conversationally, and because you will only need to recognize that it expresses a completed past action, see how well you can understand the verbs in the following exercise.

Exercice 2

Give the meaning for each verb in the *passé simple* that gives a fact about French culture.

1. Louis David <u>peignit</u> avec précision des scènes de l'histoire grecque.

2. Dominique Ingres, élève de David, <u>devint</u> le champion de la peinture académique.

3. Édouard Manet <u>fut</u> un des fondateurs de l'école impressioniste.

4. Paul Gauguin <u>partit</u> pour Tahiti pour continuer sa carrière de peintre.

5. Henri de Toulouse-Lautrec <u>fit</u> des affiches des scènes de music-hall.

6. Jean-Baptiste Lully <u>écrivit</u> de la musique pour plusieurs comédies de Molière.

7. Sous le règne de Louis XIV l'opéra <u>prit</u> naissance.

8. Jean de la Fontaine, fabuliste français, <u>naquit</u> en 1621 et <u>mourut</u> en 1695.

9. Sully Prudhomme, un poète, <u>reçut</u> le premier prix Nobel de littérature en 1901.

10. Jean-Paul Sartre <u>eut</u> une grande influence sur les autres existentialistes.

Forming and Using the *Passé Antérieur*

The *passé antérieur* is a compound tense, which means that it is made up of more than one part. The following two elements are needed to form the *passé antérieur*:

♦ The *passé simple* of the helping verb *avoir* (*eus, eus, eut, eûmes, eûtes, eurent*) or *être* (*fus, fus, fut, fûmes, fûtes, furent*), which expresses that something had taken place

♦ The past participle of the verb, which expresses what the action was

The following figure shows how the *passé antérieur* is formed:

Formation of the passé antérieur.

Passé antérieur of verb =   when + what
/   \

Passé antérieur of verb =   (what) had + happened
/   \

Passé antérieur of verb = helping verb + main verb
/   \

Passé antérieur of verb = *avoir* (to have) + past participle
être (to be)

The formula for the formation of the *passé antérieur* is as follows:

subject noun or pronoun + *avoir* (*être*) in *passé simple* + past participle

I already explained the formation of past participles in Chapter 1. Irregular past participles are listed in Table 1.3 and in Appendix H.

Note the following about the use of the *passé antérieur:*

◆ The *passé antérieur* is used mainly in literary and historical writings to show that an action or event was completed before another action (in the *passé simple*) took place.

Dès qu'ils eurent dîné, ils rentrèrent.
As soon as they had dined, they went home.

◆ The *passé antérieur* generally follows expressions such as these:

quand (*when*)
lorsque (*when*)
après que (*after*)
dès que (*as soon as*)
aussitôt que (*as soon as*)

Quand elle eut entendu les nouvelles, elle pleura.
When she had heard the news, she cried.

◆ In conversation and informal writing, the *passé antérieur* is replaced by the pluperfect or the *passé composé.*

Exercice 3

Express what happened by giving the meaning for each verb in the *passé simple* and the *passé antérieur.*

1. Quand nous <u>eûmes ouvert</u> la porte, le vendeur nous <u>salua</u>.

2. Dès que le garçon <u>eut dit</u> le mensonge, il le <u>regretta</u>.

3. Après que je lui <u>eus écrit</u> une lettre, je le <u>détruisis</u>.

4. Aussitôt que tu te <u>fus réveillé</u>, tu <u>téléphonea</u> à ton ami.

5. Lorsque vous <u>fûtes arrivé</u> à maison, vous <u>mangeâtes</u>.

6. Après que ses parents <u>furent rentrés</u>, elle <u>sortit</u>.

Récapitulation

1. The *passé simple* of regular *-er* verbs is formed by dropping the infinitive ending and adding *-ai, -as, -a, -âmes, -âtes, -èrent.*

2. The *passé simple* of regular *-ir* and *-re* verbs is formed by dropping the infinitive ending and adding *-is, -is, -it, -îmes, -îtes, -irent.*

3. In the *passé simple*, the reflexive pronoun precedes the conjugated verb.

4. In the *passé simple*, verbs ending in *-cer* change *c* to *ç* before *passé simple* endings beginning with an *a* to maintain the soft *c* sound.

5. In the *passé simple*, verbs ending in *-ger* add a silent *e* between *g* and *passé simple* endings beginning with an *a* to maintain the soft *g* sound.

6. Verbs irregular in the *passé simple* have the following endings: *-s, -s, -t, -ˆmes, -ˆtes,* and *-rent* (where the circumflex accent is placed on the vowel preceding the ending).

7. In many cases the stem of the *passé simple* of an irregular verb is similar or identical to the past participle of that verb.

8. The *passé simple* is used to express a completed past action and is used in literary, formal, and historical writings. It is not used conversationally.

9. The *passé antérieur* expresses what had occurred and is formed by conjugating *avoir* (*être*) in the *passé simple* and adding a past participle (which remains the same for all subject pronouns).

10. The *passé simple* is found only in formal literary and historical writing and is used after the expressions *quand, lorsque, après que, dès que,* and *aussitôt que.*

The Least You Need to Know

- The *passé simple* endings of regular *-er* verbs are *-ai, -as, -a, -âmes, -âtes, -èrent.*

- The *passé simple* endings of regular *-ir* and *-re* verbs are *-is, -is, -it, -îmes, -îtes, -irent.*

- *-cer* and *-ger* spelling-change verbs require changes in the *passé simple.*

- The stem for the *passé simple* of many irregular verbs is similar to or identical to the past participle of that verb.

- The *passé antérieur* is formed by taking the *passé simple* of *avoir* (*être*) and adding a past participle.

Chapter **6**

The Future and the Future Perfect

In This Chapter

◆ Using the present to express the future

◆ Using *aller* + infinitive to express the future

◆ Forming and using the future

◆ Forming and using the future perfect

In French, there are three ways to express the simple future: by using the present (as explained in Chapter 3), by using the irregular verb *aller* + an infinitive to say what the subject is *going to do* or what is *going to happen* soon, and by using the future tense to say what the subject *will do* or what *will happen* at a later date.

The future perfect is the compound equivalent of the future, and it is used to express what the subject will have done or what will have happened before another future action will have occurred. In this chapter, you'll learn when to use the "near future" or the future tense, and when to use the future perfect.

Using the Present to Express the Future

The present tense is often used to express the future when the subject is asking for instructions or is referring to an action that will take place in the immediate future:

J'y vais maintenant?   Je te rappelle dans une heure.
Shall I go there now?   *I'll call you back in an hour.*

Using *aller* + Infinitive to Express the Future

The irregular verb *aller* (to go) is used to express what is going to happen:

je vais	nous allons
tu vas	vous allez
il, elle, on va	ils, elles vont

Aller is followed by the infinitive of the verb expressing the action that the speaker is going to perform. Any negatives surround the conjugated form of *aller:*

Je vais sortir.   Nous n'allons pas étudier.
I'm going to go out.   *We aren't going to study.*

Exercice 1

Express what the different people are going to do during their free time by using *aller* + *a* + infinitive:

1. je/écouter des CD _____

2. nous/regarder la télévision _____

3. elle/lire _____

4. vous/aller en ville _____

5. tu/surfer l'Internet _____

6. ils/jouer à des jeux vidéo _____

The Future of Regular and Reflexive Verbs

The future tense in French is rather easy because all verbs, whether they have regular or irregular stems, have the same endings. All stems end in *-r* or *-rr*.

> **Attention!**
>
> For regular verbs ending in *-re,* drop the final *-e* from the infinitive for all forms of the future before adding the endings: for example, *j'attendrai* (I will wait); *nous attendrons* (we will wait).

Forming the Future of Regular Verbs

To form the future of regular verbs, add the future endings in Table 6.1 to the infinitive (the "to" form) of the verb.

Table 6.1   The Future of Regular Verbs

	-er verbs	*-ir* verbs	*-re* verbs
	parler (*to speak*)	obéir (*to obey*)	vendre (*to sell*)
Je (J')	parlerai	obéirai	vendrai
Tu	parleras	obéiras	vendras
Il, Elle, On	parlera	obéira	vendra
Nous	parlerons	obéirons	vendrons
Vous	parlerez	obéirez	vendrez
Ils, Elles	parleront	obéiront	vendront

The only difference in the formation of the future of reflexive verbs is that the reflexive pronoun must be used before the verb:

Je me coucherai de bonne heure ce soir.
I'm going to go to bed early tonight.

> **Regarde!**
>
> The future endings (*ai, as, a, -ons, -vez, ont*) resemble the present tense conjugation of *avoir* except for the *nous* and *vous* forms (where *av* must be dropped).

The Future of Verbs with Spelling Changes

Verbs ending in -*yer* and -*e* + consonant + *er* are the only verbs with spelling changes that require a change in the future.

Verbs Ending in -*yer*

Verbs ending in -*yer* change *y* to *i* for every form of the future:

j'emploierai	nous emploierons
tu emploieras	vous emploierez
il emploiera	ils emploieront

For verbs ending in -*ayer*, you have the option of changing the *y* to *i* or retaining the *y* in all forms:

j'essaierai *or* j'essayerai (I will try)

nous essaierons *or* nous essayerons (we will try)

Verbs ending in -*e* + Consonant + *er*

Verbs ending in -*e* + consonant + *er* change silent *e* to *è* or instead, where necessary, double the consonant before the infinitive ending in every form of the future (see Appendix B):

j'achèterai	j'appellerai
tu achèteras	tu appelleras
il achètera	il appellera
nous achèterons	nous appellerons
vous achèterez	vous appellerez
ils achèteront	ils appelleront

The verb *envoyer* (and its compound *renvoyer* [to send back]) has an irregular future stem: *enverr:*

j'enverrai (I will send)

nous renverrons (we will send back)

Exercice 2

Express what each person will do to complete his or her chores.

1. (jeter) Nous _____ les ordures.
2. (sortir) Alice _____ les poubelles.
3. (nettoyer) Je _____ la maison.
4. (ranger) Lucien et Paul _____ les chambres.
5. (promener) Tu _____ le chien.
6. (payer) Vous _____ les factures.
7. (tondre) Étienne _____ la pelouse.
8. (nourir) Anne et Charline _____ le chat.

The Future of Irregular Verbs

Most verbs that are irregular in the present are also irregular in the future and are shone in boldface. Some verbs that are irregular in the present have regular future forms, as shown in Table 6.2.

Table 6.2   The Future of Irregular Present Tense Verbs

Infinitive	Stem for Future
aller (to go)	**ir-**
asseoir (to seat)	**assiér-** or **assoir-**
avoir (to have)	**aur-**
battre (to beat)	battr-
boire (to drink)	boir-
conduire (to drive)	conduir-
connaître (to know)	connaîtr-
courir (to run)	**courr-**
craindre (to fear)	craindr-
croire (to believe)	croir-
cueillir (to pick)	**cueiller-**
devoir (to have to)	**devr-**

continues

Table 6.2   The Future of Irregular Present Tense Verbs   (continued)

Infinitive	Stem for Future
dire (to say, tell)	dir-
distraire (to distract)	distrair-
dormir (to sleep)	dormir-
écrire (to write)	écrir-
envoyer (to send)	**enverr-**
être (to be)	**ser-**
faire (to make, do)	**fer-**
falloir (to be necessary)	**il faudra**
fuir (to flee)	fuir-
joindre (to join)	joindr-
lire (to read)	lir-
mettre (to put)	mettr-
mourir (to die)	**mourr-**
naître (to be born)	naîtr-
offrir (to offer)	offrir-
ouvrir (to open)	ouvrir-
paraître (to seem)	paraîtr-
partir (to leave)	partir-
pouvoir (to be able to)	**pourr-**
plaindre (to pity)	plaindr-
plaire (to please)	plair-
pleuvoir (to rain)	**il pleuvra**
prendre (to take)	prendr-
recevoir (to receive)	**recevr-**
résoudre (to resolve)	résoudr-
savoir (to know)	**saur-**
sentir (to feel)	sentir-
servir (to serve)	servir-
sortir (to go out)	sortir-
suivre (to follow)	suivr-
vaincre (to defeat)	vaincr-
valoir (to be worth)	**vaudr-**
venir (to come)	**viendr-**
vivre (to live)	vivr-
voir (to see)	**verr-**
vouloir (to wish, want)	**voudr-**

Exercice 3

Complete the message left on your answering machine by filling in the correct form of the verb in the future.

Salut Christine! Ici Yvette. Je te (dire) ____1____ mes projets pour demain soir. J' (aller) ____2____ dîner au restaurant La Coquille. Je sais que ta famille et toi (vouloir) ____3____ m'y accompagner. Je (pouvoir) ____4____ passer chez toi à sept heures. Ce (être) ____5____ une bonne idée d'être tous prêts à l'avance. En route chez toi je (devoir) ____6____ m'arrêter à la pharmacie où je (faire) ____7____ des achats nécessaires. Ne t'inquiète pas! Je (venir) ____8____ chez toi bien à l'avance. (savoir) ____9____ -vous comment aller au restaurant de ta maison? Il (valoir) ____10____ la peine y arriver à l'heure parce qu'il y (avoir) ____11____ sans doute beaucoup de monde à cette heure. Je t' (envoyer) ____12____ un message par courrier électronique s'il y a des problèmes. À demain.

Using the Future

The future is used in French to express future time—what *will happen.*

> Nous voyagerons pendant l'été.
> *We will travel during the summer.*

The future is used after *quand* (when), *lorsque* (when), *dès que* (as soon as), *aussitôt que* (as soon as), *après que* (after), *tant que* (while) and *pendant que* (while) when the future is implied, even though the present may be used in English.

> Je te téléphonerai quand j'aurai le temps.
> *I'll call you when I have the time.*

> Pendant que maman se reposera papa préparera le dîner.
> *While mom is resting dad will prepare the dinner.*

Exercice 4

Express what Claudine will do when she visits her friend for the weekend.

1. Tant que tu (être) _____ occupée, je (se promener) _____.

2. Dès que je (venir) _____ chez toi, je (pouvoir) _____ t'aider avec tes devoirs.

3. Lorsque nous (aller) _____ au centre commercial j' (acheter) _____ de nouveaux vêtements.

4. Aussitôt que j' (arriver) _____ chez toi, j' (envoyer) _____ un message par courrier électronique à mes parents.

5. Quand il (pleuvoir) _____ nous (s'ennuyer) _____.

6. Pendant que tu (recevoir) _____ des coups de téléphone de tes amis, je (faire) _____ un sandwich.

Forming and Using the Future Perfect

The future perfect is a compound tense, which means that it is made up of more than one part. The following two elements are needed to form the future perfect:

♦ The future tense of the helping verb *avoir* (*aurai, auras, aura, aurons, aurez, auront*) or *être* (*serai, seras, sera, serons, serez, seront*), which expresses that something will have taken place

♦ The past participle of the verb, which expresses what the action was.

The following figure shows how the future perfect is formed:

Formation of the future perfect.

Future perfect of verb =   when + what
                                /   \
Future perfect of verb = (what) will have + happened
                              /   \
Future perfect of verb = helping verb + main verb
                            /   \
Future perfect of verb = *avoir* (to have) + past participle
                          être (to be)

The formula for the formation of the future perfect is as follows:

subject noun or pronoun + *avoir* (*être*) in future + past participle

The formation of past participles was explained in Chapter 1. Irregular past participles appear in Table 1.3 and in Appendix H.

Note the following about the future perfect tense:

♦ The future perfect expresses an action or event that will have taken place or will have been completed before another future action takes place:

J'aurai fini mon travail avant minuit.
I will have finished my work before midnight.

♦ The future perfect may be used to express probability, supposition, or conjecture in the past:

Il a fait une faute. Il aura mal compris.
He made a mistake. He must have (probably) misunderstood.

Il sera arrivé quelque chose.
Something must have (probably) happened.

♦ The future perfect is often used after *quand* (when), *lorsque* (when), *dès que* (as soon as), *aussitôt que* (as soon as), *après que* (after), *tant que* (while) and *pendant que* (while) when the future is implied, no matter what the English translation:

Aussitôt qu'il aura mangé, il sortira.
As soon as he has eaten (will have eaten), he will go out.

CAUTION   **Attention!** _____

Be careful to distinguish between "will" used to form the future and the verb "will" expressing a willingness to do something, requiring the verb *vouloir*.

M'aiderez-vous?
Will you (are you going to) help me?
Voulez-vous m'aider?
Will you (are your willing to) help me?
"Will you have," meaning "do you wish" is translated as *voulez-vous*.
Voulez-vous du café?
Will you have some coffee?

Exercice 5

Express what the following people will have done before 9 P.M.

1. (se coucher) Nous _____.

2. (dîner) Ils _____.

3. (rentrer) Je _____.

4. (se déshabiller) Christine _____.

5. (monter) Tu _____ à ta chambre.

6. (faire) Vous _____ des exercices.

Récapitulation

1. The future of regular verbs is formed by keeping the infinitive ending and adding the future endings -*ai*, -*as*, -*a*, -*ons*, -*ez*, -*ont*.

2. Verbs with -*yer* spelling changes change *y* to *i* in all forms of the future.

3. Verbs with *e* + consonant + *er* spelling changes change *e* to *è* or double their final consonant in all forms of the future.

4. All verbs that are irregular in the future have stems that end in -*r* or -*rr* and have the same endings as verbs that are regular in the future.

5. The future perfect expresses what will have occurred and is formed by conjugating *avoir* (*être*) in the future tense and adding a past participle (which remains the same for all subject pronouns).

6. The future and the future perfect are used after *quand* (when), *lorsque* (when), *dès que* (as soon as), *aussitôt que* (as soon as), *après que (after)*, *tant que* (while) and *pendant que* (while) when the future is implied, no matter what the English translation.

The Least You Need to Know

◆ The future endings -*ai*, -*as*, -*a*, -*ons*, -*ez*, -*ont* are added to the verb infinitive or to a special irregular stem.

◆ To form the future perfect, take the future of *avoir* (*être*) and add the past participle.

◆ The future and the future perfect are used after *quand*, *lorsque*, *dès que*, *aussitôt que*, *après que (after)*, *tant que*, and *pendant que* when the future is implied.

Chapter 7

The Conditional and the Conditional Perfect

In This Chapter

- ◆ Forming the conditional of regular, irregular, and reflexive verbs
- ◆ Forming the conditional of verbs with spelling changes
- ◆ Forming and using the conditional perfect
- ◆ Using conditional sentences

In French, the conditional is a mood that is generally used in the same way it is used in English: to express what *would* happen under certain circumstances. Beware of confusing the conditional with the future, whose stem it borrows; or with the imperfect, whose endings it uses.

The conditional perfect is the compound equivalent of the conditional, and it is used to express what the subject would have done or what would have happened in particular situations in the past.

Conditional sentences are used to describe real conditions and contrary-to-fact conditions. In this chapter, you'll learn how to form and use the conditional and the conditional perfect and what tenses to use in conditional sentences.

The Conditional of Regular and Reflexive Verbs

When you've mastered the future and the conditional, you'll find that the conditional mood in French is relatively simple to form because it combines the two. The stem of the conditional is the exact same stem that was used to form the future, so all verbs—regular, irregular, and those with spelling changes—will start in the same way for the conditional as they did for the future. The endings for the conditional are the exact same endings that were used for the imperfect, and all verbs have the same endings.

Définitions

The mood of a verb (also known as the mode) indicates the manner in which the action or state is conceived. The conditional mood expresses what would happen if certain circumstances prevailed. The tense of the verb tells when the action takes/took place: past, present, future.

Forming the Conditional of Regular Verbs

To form the conditional of regular verbs, add the conditional endings in Table 7.1 to the infinitive (the "to" form) of the verb.

Table 7.1   The Conditional of Regular Verbs

	-er Verbs parler (*to speak*)	*-ir* Verbs obéir (*to obey*)	*-ir* Verbs vendre (*to sell*)
Je (J')	parler**ais**	obéir**ais**	vendr**ais**
Tu	parler**ais**	obéir**ais**	vendr**ais**
Il, Elle, On	parler**ait**	obéir**ait**	vendr**ait**
Nous	parler**ions**	obéir**ions**	vendr**ions**
Vous	parler**iez**	obéir**iez**	vendr**iez**
Ils, Elles	parler**aient**	obéir**aient**	vendr**aient**

The only difference in the formation of the conditional of reflexive verbs is that the reflexive pronoun must be used before the verb:

Si j'avais le temps, je m'amuserais à faire du sport.
If I had the time, I would enjoy myself by playing sports.

The Conditional of Verbs with Spelling Changes

Verbs ending in -yer and -e + consonant + er are the only verbs with spelling changes that require a change in the future.

Verbs Ending in -yer

Verbs ending in -yer change y to i for every form of the future:

j'emploierais	nous emploierions
tu emploierais	vous emploieriez
il emploierait	ils emploieraient

Attention!

For verbs ending in -ayer, you have the option of changing the y to i or retaining the y in all forms: for example, j'essaierais or j'essayerais (I would try); nous essaierions or nous essayerions (we would try).

Verbs Ending in -e + Consonant + er

Verbs ending in -e + consonant + er change silent e to è or instead, where necessary, double the consonant before the infinitive ending in every form of the future (see Appendix B):

j'achèterais	j'appellerais
tu achèterais	tu appellerais
il achèterait	il appellerait
nous achèterons	nous appellerions
vous achèteriez	vous appelleriez
ils achèteraient	ils appelleraient

Attention!

The verb envoyer and its compound renvoyer (to send back) has an irregular stem: enverr—j'enverrais (I would send); nous renverrions (we would send back).

Exercice 1

Express what each of these people would do if they had the time:

1. (s'occuper) Nous _____ du ménage.

2. (renouveler) Je _____ ma garde-robe.

3. (finir) Tu _____ ton travail.

4. (correspondre) Ils _____ avec leurs anciens amis.

5. (nettoyer) Elle _____ la maison.

6. (emmener) Vous _____ votre frère au cinéma.

7. (ranger) Les filles _____ leurs affaires.

8. (s'acheter) Pascal _____ une nouvelle montre.

The Conditional of Irregular Verbs

Most verbs that are irregular in the present are also irregular in the conditional and are shone in boldface. Some verbs that are irregular in the present have regular conditional forms, as shown in Table 7.2.

Table 7.2   The Future of Irregular Present Tense Verbs

Infinitive	Stem for Future
aller (to go)	**ir-**
asseoir (to seat)	**assiér-** or **assoir-**
avoir (to have)	**aur-**
battre (to beat)	battr-
boire (to drink)	boir-
conduire (to drive)	conduir-
connaître (to know)	connaîtr-
courir (to run)	**courr-**
craindre (to fear)	craindr-
croire (to believe)	croir-
cueillir (to pick)	**cueiller-**
devoir (to have to)	**devr-**
dire (to say, tell)	dir-
distraire (to distract)	distrair-
dormir (to sleep)	dormir-
écrire (to write)	écrir-
envoyer (to send)	**enverr-**
être (to be)	**ser-**
faire (to make, do)	**fer-**
falloir (to be necessary)	**il faudra**
fuir (to flee)	fuir-
joindre (to join)	joindr-

Infinitive	Stem for Future
lire (to read)	lir-
mettre (to put)	mettr-
mourir (to die)	**mourr-**
naître (to be born)	naîtr-
offrir (to offer)	offrir-
ouvrir (to open)	ouvrir-
paraître (to seem)	paraîtr-
partir (to leave)	partir-
pouvoir (to be able to)	**pourr-**
plaindre (to pity)	plaindr-
plaire (to please)	plair-
pleuvoir (to rain)	**il pleuvra**
prendre (to take)	prendr-
recevoir (to receive)	**recevr-**
résoudre (to resolve)	résoudr-
savoir (to know)	**saur-**
sentir (to feel)	sentir-
servir (to serve)	servir-
sortir (to go out)	sortir-
suivre (to follow)	suivr-
vaincre (to defeat)	vaincr-
valoir (to be worth)	**vaudr-**
venir (to come)	**viendr-**
vivre (to live)	vivr-
voir (to see)	**verr-**
vouloir (to wish, want)	**voudr-**

Exercice 2

Express what might happen if there were a blackout:

1. les employés/ne pas venir au bureau _____

2. il/valoir mieux rester à la maison _____

3. nous/avoir peur _____

4. vous/ne pas aller à l'école _____

5. je/devoir aider mes parents _____

6. Carine/ne pas pouvoir envoyer son courrier électronique _____

7. tout le monde/savoir rester calme _____

8. tu/s'inquiéter _____

Using the Conditional

The conditional is used in French to express an action or event that would happen if certain circumstances existed:

S'il faisait beau j'irais au bord de la mer.
If the weather were nice I would go to the seashore.

Attention! _____

When *would* means *used to*, the imperfect is used in French: *Je faisais du vélo le dimanche.* (I would/used to go bike riding on Sundays.) When *would* means *to be willing* (to want), *vouloir* is used in the *passé composé* or the imperfect: *Je n'ai pas voulu sortir à huit heures.* (I wasn't willing [wouldn't] go out at 8 o'clock.) *Je ne voulais pas sortir.* (I wasn't willing [wouldn't] go out.)

The conditional may be used to express an action that will take place in the future from a view in the past.

Elle m'a rassuré qu'elle viendrait de bonne heure.
She reassured me that she would come early.

Elle savait qu'il mentirait.
She knew he would lie.

Attention! _____

When *could* means *was able to*, the *passé composé* or the imperfect of *pouvoir* is used: *Il a pu réparer la voiture.* (He could [was able to] repair the car.) *Elle ne pouvait pas venir.* (She couldn't [wasn't able to] come.)

The conditional is used to make a request or a demand more polite.

Je voudrais vous voir.
I would like to see you.

Pourriez-vous m'aider?
Could you help me?

Elle aimerait te parler.
She would like to speak to you.

Exercice 3

Express what these people would do if they were retired:

1. (faire) Je _____ le tour du monde.

2. (s'acheter) Tu _____ un château au Midi de la France.

3. (voyager) Nous _____ à travers les États-Unis.

4. (aller) Vous _____ souvent aux pays francophones.

5. (dormir) Il _____ jusqu'à midi tous les jours.

6. (s'amuser) Elles _____ tous les jours.

Forming and Using the Past Conditional

The conditional perfect is a compound tense, which means that it is made up of more than one part. The following two elements are needed to form the conditional perfect:

1. The conditional tense of the helping verb *avoir* (*aurais, aurais, aurait, aurions, auriez, auraient*) or *être* (*serais, serais, serait, serions, seriez, seraient*), which expresses that something will have taken place

2. The past participle of the verb, which expresses what the action was

The following figure shows how the past conditional is formed:

Past conditional of verb =   when + what

                      /   \

Formation of the past conditional.

Past conditional of verb = (what) would have + happened

                     /   \

Past conditional of verb =   helping verb + main verb

                   /   \

Past conditional of verb = *avoir* (to have) + past participle

                  être (to be)

The formula for the formation of the past conditional is as follows:

subject noun or pronoun + *avoir* (*être*) in conditional + past participle

The formation of past participles was explained in Chapter 1. Irregular past participles are listed in Table 1.3 and in Appendix F.

Note the following about the past conditional tense:

♦ The past conditional expresses an action or event that would have taken place or been completed in the past had something else occurred:

Je les aurais avertis si j'avais su les conséquences.
I would have warned them had I known the consequences.

Je l'aurais salué mais je ne l'ai pas reconnu.
I would have greeted him but I didn't recognize him.

♦ The past conditional may be used to express a possibility or an eventuality:

Elle aurait été heureuse de savoir cela.
She would have been happy to know that.

Exercice 4

Express what the following people would have done had they had the money:

1. (faire) Ils _____ un safari.

2. (s'acheter) Je _____ une voiture de sport.

3. (prendre) Nous _____ le Concorde pour traverser l'Océan Atlantique.

4. (aller) Elle _____ à Saint Martin.

5. (se retirer) Vous _____ des affaires.

6. (devenir) Tu _____ médecin.

Conditional Sentences

A conditional sentence consists of a condition, an "if" clause (*si* clause) and a result (result or main clause). Two basic conditions exist: "real" conditions and "unreal" or "contrary-to-fact" conditions.

Real Conditions

Real conditions address situations that exist, that are certain, or that are likely to occur. The present indicative is used after *si* to express a real condition. The result clause is in the present, future, or imperative.

Si tu veux, tu peux rester ici.
If you want, you can stay here.

Si vous étudiez beaucoup, vous apprendrez vite.
If you study a lot, you will learn quickly.

Si tu as besoin de quelque chose, dis-le moi.
If you need anything, tell me.

CAUTION

Attention!

Si becomes *s'* only before *il* and *ils*. For example: *S'il fait mauvais, je resterai à la maison.* (If the weather is bad, I will stay home.)

Exercice 5

Express what will happen to each person under certain circumstances:

Exemple:
(avoir/quitter) Si vous ___ chaud, vous ____ votre pull. Si vous avez chaud, vous quitterez votre pull.

1. (recevoir/avoir) Tu _____ un cadeau, si tu _____ de bonnes notes.

2. (être/obtenir) Si je _____ diligent, j' _____ un bon poste.

3. (comprendre/étudier) Vous ___ tout, si vous ____ davantage.

4. (travailler/gagner) Si elles _____ dur, elles ____ beaucoup.

5. (faire/réussir) Si nous _____ de notre mieux, nous _____.

6. (devenir/s'appliquer) Il _____ riche, s'il _____ à ses études.

Contrary-to-Fact Conditions

Contrary-to-fact conditions address situations that do not actually exist, that have not occurred, or that are unlikely to happen. To express something that is contrary to fact (not true) at the present time, a contrary-to-fact condition, French uses the imperfect in the *si* clause and the conditional in the result clause or the pluperfect (compound imperfect) in the *si* clause and the conditional perfect (compound imperfect) in the result clause, as shown in Table 7.3.

Table 7.3   Contrary-to-Fact Conditions

When?	Tense of *si* Clause	Tense of Result Clause
Present	Imperfect	Conditional
Past	Pluperfect	Past Conditional

Si elle avait assez d'argent, elle achèterait une nouvelle voiture.
If she had enough money, she would buy a new car.
(*She doesn't earn much money.*)

S'il avait reçu votre message, il y aurait répondu.
If he had received your message, he would have responded to it.
(*He didn't receive the message.*)

Si always means "if" in conditional sentences. When *si* means "whether," it may be followed by any tense, just as it is in English.

Je ne sais pas s'il a fini ses tâches.
I don't know if he has finished his chores.

Exercice 6

Complete the sentence expressing what each person would do in the following situations by filling in the correct form of the verb:

1. (oublier) Si vous _____ un rendez-vous avec moi, je t'aurais téléphoné.

2. (être) Je t'aiderais si tu _____ malade.

3. (avoir) Si elles _____ faim, je leur préparerais quelque chose à manger.

4. (aller) Si nous avions gagné le gros lot, nous _____ en France.

5. (faire) Tu _____ ce travail si tu voulais le faire.

6. (se marier) Elle _____ si elle avait été amoureuse de Guy.

Récapitulation

1. The conditional of regular verbs is formed by keeping the infinitive ending and adding the conditional endings *-ais*, *-ais*, *-ait*, *-ions*, *-iez*, *-aient*.

2. Verbs with *-yer* spelling changes change *y* to *i* in all forms of the conditional.

3. Verbs with -*e* + consonant + *er* spelling changes change *e* to *è* or double their final consonant in all forms of the conditional.

4. All verbs that are irregular in the conditional have stems that end in -*r* or -*rr* and have the same endings as verbs that are regular in the conditional.

5. The conditional perfect expresses what would have occurred under certain conditions and is formed by conjugating *avoir* (*être*) in the conditional and adding a past participle (which remains the same for all subject pronouns).

6. A conditional sentence consists of a condition, an "if" clause (*si* clause) and a result (result or main clause).

7. Real conditions address situations that exist, that are certain, or that are likely to occur and require the indicative after *si*. The present is used after *si*, whereas the present, future, or imperative is used in the result or main clause.

8. Contrary-to-fact conditions address past situations that do not actually exist or that have not occurred. The imperfect (pluperfect) is used after *si*, whereas the conditional (past conditional) is used in the result or main clause.

9. *Si* may be followed by any tense when it expresses "whether."

The Least You Need to Know

◆ The conditional endings -*ais*, -*ais*, -*ait*, -*ions*, -*iez*, -*aient* are added to the verb infinitive or to a special irregular stem.

◆ To form the past conditional, take the conditional of *avoir* or *être* and add the past participle.

◆ Conditional sentences may express real conditions and use the present after *si* and either the present, the future, or the imperative in the main or result clause.

◆ Conditional sentences may express contrary-to-fact conditions and use the imperfect (pluperfect) after *si* and the conditional (past conditional) in the main or result clause.

Chapter 8

The Subjunctive and the Past Subjunctive

In This Chapter

- Forming the subjunctive of regular, irregular, and reflexive verbs
- Forming the subjunctive of verbs with two stems
- When to use the subjunctive
- Forming and using the past subjunctive
- Recognizing the imperfect and pluperfect subjunctive

The subjunctive, used far more frequently in French than in English, allows speakers to express and describe various attitudes through the use of different verb forms and constructions.

Whereas the indicative mood states a factual condition or situation and expresses certainty or reality, the subjunctive mood expresses unreal, hypothetical, or unsubstantiated conditions or situations involving doubt, wishes, needs, desires, speculation, and supposition.

The past subjunctive is the compound equivalent of the present subjunctive and is used to express an attitude towards an action that has already taken place.

The imperfect and pluperfect subjunctive are only seen in literary and historical works and will be taught for recognition purposes only.

In this chapter, you'll learn how to form and when to use the present and the past subjunctive and how to avoid using the subjunctive when possible.

The Present Subjunctive of Regular and Reflexive Verbs

The present subjunctive of regular verbs is formed by dropping the *-ent* ending of the third person plural form of the present indicative (*ils*) and adding the endings shown in Table 8.1.

Table 8.1 The Present Subjunctive of Regular Verbs

	-er Verbs	*-ir* Verbs	*-re* Verbs
Ils form of present	aid~~ent~~ (*They help*)	finiss~~ent~~ (*They finish*)	vend~~ent~~ (*They sell*)
Je (J')	aid**e**	finiss**e**	vend**e**
Tu	aid**es**	finiss**es**	vend**es**
Il, Elle, On	aid**e**	finiss**e**	vend**e**
Nous	aid**ions**	finiss**ions**	vend**ions**
Vous	aid**iez**	finiss**iez**	vend**iez**
Ils, Elles	aid**ent**	finiss**ent**	vend**ent**

Because the subjunctive is not a tense (a verb form indicating time), the present subjunctive can be used to refer to actions in the present or in the future:

> Il est essentiel que tu ne perdes pas ton argent.
> *It is essential that you not lose your money.*

> Il est possible que nous finissions vite ce travail.
> *It is possible that we will finish this work quickly.*

Regarde! _____

Note that the subjunctive endings are the same for all verbs except *être*.

In the subjunctive, the reflexive pronoun precedes the conjugated verb:

> Il est important que vous réveilliez tôt.
> *It is important that you wake up early.*

Exercice 1

Express what it is necessary for each person to do to be a good student:

Exemple:
ce garçon/écouter attentivement
Il est nécessaire que ce garçon écoute attentivement.

1. cette fille/finir ses devoirs chaque soir _____

2. je/répondre à beaucoup de questions en classe _____

3. tous les élèves/participer consciencieusement _____

4. tu/réfléchir avant de parler _____

5. nous/s'occuper seulement de nos affaires _____

6. vous/défendre vos opinions _____

The Subjunctive of Verbs with Two Stems

Some irregular verbs and most verbs with spelling changes use two different stems to form the present subjunctive:

◆ They use the *ils* stem of the present indicative for *je, tu, il/elle/on,* and *ils/elles* forms of the present subjunctive.

◆ They use the *nous* form of the present indicative for the *nous* and *vous* forms of the present subjunctive.

Table 8.2 lists irregular verbs and verbs with spelling changes that require two different stems. Keep in mind that any compound forms of the verbs or related verbs use these same stems.

Regarde!

Verbs that end in -cer have no change in the subjunctive, because c followed by e or i always produces a soft sound. Verbs that end in -ger drop the -e from the nous form of the verb before adding the -ions present subjunctive ending, because g followed by i produces a soft sound.

… que je commence   … que nous commencions

… que je mange   … que nous mangions

Table 8.2   The Subjunctive of Verbs with Two Stems

Verb	Meaning	*Ils* Stem	*Nous* Stem
boire	to drink	**boiv-**	**buv-**
croire	to believe	**croi-**	**croy-**
devoir	to have to	**doiv-**	**dev-**
mourir	to die	**meur-**	**mour-**
prendre	to take	**prenn-**	**pren-**
recevoir	to receive	**reçoiv-**	**recev-**
venir	to come	**vienn-**	**ven-**
voir	to see	**voi-**	**voy-**
envo**y**er	to send	**envoi-**	**envoy-**
ach**et**er	to buy	**achèt**	**achet-**
app**el**er	to call	**appell-**	**appel-**
préf**ér**er	to prefer	**préfèr-**	**préfér-**

Exercice 2

Express what is important for each person to do:

Exemple:
je/amener ma soeur à l'école
Il est important que j'amène ma soeur à l'école.

1. nous/manger bien _____

2. elles/recevoir de bonnes notes _____

3. tu/employer un ordinateur pour faire tes devoirs _____

4. il/achever son travail _____

5. vous/boire beaucoup d'eau _____

6. elle/épeler bien les verbes _____

7. ils/répéter les mots de vocabulaire _____

8. je/prendre le temps de bien faire mes devoirs _____

The Subjunctive of Irregular Verbs

A few high-frequency verbs that are irregular in the present (including the helping verbs, *avoir* and *être*) also have irregular subjunctive forms, some with one stem and others with two stems, as shown in Table 8.3.

Table 8.2   The Subjunctive of Irregular Verbs

Verb	Meaning	Subjunctive Forms
		Verbs with one stem
faire	to make, do	je fasse, tu fasses, il fasse, nous fassions, vous fassiez, ils fassent
pouvoir	to be able to, can	je puisse, tu puisses, il puisse, nous puissions, vous puissiez, ils puissent
savoir	to know	je sache, tu saches, il sache, nous sachions, vous sachiez, ils sachent
falloir	to be necessary	il faille
pleuvoir	to rain	il pleuve
		Verbs with two stems
aller	to go	j'**aille**, tu **aille**s, il **aille**, nous **all**ions, vous **all**iez, ils **aillent**
avoir	to have	j'**aie**, tu **aie**s, il **ait**, nous **ay**ons, vous **ay**ez, ils **aient**
être	to be	je **sois**, tu **sois**, il **soit**, nous **soyons**, vous **soyez**, ils **soient**
valoir	to be worth	je **vaille**, tu **vaille**s, il **vaille**, nous **val**ions, vous **val**iez, ils **vaillent**
vouloir	to wish, want	je **veuille**, tu **veuille**s, il **veuille**, nous **voul**ions, vous **voul**iez, ils **veuillent**

All other verbs that are normally irregular in the present indicative form the subjunctive according to the rules for regular verbs, as shown in Table 8.3.

Table 8.3   The Subjunctive of Irregular Present Tense Verbs

Infinitive	Stem for *Subjunctive*
battre (to beat)	batt-
conduire (to drive)	conduis-
connaître (to know)	connaiss-
courir (to run)	cour-

continues

Table 8.3 The Subjunctive of Irregular Present Tense Verbs (continued)

Infinitive	Stem for *Subjunctive*
craindre (to fear)	craign-
cueillir (to pick)	cueill-
dire (to say, tell)	dis-
distraire (to distract)	distrai-
dormir (to sleep)	dorm-
écrire (to write)	écriv-
fuir (to flee)	fui-
joindre (to join)	joign-
lire (to read)	lis-
mettre (to put)	mis-
naître (to be born)	naiss-
offrir (to offer)	offr-
ouvrir (to open)	ouvr-
paraître (to seem)	paraiss-
partir (to leave)	part-
plaindre (to pity)	plaign-
plaire (to please)	plais-
résoudre (to resolve)	résolv-
sentir (to feel)	sent-
servir (to serve)	serv-
sortir (to go out)	sort-
suivre (to follow)	suiv-
vaincre (to defeat)	vainqu-
vivre (to live)	viv-

Exercice 3

Express what is doubtful:

Exemple:
nous/aller au cinéma
Il est douteux que nous allions au cinéma.

1. Janine et Lise/être en retard _____

2. tu/vouloir travailler dimanche _____

3. vous/pouvoir nous accompagner au musée _____

4. ils/savoir jouer du piano _____

5. elle/devenir ingénieur _____

6. je/avoir tort _____

7. Jacques/se plaindre de son problème _____

8. nous/faire un voyage cet été _____

Using the Subjunctive

The subjunctive is used when the following conditions are met:

◆ Two different clauses exist with two different subjects.

◆ The two clauses are joined by *que* (that) or in special instances, by *qui*, which is followed by the clause in the subjunctive.

◆ One of the clauses must show, among other things, wishing, wanting, need, necessity, emotion, or doubt.

Définitions _____

A clause is a group of words that contains a verb and its subject and is used as a part of a sentence. A clause may be main or independent, which means that it can stand by itself as a simple sentence. A clause may also be subordinate or dependent, which means that it cannot stand alone and is used as a noun, an adjective, or an adverb.

The Subjunctive After Impersonal Expressions

The subjunctive is used in French after impersonal expressions that show need, necessity, doubt, uncertainty, possibility, probability, and emotion, among others, as shown in Table 8.4.

Table 8.4   Impersonal Expressions Taking the Subjunctive

Expression	French
It could be that	Il se peut que
It is a pity that	Il est dommage que
It is absurd that	Il est absurde que
It is amazing that	Il est étonnant que
It is amusing that	Il est amusant que
It is better that	Il vaut mieux que
It is strange that	Il est curieux que
It is doubtful that	Il est douteux que
It is enough that	Il suffit que
It is essential that	Il essentiel que
It is fair that	Il est juste que
It is fitting that	Il convient que
It is good that	Il est bon que
It is imperative that	Il est impératif que
It is important that	Il est important que
It is impossible that	Il est impossible que
It is improbable that	Il est improbable que
It is incredible that	Il est incroyable que
It is indispensable that	Il est indispensable que
It is interesting that	Il est intéressant que
It is ironic that	Il est ironique que
It is natural that	Il est naturel que
It is necessary that	Il est nécessaire que Il faut que
It is nice that	Il est bien que
It is normal that	Il est normal que
It is possible that	Il est possible que
It is preferable that	Il est préférable que
It is rare that	Il est rare que
It is reasonable that	Il est raisonnable que
It is remarkable that	Il est remarquable que
It is regrettable that	Il est regrettable que
It is sad that	Il est triste que
It is strange that	Il est étrange que
It is surprising that	Il est surprenant que

Expression	French
It is time that	Il est temps que
It is unfair that	Il est injuste que
It is urgent that	Il est urgent que
It is useful that	Il est utile que
It seems that	Il semble que

Note how the subjunctive is used in the clause following an impersonal expression, even if the impersonal expression is negated:

Il est surprenant que tu ne veuilles pas aller au théâtre.
It is surprising that you don't want to go to the theater.

Il ne convient pas qu'ils viennent à cette heure.
It isn't appropriate that they come at that time.

The following impersonal expressions show probability or certainty and, therefore, require the indicative:

it appears	il paraît
it is certain (sure)	il est certain
it is clear	il est clair
it is evident	il est évident
it is exact	il est exact
it is probable	il est probable
it is sure	il est sûr
it is true	il est vrai

Il est certain qu'elle ira en Europe.
It is certain that she is going to Europe.

Il est évident qu'il veut travailler.
It is evident that he wants to work.

In the negative, however, these expressions show doubt or denial and require the subjunctive:

Il n'est pas certain qu'elle aille en Europe.
It is not certain that she is going to Europe.

Il n'est pas évident qu'il veuille travailler.
It is not evident that he wants to work.

Exercice 4

Express opinions about a picnic that you and a friend are planning by using the correct form of the indicative or the subjunctive:

1. (venir) Il est possible que Sylvie ne _____ pas.

2. (faire) Il est douteux qu'il _____ mauvais ce jour-là.

3. (acheter) Il est certain que nous _____ assez de provisions.

4. (se réunir) Il est important que tout le monde _____ chez moi à onze heures.

5. (conduire) Il est nécessaire que nos parents nous _____ au parc.

6. (attend) Il est clair que vous _____ le jour du pique-nique avec impatience.

Attention! _____

Although we often omit the word *that* when using the subjunctive in English, in French *que* must always be used to join the two clauses:

Il est important que tu fasses de ton mieux.
It's important (that) you do your best.

Je veux que vous étudiiez encore plus.
I want you to study more.

Using the Subjunctive After Certain Verbs

The subjunctive is used in the dependent clause introduced by *que* when the main clause expresses advice, command, demand, desire, emotion, hope, permission, preference, prohibition, request, suggestion, wishing, and wanting, as shown in Table 8.5.

Table 8.5   Verbs of Wishing, Emotion, and Doubt

French Verb	Meaning
aimer mieux	to prefer
commander	to command, order

French Verb	Meaning
consentir	to consent
craindre	to fear
défendre	to forbid
désirer	to desire, want
douter	to doubt
empêcher	to prevent
exiger	to require, demand
insister	to insist
interdire	to prohibit
ordonner	to order
permettre	to permit
préférer	to prefer
reclamer	to demand, ask for
regretter	to be sorry, to regret
souhaiter	to wish
suggérer	to suggest
vouloir	to wish, want

Son père défend qu'il sorte ce soir.
His father forbids him to go out tonight.

Je veux que vous vous comportiez bien.
I want you to behave well.

When There's No Doubt About It

When an event or an opinion is questioned, doubt exists and the subjunctive is used. When doubt is negated, certainty or probability exists and the indicative is used, as shown in Table 8.6.

Table 8.6   Doubt and the Indicative vs. the Subjunctive

Indicative (Certainty)	Subjunctive (Uncertainty)
Je crois … *I believe*	Crois-tu …? (Croyez-vous …?) *Do you believe …?*
	Je ne crois pas. *I don't believe.*

continues

Table 8.6   Doubt and the Indicative vs. the Subjunctive   (continued)

Indicative (Certainty)	Subjunctive (Uncertainty)
Je suis sûr(e) ... *I'm sure*	Es-tu/Êtes-vous sûr(e)? *Are you sure ...?*
	Je ne suis pas sûr(e) *I'm not sure ...*
Je ne doute pas ... *I don't doubt*	Doutes-tu? (Doutez-vous?) *Do you doubt ...?*
	Je doute *I doubt ...*
J'espère ... *I hope*	Espères-tu? (Espérez-vous?) *Do you hope ...?*
	Je n'espère pas ... *I don't hope ...*
Je pense ... *I think*	Penses-tu? (Pensez-vous?) *Do you think ...?*
	Je ne pense pas *I don't think ...*

Penses-tu qu'elle le fasse?
Do you think she will do it?

Je ne pense pas qu'elle le fasse.
I don't think she will do it.

Je pense qu'elle le fera.
I think she will do it.

After verbs of opinion or knowledge used affirmatively, the indicative is generally used to show belief, conviction, or knowledge on the part of the speaker. When these verbs are used negatively or interrogatively, the subjunctive is generally used if the speaker is implying doubt (which is not necessarily always the case). When used in the negative interrogative, these verbs imply certainty and take the indicative.

Je crois qu'il viendra.
I believe he will come.

Croyez-vous qu'il vienne.
Do you believe he will come? (Doubt is implied.)

(Ne) Croyez-vous (pas) qu'il viendra?
Do(n't) you believe he will come? (The speaker has little doubt that he will come and is merely asking for someone else's opinion.)

Je ne crois pas qu'il vienne.
I don't believe he is coming. (Doubt is implied.)

Exercice 5

Express what each person wants by completing the sentence with the correct form of the subjunctive or the indicative:

1. (s'apercevoir) Le professeur préfère que les élèves _____ de leurs erreurs.

2. (prendre) Ses parents aiment mieux qu'il _____ un taxi.

3. (finir) Papa insiste que nous _____ nos devoirs avant de sortir.

4. (lire) Je voudrais que vous _____ cet article intéressant.

5. (résoudre) Espère-t-il que tu _____ le probléme tout de suite?

6. (être) Mon frère exige que je _____ plus responsable.

7. (répondre) Elle est sûre que vous _____ à sa lettre.

8. (mettre) Mes parents demandent que je _____ la table chaque soir.

Using the Subjunctive After Certain Adjectives

The subjunctive is also used after adjectives (that follow the verb *être*) that express feelings, as shown in Table 8.6.

Table 8.6 Adjectives Expressing Feelings

Spanish	Adjective
agacé(e)	annoyed
content(e)	happy
désolé(e)	sorry
embarrassé(e)	embarrassed
enchanté(e)	delighted
énervé(e)	irritated
ennuyé(e)	bothered
étonné(e)	astonished, surprised
fâché(e)	angry

continues

Table 8.6 Adjectives Expressing Feelings (continued)

Spanish	Adjective
fier (fière)	proud
flatté(e)	flattered
furieux (furieuse)	furious
gêné(e)	embarrassed
heureux (heureuse)	happy
irrité(e)	irritated
malheureux (malheureuse)	unhappy
mécontent(e)	displeased
ravi(e)	delighted
surpris	surprised
triste	sad

Nous sommes contents qu'il apprenne à lire vite.
We are happy that he is learning to read quickly.

Je suis ravi que tu reçoives une bourse.
I am delighted that you will receive a scholarship.

Regarde! _____

The subjunctive is also used after nouns (that follow the verb *avoir*) that express feelings: *avoir + crainte* (to be afraid), *+ honte* (to be ashamed), or *+ peur* (to be afraid) *+ que*. Note that expressions of fear take *ne* with the subjunctive, and the *ne* has no meaning.

As-tu peur qu'il ne découvre le secret?
Are you afraid that he will discover the secret?

Il craint que tu ne lui dises des mensonges.
He is afraid that you will tell him lies.

Exercice 6

Express how these people feel:

1. (sortir) Je suis contente que mon ami _____ avec moi ce soir.

2. (recevoir) Ma mère est heureuse que je _____ tant de compliments de mes amis.

3. (savoir) Je suis surpris que vous _____ cuisiner.

4. (suivre) Leur père est content qu'ils _____ un cours de judo.

5. (courir) Pourquoi es-tu étonnée que je _____ si vite.

6. (faire) Le directeur est ravi que ses élèves _____ tant de progrès.

The Subjunctive After Conjunctions

The subjunctive is used after certain conjunctions when uncertainty, doubt, purpose, anticipation, or indefiniteness is implied.

Définitions

A conjunction is a part of speech that connects and relates words, phrases, or clauses. Coordinating conjunctions, such as *and, but, or, nor,* and *for,* connect words, phrases, and clauses of equal importance. Subordinating conjunctions, such as *if, although, since, in order that, as, because, unless, after, before, until, when, whenever, where, while, wherever,* and so on, connect dependent clauses with independent clauses.

The subjunctive is used with the following conjunctions that express time, purpose, concession, condition or restriction, negation, and fear:

◆ Conjunctions that express time:

until   *en attendant que*
until   *jusqu'à ce que*
before   *avant que*

Nous attendrons jusqu'à ce que vous arriviez.
We will wait until you arrive.

◆ Conjunctions that express purpose:

so that, in order that   *pour que*
in order that   *afin que*
so that   *de sorte que*
so that   *de manière que*
so that   *de façon que*

Elle parle lentement pour que je puisse la comprendre.
She speaks slowly so that I can understand her.

♦ Conjunctions that express concession:

although   *bien que*
although   *quoique*
in spite of the fact that   *malgré que*

Quoiqu'il ne soit pas très riche, il est très généreux.
Although he is not very rich, he is very generous.

♦ Conjunctions that express condition or restriction:

provided that, as long as   *pourvu que*
unless   *à moins que*
in case (that)   *au(en) cas que*
on condition that, as long as   *à condition que*

Je le ferai pourvu que vous m'aidiez.
I will do it provided that you help me.

♦ Conjunctions that express negation:

without   *sans que*

Il sort sans que je le voie.
He leaves without my seeing it.

♦ Conjunctions that express fear:

for fear that   *de peur que*
for fear that   *de crainte que*

Elle ne sortira pas de crainte qu'il (ne) lui téléphone.
She will not go out for fear that he will call her.

Regarde!

À moins que, avant que, de peur que, and *de crainte que* may or may not be followed by *ne,* which has no meaning.

Je te rappellerai la date de crainte que tu (ne) l'oublies.
I will remind you of the date for fear that you will forget it.

Attention!

Do not confuse the conjunctions *pour que, afin que, avant que, malgré que, jusqu'à ce que,* and *sans que* with the prepositions *pour, afin, avant, malgré, jusqu'à,* and *sans,* which are used before an infinitive when the infinitive's subject is the same as that of the main verb.

Je te parlerai avant que tu partes.
I will speak to you before you leave.

Je te parlerai avant de partir.
I will speak to you before leaving.

The following conjunctions use the indicative:

> *après que* (after)
> *aussitôt que* (as soon as)
> *dès que* (as soon as)
> *parce que* (because)
> *pendant que* (while)
> *peut-être que* (perhaps)
> *puisque* (since)
> *tandis que* (while)

Je le ferai parce que c'est une bonne idée.
I will do it because it is a good idea.

Exercice 7

Express that the members of the Dupont family do the following things.

Exemple:
Maman nous réveille/afin que/nous/arriver au bureau à l'heure.
Maman nous réveille afin que nous arrivions au bureau à l'heure.

1. Papa donne de l'argent à Mirelle/pour que/elle/s'acheter de nouveaux vêtements

   _____

2. Rose fait tant de bruit/parce que/elle/apprendre à jouer de la guitare

   _____

3. Je prépare le dîner/avant que/ma mère/pouvoir me le demander

   _____

4. Thomas regarde la télévision/malgré que/il/avoir beaucoup de devoirs à faire

   _____

5. Lucien écoute des CDs/pendant que/nous/jouer aux échecs

   _____

6. Je lis le journal/en attendant que/vous/m'aider

   _____

The Subjunctive in Relative Clauses

The subjunctive is used in relative clauses if the person or thing in the main clause is indefinite, desired but not yet attained, is nonexistent, or if its existence is doubtful:

> Je cherche un appartement qui soit grand.
> *I'm looking for an apartment that is big.*
> (Does such an apartment exist?)

> J'ai trouvé appartement qui est grand.
> *I found a big apartment.*
> (Such an apartment exists.)

Regarde! _____

In relative clauses, *que* (that), which usually joins the clauses, is replaced by *qui* (that).

> Je cherche un docteur qui puisse m'aider.
> *I'm looking for a doctor who can help me.*

The Subjunctive in Third Person Commands

The subjunctive is used in third person singular or plural commands expressing a wish:

> Qu'elle vive longtemps!
> *May she live a long time.*

> Qu'ils soient heureux.
> *Let them be happy.*

> Vive la république!
> *Long live the republic!*

The Subjunctive After Superlative Expressions

The subjunctive is used after superlative expressions, generally showing an opinion, a feeling, or an emotion: *le premier* (the first), *le dernier* (the last), *le meilleur* (the best), *le seul* (the only), *l'unique* (the only), and *ne … que* (only).

> C'est la meilleure marque qu'on puisse acheter.
> *It's the best brand you can buy.*

The indicative is used after a superlative when a fact is stated and there is no opinion given by the speaker.

> C'est son meilleur ami qui l'aide.
> *It's his best friend who is helping him.*

The indicative is used after the superlative of an adverb:

Je marche le plus vite que je peux.
I'm walking as fast as I can.

Exercice 8

Complete each person's thought with the correct form of the indicative or the superlative:

1. (avoir) Je connais une femme qui _____ dix enfants.

2. (être) Ses conseils sont les seuls qui _____ raisonnables.

3. (connaître) Le patron cherche un employé qui _____ la comptabilité.

4. (pouvoir) C'est la meilleure glace qu'on _____ acheter.

5. (savoir) Janine est la seule personne qui _____ faire ce travail.

6. (partir) Qu'il_____ immédiatement!

Forming and Using the Past Subjunctive

The past subjunctive is a compound tense, which means that it is made up of more than one part. The following two elements are needed to form the past subjunctive:

1. The present subjunctive of the helping verb *avoir* (*aie, aies, ait, ayons, ayez, aient*) or *être* (*sois, sois, soit, soyons, soyez, soient*), which expresses that something took place in the past

2. The past participle of the verb, which expresses what the action was

The following figure shows how the past subjunctive is formed:

Past subjunctive of verb =   when + what   *Formation of the past*
                             /   \   *subjunctive.*
Past subjunctive of verb = (what) has + happened
                             /   \
Past subjunctive of verb = helping verb + main verb
                             /   \
Past subjunctive of verb = *avoir* (to have) + past participle
                   être (to be)

The formula for the formation of the past subjunctive is as follows:

subject noun or pronoun + *avoir* (*être*) in present subjunctive + past participle

The formation of past participles was explained in Chapter 1. Irregular past participles appear in Table 1.3 and in Appendix H.

Je suis heureux que tu m'aies rendu visite.
I'm happy you visited me.

Tout le monde regrette que vous soyez arrivé(e)(s) trop tard.
Everyone regrets that you arrived too late.

Exercice 9

Express what happened by using the past subjunctive:

1. (s'égarer) Croyez-vous qu'elle _____.

2. (apprendre) Il est important que M. Leduc _____ à son fils à lire.

3. (devenir) Il est juste qu'Henri _____ chef de son équipe.

4. (découvrir) Il est surprenant que Mme Louise _____ l'amour à l'âge de 80 ans.

5. (s'arrêter) Il est bien étonnant que vous _____ de fumer si facilement.

6. (naître) Il est amusant que Martine _____ le même jour que moi.

Avoiding the Subjunctive

It is generally preferable to avoid the subjunctive whenever possible. Until this point, the verbs in the dependent clause (where the subjunctive is used) and the verbs in the main clause (need, necessity, wishing, wanting, and so on) have different subjects. If the subjects in both clauses are the same, *que* is omitted and the infinitive replaces the subjunctive:

Elle préfère que je la conduise en ville.
She prefers me to drive her to the city.

Elle préfère conduire en ville.
She prefers driving in the city.

Wherever possible, use the verb *devoir* + infinitive to avoid using the subjunctive.

Il faut que tu fasses les courses.
Tu dois faire les courses.
You have to go shopping.

Exercice 10

Express what certain people have to do:

Exemple:
Il faut qu'il garde les enfants.
Il doit garder les enfants.

1. Il faut que M. Legrand fasse un voyage en Italie.

   _____

2. Il faut que j'écrive une lettre à ma correspondante.

   _____

3. Il faut que nous lisions un recueil de poèmes.

   _____

4. Il faut que Claire et Madeleine prennent le métro.

   _____

5. Il faut que vous restiez à la maison pendant le week-end.

   _____

6. Il faut que tu te réveilles tôt demain matin.

   _____

Exercice 11

For each sentence, decide whether to use the subjunctive or the indicative to describe what happens in school:

1. (traduire) Le professeur de français veut bien que nous _____ les phrases.

2. (venir) Le directeur ne croit pas que je _____ à l'école à l'heure tous les jours.

3. (choisir) Il est bon que les élèves _____ les réponses correctes.

4. (écrire) Il est certain que vous n' _____ pas vos devoirs en classe.

5. (avoir) Nous cherchons une grammaire qui _____ toutes les règles de la langue française.

6. (perdre) Il est nécessaire que tu ne _____ pas ton manuel scolaire.

7. (dormir) Il est vrai que nous ne _____ pas en classe.

8. (réussir) Il faut que nous _____.

9. (être) Tous les élèves sont contents que le professeur d'histoire ne _____ pas absent aujourd'hui.

10. (attendre) Il vaut mieux que j' _____ mes amis à la bibliothèque pour étudier.

11. (agir) Croyez-vous que j' _____ comme un enfant?

12. (connaître) Suzanne est l'élève la plus sportive que je _____.

13. (se servir) J'ai un professeur qui ne _____ pas de notes quand il parle.

14. (savoir) Est-il possible que nous _____ tous les mots de vocabulaire?

15. (aller) Le directeur exige que tous les élèves _____ à l'école tous les jours.

16. (faire) Il n'est pas clair que tous les élèves _____ le travail scolaire.

17. (suivre) Il est important que je _____ un cours d'art.

18. (répéter) Je pense que Robert _____ toujours la même chose.

19. (appeler) Les professeurs ordonnent que nous _____ nos amis quand nous sommes absents.

20. (pouvoir) Le professeur explique les devoirs pour que nous _____ les faire facilement à la maison.

Recognizing the Imperfect and Pluperfect Subjunctive

The imperfect and pluperfect subjunctive will only be found in literary and historical writings. For this reason, you only need to be able to recognize them. They are listed in the verb charts in Appendix B.

For the imperfect subjunctive, drop the *passé simple* endings and add the imperfect subjunctive endings as indicated in the following list:

- For verbs with a *passé simple* stem ending in -a (*è*):

  Drop: *-ai, -as, -a, -âmes, -âtes, -èrent*

  Add: *-asse, -asses, -ât, -assions, -assiez, -assent*

  Exemple: je parlasse, tu parlasses, il parlât, nous parlassions, vous parlassiez, ils parlassent

  je parlasse
  I spoke (might have spoken)

- For verbs with a *passé simple* stem ending in -i:

  Drop: *-is, -is, -it, -îmes, -îtes, -irent*

  Add: *-isse, -isses, -ît, -issions, -issiez, -issent*

  Exemple: je finisse, tu finisses, il finît, nous finissions, vous finissiez, ils finissent

  je finisse
  I finished (might have finished)

- For verbs with a *passé simple* stem ending in -u:

  Drop: *-us, -us, -ût, -ûmes, -ûtes, -urent*

  Add: *-usse, -usses, -ût, -ussions, -ussiez, -ussent*

  Exemples:

  (avoir) j'eusse, tu eusses, il eût, nous eussions, vous eussiez, ils eussent

  j'eus I had (might have)

  (être) je fusse, tu fusses, il fût, nous fussions, vous fussiez, ils fussent

  je fusse I was (might be)

To form the pluperfect subjunctive, take the imperfect subjunctive of the appropriate helping verb *avoir* or *être* (shown directly above) and add the past participle:

il eut travaillé
he had worked

elle fût rentrée
she had returned

Récapitulation

1. The subjunctive of most verbs is formed by dropping the *-ent* from the *ils* form of the present indicative and adding the appropriate subjunctive ending.

2. The subjunctive endings for all verbs except *être* are *-e, -es, -e, -ions, -iez, -ent.*

3. Verbs with two subjunctive forms are as follows:

boire (to drink)	**boiv-**	buv-
croire (to believe)	croi-	croy-
devoir (to have to)	doiv-	dev-
mourir (to die)	meur-	mour-
prendre (to take)	**prenn-**	pren-
recevoir (to receive)	reçoiv-	recev-
venir (to come)	**vienn-**	ven-
voir (to see)	voi-	voy-

4. Verbs with the highlighted endings have two forms due to spelling changes in the subjunctive:

envo**y**er (to send)	envoi-	envoy-
ache**t**er (to buy)	achèt-	achet-
appe**l**er (to call)	appell-	appel-
préf**ér**er (to prefer)	préfèr-	préfér-

5. The following verbs are irregular in the subjunctive and must be memorized:

Verbs with one stem

faire (to make, do): je fasse, tu fasses, il fasse, nous fassions, vous fassiez, ils fassent

pouvoir (to be able to, can): je puisse, tu puisses, il puisse, nous puissions, vous puissiez, ils puissent savoir (to know): je sache, tu saches, il sache, nous sachions, vous sachiez, ils sachent

falloir (to be necessary): il faille

pleuvoir (to rain): il pleuve

Verbs with two stems

aller (to go): j'**aille**, tu **aill**es, il **aill**e, nous **all**ions, vous **all**iez, ils **aill**ent

avoir (to have): j'**aie**, tu **ai**es, il **ait**, nous **ay**ons, vous **ay**ez, ils **aient**

être (to be): je **sois**, tu **sois**, il **soit**, nous **soyons**, vous **soyez**, ils **soient**

valoir (to be worth): je **vaill**e, tu **vaill**es, il **vaill**e, nous **val**ions, vous **val**iez, ils **vaill**ent

vouloir (to wish, want): je **veuill**e, tu **veuill**es, il **veuill**e, nous **voul**ions, vous **voul**iez, ils **veuill**ent

6. In the subjunctive, the reflexive pronoun precedes the conjugated verb.

7. The subjunctive is used to express the present and the future.

8. The subjunctive is used in sentences where there are two clauses with different subjects and that are joined by *que*. One of the clauses must express need, necessity, doubt, uncertainty, possibility, probability, emotion, advice, command, demand, desire, emotion, hope, permission, preference, prohibition, request, suggestion, wishing, or wanting.

9. The subjunctive is used after certain conjunctions when uncertainty, doubt, purpose, anticipation, or indefiniteness is implied.

10. The subjunctive is used in relative clauses if the person or thing in the main clause is indefinite, desired but not yet attained, or if it is nonexistent or its existence is doubtful.

11. The subjunctive is used in third person singular or plural commands expressing a wish or hope.

12. The superlative is used after superlative expressions to show an opinion, a feeling, or an emotion.

13. The past subjunctive expresses what has occurred in the past and is formed by conjugating *avoir* (*être*) in the subjunctive and adding a past participle (which remains the same for all subject pronouns).

14. The subjunctive may be avoided if the subjects in both clauses are the same; *que* is omitted and the infinitive replaces the subjunctive.

15. The imperfect subjunctive need only be learned for recognition because it is only used in formal literary writing. It is formed by dropping the *-a (è)*, *-i*, or *-u* ending from the *passé simple* and adding *-asse*, *-asses*, *-ât*, *-assions*, *-assiez*, *-assent*; *-isse*, *-isses*, *-ît*, *-issions*, *-issiez*, *-issent*; or *-usse*, *-usses*, *-ût*, *-ussions*, *-ussiez*, *-ussent*.

16. The pluperfect subjunctive need only be learned for recognition because it is only used in formal literary writing. It is formed by using the imperfect subjunctive of the appropriate helping verb *avoir* or *être* plus a past participle.

The Least You Need to Know

♦ To form the present subjunctive, take the present tense *ils* form of the indicative, drop the *-ent*, and add *-e*, *-es*, *-e*, *-ions*, *-iez*, *-ent* for all verbs except *être*.

♦ Some irregular verbs and spelling change verbs have two forms in the subjunctive.

♦ The past subjunctive is formed by taking the subjunctive of *avoir* (*être*) and adding a past participle.

♦ The subjunctive is used after certain verbs and expression expressions showing wishing, wanting, need, necessity, emotion, doubt, and the like.

♦ The subjunctive is also used after certain conjunctions, in relative clauses, in third person commands, and in superlative sentences when there is wishing, emotion, or doubt.

♦ The imperfect and pluperfect subjunctive need only be learned for recognition in formal literary works.

Part 3

Verbal Distinctions and Expressions

The goal of a second language learner is to achieve a degree of fluency that mimics the way a native speaker uses language idiomatically. In French, the knowledge of just a few irregular verbs will help you accomplish this task.

Part 3 offers an extensive foundation for effective, idiomatic communication as well as an understanding of the differences between active and passive voice. It also explains the difference between expressing a thought in English, which requires only one simple verb, and in French, in which different connotations require the use of different verbs with different conjugations. By the end of this part, after you've worked earnestly and conscientiously, you'll be well equipped and prepared to use French verbs proficiently.

Chapter 9

Common Verbal Distinctions

In This Chapter

◆ Special uses of verbs

◆ Verbs with different meanings when reflexive

◆ Verbs with different connotations

In French, some verbs have different meanings depending upon how they are used in a sentence. Other verbs change meaning in different tenses. To speak and write good, authentic French, it is essential to know how to use these verbs correctly.

There are verbs that mean one thing when they are used nonreflexively and another when they become reflexive. Knowing when to use these verbs with or without their reflexive pronouns will enable you to convey your thoughts properly and will undoubtedly increase your fluency.

Lastly, there are verbs that have the same meanings but connote different ideas. Although we use only one verb in English to get our meaning across, French requires different verbs to express these nuances.

This chapter explains the special uses of certain verbs, when it's necessary to make a verb reflexive, and when different verbs are required to make yourself properly understood.

Special Uses of Verbs

The following high-frequency irregular verbs have special uses and meanings according to the tense being used.

devoir

In the present tense the irregular verb *devoir* follows the "shoe" pattern (see Chapter 2), where changes are made to the *je*, *tu*, *il*, and *ils* forms of the verb, and where the *nous* and *vous* forms are taken from the infinitive:

je **dois**	nous devons
tu **dois**	vous devez
il **doit**	ils **doivent**

Devoir is used to express the following:

♦ **Obligation.** *Devoir* shows that the subject "must," "has to," or "is supposed to" do something. *Devoir* + an infinitive is often used to avoid the subjunctive:

Il doit venir me voir.
He has to come see me.

Il devait venir me voir mais il était occupé.
He was supposed to come see me but he was busy.

Il devra venir me voir.
He will have to come see me.

In the conditional, *devoir* means "ought to" or "should (have)":

Il devrait venir me voir.
He should (ought to) come see me.

Il aurait dû venir me voir.
He should have (ought to have) come see me.

♦ **Probability or supposition.** *Devoir* expresses a conjecture, a probable action or event, or an intended or scheduled happening:

Il doit être heureux.
He must be happy.

Elle a dû oublier l'heure du rendez-vous.
She must have forgotten the time of the meeting.

♦ **Debt.** When followed by a noun, *devoir* indicates that the subject "owes" something:

Tu me dois vingt dollars.
You owe me twenty dollars.

faire

Faire can be used in a causative construction to show that the subject causes an action to be done by someone or something else. The English equivalent is "to have (make) someone do something" or "to have something done." *Faire* is followed by the infinitive expressing the action to be completed:

Tu me fais rire.
You make me laugh.

M. Gérard fait faire un complet.
Mr. Gérard is having a suit made.

Mon mari et moi avons fait construire une maison.
My husband and I had a house built.

Note the following about the use of the causative *faire*:

♦ *Faire* + infinitive forms a unit that is generally not separated. Nouns follow the infinitive and object pronouns precede *faire*. When *faire* + infinitive is followed by two objects, the object of the infinitive is the direct object and the object of *faire* is the indirect object. Both object pronouns precede *faire*:

Mme Clermont fait planter les fleurs par le jardinier.
Mrs. Clermont has the gardener plant the flowers.

Elle les fait planter au jardinier.
She has the gardener plant them.

Elle lui fait planter les fleurs.
She has him plant the flowers.

Elle les lui fait planter.
She has him plant them.

♦ The person or thing performing the action can be introduced by *par* instead of *à* to avoid ambiguity:

Il fait envoyer le chèque à son fils.
He has his son send the check.
He has the check sent to his son.

Il fait envoyer le chèque par son fils.
He has his son send the check.

Regarde! _____

In compound tenses, the past participle of *faire* + infinitive does not agree with a preceding direct object:

Le garçon a fait pleurer la fille.
The boy made the girl cry.

Il l'a fait pleurer.
He made her cry.

◆ A reflexive verb (whose reflexive pronoun serves as an indirect object) can be used in a causative *faire* construction. *Se faire* + infinitive shows that the subject is having something made or done for himself/herself:

Je me suis fait laver la voiture.
I had my car washed.

Je me la suis fait laver.
I had it washed.

falloir

Falloir is an impersonal verb that is used only in the third person singular form (*il*). Like *devoir*, *falloir* usually expresses necessity, although it is stronger than *devoir*:

Vous devez travailler dur.
Il faut que vous travailliez dur. } *You have to work hard.*
Il vous faut travailler dur.

Falloir is used as follows:

◆ With the infinitive:

Il faut l'accepter.
It is necessary (One must) accept it.
It has to be accepted.

Il ne faudrait pas le faire.
One/you/we shouldn't do it.

◆ With the infinitive and an indirect object pronoun:

Il lui faudra partir tout de suite.
He (She) will have to leave immediately.

Il me fallait attendre longtemps.
I had to wait a long time.

◆ With *que* + subjunctive:

Il a fallu que nous obéissions.
We had to obey.

Il aurait fallu que vous écoutiez.
You should have listened.

◆ After a noun to express need:

Il me faut une règle.
I need a ruler.

Il lui faut cent dollars.
He (She) needs a hundred dollars.

pouvoir

In the present tense the irregular verb *pouvoir* follows the "shoe" pattern (see Chapter 2), where changes are made to the *je*, *tu*, *il*, and *ils* forms of the verb and where the *nous* and *vous* forms are taken from the infinitive:

je **peux**	nous pouvons
tu **peux**	vous pouvez
il **peut**	ils **peuvent**

Pouvoir is used:

◆ To express ability or success, lack of either, or doubt about either:

Elle ne peut pas cuisiner.
She can't cook.

Il n'a pas pu trouver la réponse correcte.
He couldn't find the correct answer.

Pourrez-vous comprendre le problème.
Will you be able to understand the problem?

◆ To express permissibility or possibility:

Est-ce que je peux aller au cinéma ce soir?
May I go (Am I allowed to go) to the movies tonight?

Je pourrai t'aider demain.
I may be able to help you tomorrow.

◆ To express a suggestion:

Il pourrait t'emmener à la fête.
He could take you to the party.

◆ To express obligation when an infinitive is negated:

Vous pouvez ne pas nous accompagner.
You don't need to (You aren't obligated) to accompany us.

◆ To express "might" or "could" when it is used in the conditional:

Pourriez-vous me montrer cette chemise?
Could you (Might you) show me that shirt?

◆ Idiomatically:

Je n'en peux plus.
I'm exhausted.

Je n'y peux rien.
I can't help it. (It's out of my control.)

savoir

The verb *savoir* expresses knowledge gained through mental ability or know-how, memorization, or learning and demonstrates knowledge of facts or reasons about things:

Il sait jouer au golf.
He knows how to play golf.

Je ne sais pas ton nom.
I don't know your name.

Il est trop jeune pour savoir marcher.
He's too young to know how to walk.

Savoir is used as follows:

◆ To express "to find out" or "to learn about something" when used in the *passé composé:*

Il l'a su trop tard.
He found out about it too late.

◆ Idiomatically to express "could" or "would":

Elle ne saurait pas exprimer sa joie.
She couldn't possibly (wouldn't know how to) express her joy.

vouloir

In the present tense the irregular verb *vouloir* follows the "shoe" pattern (see Chapter 2), where changes are made to the *je, tu, il,* and *ils* forms of the verb, and where the *nous* and *vous* forms are taken from the infinitive:

je **veux**	nous voulons
tu **veux**	vous voulez
il **veut**	ils **veulent**

Vouloir is used to express the following:

◆ Strong will (similar to a command) when used in the present:

Je ne veux pas le faire.
I don't want to do it.

◆ A wish or a desire in a more courteous manner when used in the conditional:

Je ne voudrais pas y aller.
I wouldn't like to go there.

◆ An attempt or a refusal to do something in the *passé composé:*

Elle a voulu faire de son mieux.
She tried to do her best.

Il n'a pas voulu le faire.
He refused to do it.

◆ A polite command when used in the imperative:

Veuillez ouvrir la porte.
Please open the door.
Would you please open the door?

◆ Idiomatically followed by *bien* to express "to be good enough to" or "to be willing to":

Voulez-vous bien nous attendre?
Will you be good enough to wait for us?
Are you willing to wait for us?

Exercice 1

Complete each sentence with the correct form of the verb that is missing:

1. (must be) Elle _____ être jalouse.

2. (need) Il me _____ une nouvelle voiture.

3. (had) Je _____ couper les cheveux.

4. (weren't able to) Ils _____ rester longtemps.

5. (know) _____ -tu que j'étudie la musique?

6. (would like) Nous _____ aller à la campagne.

7. (makes) Le père _____ chanter sa fille.

8. (owe) Vous me _____ dix dollars.

9. (could) Ta soeur _____ être malade.

10. (kindly) _____ m'excuser.

Verbs with Special Reflexive Meanings

Some French verbs change meanings when used reflexively, so be careful to choose the verb that best expresses exactly what you would like to say. Use the following list as a guide:

Basic Meaning	Reflexive Meaning
agir *to act*	s'agir de *to be a question of*
apercevoir *to see, notice*	s'apercevoir *to realize*
asseoir *to seat*	s'asseoir *to sit*
attendre *to wait for*	s'attendre à *to expect*
battre *to beat*	se battre *to fight*
cacher *to hide something*	se cacher *to hide oneself*
changer *to replace, alter*	se changer *to change clothes*
conduire *to drive, conduct*	se conduire *to behave*
coucher *to put to bed*	se coucher *to go to bed/sleep*
demander *to ask*	se demander *to wonder*
douter de *to doubt, question*	se douter de *to suspect*
endormir *to put to sleep*	s'endormir *to fall asleep*
ennuyer *to bore (someone)*	s'ennuyer *to become bored*
laver *to wash*	se laver *to wash oneself*
lever *to raise, lift*	se lever *to get up*
occuper *to occupy*	s'occuper de *to take care of*

passer	se passer de
to pass, spend time	*to do without*
plaindre	se plaindre
to pity	*to complain*
rappeler	se rappeler
to call again	*to remember, recall*
servir	se servir de
to serve	*to use*
tromper	se tromper
to deceive	*to make a mistake*

Note the difference in meaning in the following examples:

Elle a trompé son amie.	Elle s'est trompée.
She deceived her friend.	*She made a mistake.*
Il lève la tête.	Il se lève.
He raises his head.	*He gets up.*
Elle couchera l'enfant.	Elle se couchera.
She will put the child to bed.	*She will go to bed/sleep.*

Exercice 2

Use the correct form of the present tense to complete each sentence:

1. (endormir/s'endormir) Maman _____ les enfants et après elle _____ .

2. (conduire/se conduire) Thierry _____ d'une façon responsable quand il _____ la voiture de ses parents.

3. (servir/se servir de) Papa _____ un plateau quand il _____ le dîner.

4. (lever/se lever) Carine _____ la main et puis elle _____ afin de parler à toute la classe.

5. (demander/se demander) Jean _____ pourquoi son frère lui _____ la permission de sortir.

6. (attendre/s'attendre à) Louise _____ à recevoir de bonnes notes et pour cette raison elle _____ les résultats de ses examens.

7. (agir/s'agir) Luc _____ respectueusement parce qu'il _____ de faire une bonne impression au chef du bureau.

8. (apercevoir/s'apercevoir) Annick _____ que tout va bien quand elle _____ que tout le monde s'amuse.

Different Verbs with Different Connotations

In French, sometimes it's necessary to use different verbs where English connotations differ. It is important to use these verbs correctly to get the proper meaning across.

connaître and *savoir*

Connaître and *savoir* both mean "to know." Selecting the correct word to use is really quite simple:

◆ *Connaître* means "to know" in the sense of being acquainted with a person, place, or thing. If you can substitute the words "acquainted with" for the word "know," then use *connaître:*

Elle connaît cet homme.
She knows (She is acquainted with) that man.

Nous connaissons bien Paris.
We know (are well aquainted with) Paris.

Je connais ce poème.
I know (am acquainted with) that poem.
(I've heard of it but don't know it by heart!)

◆ *Savoir* means "to know a fact" or "to know how to do something" when followed by an infinitive:

Je ne sais pas ton adresse.
I don't know your address.

Nous savons faire de la peinture.
We know how to paint.

Savez-vous qu'il est canadien?
Do you know he is Canadian?

Note the difference in connotation between *connaître* and *savoir* in the following sentences:

>Vous connaissez cette chanson.
>*You know that song.*
>*(You are acquainted with it.)*

>Vous savez cette chanson.
>*You know that song.*
>*(You know the words and can sing it.)*

désirer and *souhaiter*

Désirer means to wish in the sense of desiring or wanting something, whereas *souhaiter* means to make a wish or to anticipate hopefully:

>Il désire te montrer son dessin.
>*He wants to show you his drawing.*

>Je te souhaite Joyeux Noël.
>*I wish you a Merry Christmas.*

dépenser and *passer*

Dépenser expresses "to spend money" or to spend in the sense of using something up, whereas *passer* expresses "to spend time":

>Elle a dépensé cent dollars en une heure.
>*She spent a hundred dollars in an hour.*

>Il a dépensé tout son énergie.
>*He spent (used up) all his energy.*

>J'ai passé deux semaines en France.
>*I spent two weeks in France.*

partir, sortir, quitter, and *laisser*

Partir means "to go away," "to leave (from, for)," or "to depart." Because it is an intransitive verb, it cannot be followed by a direct object:

>Nous partons pour la France demain.
>*We are leaving for France tomorrow.*

Quitter is a transitive verb meaning "to leave (a place or a person)" and must be followed by a direct object:

> Il a quitté l'hôtel et après il a quitté son ami.
> *He left the hotel and afterward he left his friend.*

Laisser, also transitive, means "to leave behind," "to abandon," or "to leave something/someone somewhere":

> Elle a laissé ses clefs à l'intérieur de sa voiture.
> *She left her keys inside her car.*

Sortir means "to go out" or "to take out." As an intransitive verb it is used with *être* in compound tenses and as a transitive verb it is used with *avoir* in compound tenses:

> J'ai sorti mon argent et je suis sorti.
> *I took out my money and I went out.*

Définitions

A transitive verb can be used in the passive or in the active voice with a direct object to complete its meaning.

An intransitive verb cannot be used in the passive and does not have an object.

rendre, retourner, revenir, and rentrer

Rendre means "to return" in the sense of "to give back":

> Rends-moi mon stylo, s'il te plaît.
> *Please return (give me back) my pen.*

Retourner means "to go back" to a place mentioned:

> Elle a envie de retourner en France.
> *She wants to go back to France.*

Revenir means "to come back" to or from a place:

> Il est revenu aux États-Unis la semaine passée.
> *He came back to the United States last week.*

> Elle est revenue du Canada.
> *She came back from Canada.*

Rentrer means "to come (back) home," "to come back in," or "to go (back) home":

> Ils sont rentrés tôt.
> *They came home early.*

porter and *mener*

Porter and any of its compounds (*apporter, emporter*) can only be used in the sense of "carrying":

> Portez ce livre à la bibliothèque.
> *Take this book to the library.*

> Apporte-moi une tasse de thé, s'il te plaît.
> *Please bring me a cup of tea.*

> Il a emporté les documents avec lui.
> *He took the documents (away) with him.*

Regarde!

The prefixes *a* and *ap* before *mener* and *porter* indicate that the subject is bringing or taking something along with him. The prefix *em* shows that the subject is taking something away with him:

> Il amène (emmène) son frère au cinéma.
> *He brings (takes) his brother along (away) to the movies.*

> Il apporte (emporte) des bonbons avec lui.
> *He brings (takes) along (away) candies.*

Mener and any of its compounds (*amener, emmener*) can only be used in the sense of "leading" or "accompanying" and usually only apply to persons, animals, and objects of motion:

> Menez Robert chez le dentiste.
> *Take Robert to the dentist's.*

> J'amènerai mes amis à la foire.
> *I will bring my friends to the fair.*

> Il m'emmènera au théâtre.
> *He will take me (with him) to the theater.*

pouvoir and *savoir*

Use *savoir* when can means "to know how":

> Il sait bien danser.
> *He knows how to dance well.*

In all other cases, can (to be able to, to have permission to) is translated by *pouvoir*:

Tu peux rester.
You can (may) stay.

Elles ne pouvaient pas venir.
They couldn't come.

penser à and penser de

Penser à is used when "to think of" means "to think about" or "to bear in mind":

Elle pense toujours à ses enfants.
She is always thinking of (about) her children.

Penser de is used when "to think of" means "to have an opinion of":

Que penses-tu de cette voiture?
What do you think of this car?

Songer à is often used instead of *penser à* and means "to contemplate or consider doing something":

Nous songeons à aller en ville.
We are thinking about going to the city.

Réfléchir à is used when "to think (about)" means "to reflect," or "to think over":

Ne parlez pas sans réfléchir.
Don't speak without thinking (over what you will say).

jouer à and jouer de

Jouer à means "to play games (sports)":

Joue-t-il au tennis?
Does he play tennis?

Jouer de means "to play a musical instrument":

Je joue du piano.
I play the piano.

habiter (demeurer) and vivre

Habiter and *demeurer* (to live) are used interchangeably to designate the actual town or residence. *Habiter* may or may not be followed by the preposition *à*, which always follows *demeurer*:

> Je demeure à New York.
> J'habite (à) New York.
> *I live in New York.*

Regarde! _____

Habiter may be followed by a direct object or a preposition. *Demeurer* and *vivre* may only be followed by a preposition:

J'habitais un bel apartement.
I lived in a beautiful apartment.

Je demeurais dans un bel apartement.
I lived in a beautiful apartement.

J'ai vécu à Nice.
I lived in Nice.

A distinction is not always made between *habiter* (*demeurer*) and *vivre*, although *vivre* means "to be alive" or "to live" when referring to the place in which the subject spends his life (and not the actual residence):

> Il vit bien.
> *He lives well.*

> Il a vécu dix ans en France. Il habitait (à) Paris.
> *He lived in France for ten years. He lived in Paris.*

Exercice 3

Complete each sentence with the correct form of the proper verb in the present tense:

1. (jouer à/jouer de) Quand il pleut Paulette _____ piano et ses deux frères _____ aux cartes.

2. (penser à/penser de) Je _____ me retirer des affaires. Qu'est-ce que vous _____ de cette idée?

3. (habiter/vivre) Je (J') _____ en Floride et je (j') _____ une maison près de la côte.

4. (pouvoir/savoir) Tu _____ employer mon ordinateur si tu _____ taper.

5. (quitter/sortir) Quand Joseph _____ il _____ ses frères.

6. (rendre/rentrer) Je te _____ ton pull quand je _____ cet après-midi.

7. (dépenser/passer) Clara _____ une heure dans sa boutique favorite où elle _____ beaucoup d'argent.

8. (connaître/savoir) Nous ne _____ pas si tu _____ notre soeur.

9. (laisser/partir) Sylvie _____ son livre à l'école quand elle _____ .

10. (amener/apporter) Mme Lawrence _____ toujours des sandwiches avec elle quand elle _____ ses enfants au grand magasin.

Récapitulation

1. *Devoir* expresses obligation, probability or supposition, or debt.

2. The causative *faire* shows that the subject causes an action to be done by someone or something else.

3. The impersonal *falloir* expresses necessity.

4. *Pouvoir* expresses ability or success, permissibility or possibility, a suggestion, an obligation, or "might" or "could."

5. *Savoir* is used to express knowledge gained through learning or shows knowledge of facts or reasons.

6. *Vouloir* expresses strong will in the present, a wish or desire in the conditional, an attempt or refusal to do something in the *passé composé*, or a polite command in the imperative.

7. *Connaître* expresses "to be acquainted with," whereas *savoir* expresses knowing a fact or how to do something.

8. *Désirer* expresses desire, whereas *souhaiter* means "to wish" or "to anticipate hopefully."

9. Use *dépenser* when spending money and *passer* when spending time.

10. *Partir* expresses "to go away." *Quitter* (to leave) must be followed by a direct object. *Laisser* means "to leave behind," and *sortir* means "to go out."

11. Use *rendre* to express "to give back," *retourner* to express "to go back to a place," *revenir* to express "to come back, and *rentrer* to express "to come home."

12. *Savoir* means "to know how," whereas *pouvoir* means "to be able to" or "to have permission to."

13. *Penser à* means "to think about," whereas *penser de* means "to have an opinion of." *Songer à* often replaces *penser à*. *Réfléchir à* means "to think over."

14. Use *jouer* + *à* when playing a sport or game and *jouer de* when playing a musical instrument.

The Least You Need to Know

◆ Certain French verbs have special uses.

◆ Other French verbs have different meanings when they are used reflexively.

◆ Although English may use only one word to convey a meaning, distinctions are made in French and these verbs must be learned to avoid confusion.

Chapter 10

Common Verbal Expressions and Usages

In This Chapter

- ◆ Using idioms
- ◆ Recognizing verbs frequently used idiomatically
- ◆ Using other verbal expressions
- ◆ The passive voice

If you want to speak and understand French as if you were a native speaker, it is important to acquire a good working knowledge of its idioms. Idioms add flavor and color to any language and are an essential part of its own, very individual beauty. Without them, languages would have no life.

Certain French verbs, especially a few high-frequency irregular verbs, lend themselves to idiomatic use. For this reason, it is essential to focus on learning these verbs in all tenses. Their recurrent, everyday use in a wide variety of situations forces you to pause and commit them to memory. If you practice using them conscientiously, you'll find that you'll be able to use them with ease and confidence rather quickly.

Some French verbs are less frequently used idiomatically, but they still add their own special flavor to the language. A quick look at some of them is worth the effort.

A few verbs such as *falloir* follow special rules. A closer look will make these verbs easier to conjugate.

The passive voice, while not used very often, pops up from time to time and it is important to recognize it and understand how it is used.

In this chapter, you will learn how to use idioms effectively, how to recognize the French verbs most commonly used in everyday idioms and expressions, and how to use the passive voice.

What Is an Idiom?

An idiom (referred to as *un idiotisme* or *un gallicisme*, in French) is a word or expression whose meaning cannot be readily understood by analyzing its component words. It is, however, still considered an acceptable part of the standard vocabulary of the language. We use English idioms all the time without even realizing it. Here are some common examples:

> She let her hair down!
> Can you bring me up to speed?
> It's raining cats and dogs!
> He eats like a horse!

Idioms and slang are different. *Slang* refers to colorful, popular, informal words or phrases that are *not* part of the standard vocabulary of a language. Slang is considered unconventional. It has evolved to describe particular items or situations in street language and is composed of coinages, arbitrarily changed words, and extravagant, forced, or facetious figures of speech. Some common examples of slang are:

> It's no biggie.
> She's an airhead.
> You're wearing cheesy clothes.
> He's a geek!

Idioms are acceptable in oral and written phrases; slang, although freely used in informal conversations, is generally considered substandard in formal writing and speaking. Much slang is, at best, X-rated, and will not appear in this book.

Idioms with Regular Verbs

A few idiomatic expressions are formed with regular verbs, some of which are also reflexive and require the use of a reflexive pronoun that agrees with the subject being used. Table 10.1 lists popular phrases with verbs in this category.

Table 10.1   Idioms with Regular Verbs

Idiom	Meaning
abandonner la partie	to throw in the cards/towel
accueillir quelqu'un à bras ouverts	to welcome with open arms
bâtir des châteaux en Espagne	to build castles in the air
brasser du vent	to speak without saying anything important
briser le coeur à quelqu'un	to break someone's heart
brûler la chandelle par les deux bouts	to burn the candle at both ends
brûler ses ponts	to burn one's bridges
casser du sucre sur le dos de quelqu'un	to talk about someone behind his back
casser les pieds à quelqu'un	to get on someone's nerves, break someone's back
changer son fusil d'épaule	to change one's opinion
chercher la petite bête	to nitpick, be excessively meticulous
chercher midi à quatorze heures	to make a simple thing complicated
couper la poire en deux	to meet halfway
couper le sifflet à quelqu'un	to interrupt someone
couper les cheveux en quatre	to split hairs
coûter les yeux de la tête	to cost an arm and a leg
dépenser sans compter	to spare no expense
donner un coup de main	to lend a helping hand
écraser quelque chose dans l'oeuf	to nip something in the bud
ficher le camp	to leave, shove off
filer à l'anglaise	to sneak out
fondre comme neige au soleil	to disappear very quickly
jouer la fille de l'air	to flee
marcher sur des oeufs	to walk on egg shells
ne pas mâcher ses mots	to not mince words
parler français comme une vache espagnole	to speak French rather poorly
passer devant la glace	to arrive too late to get something
passer sur le billard	to be operated on

continues

Table 10.1   Idioms with Regular Verbs   (continued)

Idiom	Meaning
passer un savon à quelqu'un	to reprimand vigorously
pêcher en eau trouble	to fish in troubled waters
piquer un fard	to blush
pleurer un bon coup	to have a good cry
porter le chapeau	to be responsible for something
pousser comme un champignon	to mushroom
raser les murs	to keep a low profile
regarder quelqu'un de travers	to look at someone with suspicion or hostility
regarder voler les mouches	to be lazy
remuer ciel et terre	to move heaven and earth
rendre à quelqu'un la monnaie de sa pièce	to give someone a taste of his own medicine
rester bouche bée	to remain open-mouthed, to gape
retourner sa veste	to quickly change one's mind or opinion
réussir les doigts dans le nez	to win (succeed) very easily
s'entendre comme chien et chat	to argue, fight like cats and dogs
s'occuper de ses oignons	to mind one's own business
saisir le taureau par les cornes	to take the bull by the horns
sauter aux yeux	to be evident
sauter du coq à l'âne	to jump from one topic to another
se creuser la tête	to rack one's brains
se fendre la pêche	to laugh one's head off
se fourrer le doigt dans l'oeil	to be completely mistaken
se laisser aller	to let one's hair down
se taper la tête contre le mur	to knock one's head against the wall
se trouver nez à nez avec quelqu'un	to find oneself unexpectedly face to face with someone
se vendre comme des petits pains	to sell like hotcakes
taper le carton	to play cards
taper sur les nerfs de quelqu'un	to get on one's nerves
tirer les plans sur la comète	to count one's chickens before they've hatched
tirer les vers du nez de quelqu'un	to drag information out of someone
tomber dans le panneau	to allow oneself to be easily tricked, fall for a trick
tomber dans les pommes	to faint
tomber sur un os	to hit a snag

Idiom	Meaning
tourner autour du pot	to beat around the bush
tourner de l'oeil	to faint
tourner les talons	to turn on one's heels

N'abandonnez pas la partie si facilement!
Don't throw in the cards so fast!

Pourquoi Georges cherche-t-il toujours la petite bête.
Why does Georges always nitpick?

Ils fichent le camp.
They shove off.

Je me suis trouvé nez a nèz avec mon adversaire.
I found myself face to face with my opponent.

Exercice 1

Complete each sentence by using a phrase found in the word bank:

coûter les yeux de la tête	rester bouche bée
donner un coup de main	retourner sa veste
passer devant la glace	sauter aux yeux
piquer un fard	sauter du coq à l'âne
pleurer un bon coup	s'entendre comme chien et chat
porter le chapeau	se creuser la tête
pousser comme un champignon	s'occuper de ses oignons
regarder voler les mouches	tomber dans le panneau

1. Si une solution est évidente il _____.

2. Janine ne se mêle jamais aux affaires des autres. Elle _____.

3. Hervé et son frère ont toujours des disputes. Ils _____ tout le temps.

4. M. Picard change constamment d'opinion. Il _____.

5. Liliane est embarrassée et pour cette raison elle _____.

6. Mme Renaud a de plus en plus de problèmes. On peut dire que ses problèmes _____.

7. Édouard ne croit pas ce qu'il entend. Il est complètement stupéfait. Pour cette raison il ouvre sa bouche et il _____.

8. Christian rompt avec Laure. Elle est très triste et elle _____.

9. Les Poireau ont payé cinquante mille euros leur nouvelle voiture. Cette auto _____.

10. Christine aide son amie, Charlotte. Elle lui _____.

11. Thérèse arrive toujours en retard pour obtenir ce qu'elle veut. On peut dire qu'elle _____.

12. M. Latour est le chef de son département. C'est lui qui _____.

13. Serge ne travaille jamais. Il _____.

14. Danielle cherche la réponse à une question importante. Pour cette raison elle _____.

15. D'abord Jean parle de la politique. Ensuite il parle des films. On peut dire qu'il _____.

16. Quand on est naïf on risque de _____.

Idioms with Irregular Verbs

Many idiomatic expressions are formed with irregular verbs and those with spelling changes. Table 10.2 lists phrases that begin with these most high-frequency French verbs.

Table 10.2 Idioms with Irregular Verbs and Verbs with Spelling Changes

Idiom	Meaning
avancer à toute vapeur	to go full steam ahead
avoir d'autres chats à fouetter	to have bigger fish to fry
avoir de l'argent à jeter par la fenêtre	to have money to burn
avoir l'air d'une poule qui a trouvé un couteau	to look puzzled or confused
avoir la belle vie	to have an easy time of it

Idiom	Meaning
avoir la chair de poule	to have goose pimples
avoir le beurre et l'argent du beurre	to have one's cake and to eat it too
avoir le bras long	to have influence
avoir le cafard	to be down in the dumps
avoir le coeur sur la main	to give the shirt off one's back
avoir mal au coeur	to be sick to one's stomach
avoir mangé du lion	to have a lot of energy
avoir un chat dans la gorge	to have a frog in one's throat
avoir une carte maîtresse en réserve	to have an ace up one's sleeve
avoir une dent contre quelqu'un	to have resentment towards someone
avoir une faim de loup	to be very hungry
avoir une mémoire d'éléphant	to have a good memory
dire son fait à quelqu'un	to give someone a piece of one's mind
dormir comme une souche	to sleep like a log
être à peine sorti de l'oeuf	to be wet behind the ears
être au four et au moulin	to be in two places at once
être branché(e)	to be trendy
être comme un poisson dans l'eau	to be at ease
être complètement allumé(e)	to be crazy
être cousu d'or	to be made of money
être dans les nuages	to have one's head in the clouds
être du gâteau	to be a piece of cake
être facile comme tout	to be as easy as pie
être la barbe	to be boring
être la goutte d'eau qui fait déborder le vase	to be the last straw
être muet(te) comme une carpe	to be capable of keeping a secret
être naïvement plein d'espoir	to have stars in one's eyes
être sauvé(e) par le gong	to be saved by the bell
être sur la bonne piste	to be hot on the trail, on the right track
être toujours sur la brèche	to be always on the go
être une vraie girouette	to keep changing one's mind
faire à sa tête	to do as one pleases
faire d'une pierre deux coups	to kill two birds with one stone
faire des pieds et des mains	to move heaven and earth
faire du lèche-vitrines	to go window shopping

continues

Table 10.2 Idioms with Irregular Verbs and Verbs with Spelling Changes (continued)

Idiom	Meaning
faire l'âne pour avoir du son	to play dumb
faire la sourde oreille	to turn a deaf ear
faire le lézard	to soak up some sun
faire le poireau	to hang out
faire le pont	to have a long weekend
faire son cinéma de	to make a big deal about
faire une montagne d'une taupinière	to make a mountain out of a molehill
jeter de l'huile sur le feu	to add fuel to the fire
jeter des fleurs à quelqu'un	to speak highly of someone
jeter l'argent par les fenêtres	to waste money
jeter un coup d'oeil	to take a look
manger comme quatre	to eat like a horse
manger sur le pouce	to eat on the run
mener grand train	to live in great style
mener par le bout du nez	to lead someone around
mener quelqu'un en bateau	to take someone for a ride
mettre tous ses oeufs dans le même panier	to put all one's eggs in one basket
n'en pouvoir plus	to be exhausted
obtenir quelque chose à l'oeil	to get something for free
pleuvoir des cordes	to rain cats and dogs
prendre ses jambes à son cou	to make a dash for it
se faire du cinéma	to delude oneself
se mettre le doigt dans l'oeil	to be completely mistaken
tenir la jambe à quelqu'un	to inconvenience someone with idle conversation
voir le monde par le petit bout de la lorgnette	to exaggerate about oneself
voir trente-six chandelles	to see stars

Il pleut des cordes.
It's raining cats and dogs.

Pour éviter l'orage elle a pris ses jambes à son cou.
To avoid the storm she made a dash for it.

Quand il est tombé il a vu trente-six chandelles.
When he fell he saw stars.

Elle admire son amie et elle lui jette des fleurs.
She admires her friend and she speaks highly of her.

Exercice 2

Match the expressions that convey the same meanings:

1. être triste	a. avoir mal au coeur
2. être riche	b. avancer à toute vapeur
3. avoir de l'énergie	c. faire la sourde oreille
4. être ennuyeux	d. manger sur le pouce
5. être à la mode	e. faire à sa tête
6. être facile	f. avoir le cafard
7. aller vite	g. être branché(e)
8. faire ce qu'on veut	h. faire le lézard
9. déjeuner vite	i. être la barbe
10. avoir mal au ventre	j. être du gâteau
11. rester au soleil	k. avoir mangé du lion
12. ne pas écouter	l. être cousu d'or

Common Verbal Expressions

The irregular verbs *avoir* (to have) and *faire* (to make, do) are used in many expressions that are frequently used in everyday conversations. For this reason, it is important to make sure that you know these two verbs well in all their tenses.

Expressions with *avoir*

Avoir (to have) is frequently used in expressions that show physical conditions and emotions where English uses "to be." Table 10.3 lists the most common expressions with this irregular verb.

Table 10.3   Expressions with *avoir*

Expression	Meaning
avoir beau + inf.	to do (something) in vain
avoir besoin de	to need
avoir chaud (froid)	to be hot (cold)
avoir de la chance	to be lucky
avoir de quoi + inf.	to have the means to
avoir envie de + inf.	to feel like
avoir faim (soif)	to be hungry (thirsty)
avoir hâte (de) + inf.	to be in a hurry to
avoir honte (de) + inf.	to be ashamed (of)
avoir l'air + adjective	to appear, to look
avoir l'air de + inf.	to seem to, to look as if
avoir l'habitude de + inf.	to be accustomed to
avoir l'idée de + inf.	to have the idea to
avoir l'intention de + inf.	to intend to
avoir l'occasion de + inf.	to have the opportunity to
avoir la parole	to have the floor (as a speaker)
avoir le temps de + inf.	to have the time to
avoir lieu	to take place
avoir mal à	to have an ache/pain in
avoir peur	to be afraid of
avoir quelque chose	to have something wrong
avoir raison (tort)	to be right (wrong)
avoir sommeil	to be sleepy
avoir … ans	to be … years old

As-tu chaud (froid, faim, soif, raison, tort, sommeil, de la chance, honte)?
Are you hot (cold, hungry, thirsty, right, sleepy, lucky, ashamed)?

Je n'ai peur de rien.
I'm not afraid of anything.

Avez-vous mal à la tête?
Do you have a headache?

J'ai besoin d'un couteau.
I need a knife.

Ont-ils envie d'aller en ville?
Do they feel like going to the city?

Sa fête aura lieu samedi soir.
Her party will take place Saturday night.

J'ai hâte de finir mon travail.
I'm in a hurry to finish my work.

Tu as l'air fatigué.
You look tired.

Exercice 3

Match the verb with the sentence it completes:

1. (passé composé) Hier il ___ mal à la gorge.   a. eut
2. (future) L'enfant ___ sommeil bientôt.   b. aies
3. (imperfect) Marthe ___ envie de sortir.   c. ait
4. (passé simple) Ce garçon ___ de la chance.   d. aurait
5. (present) François ___ dix-huit ans.   e. aura
6. (conditional) ___-il de bonnes idées?   f. a
7. (subjunctive) Il es possible qu'il ___ tort.   g. a eu
8. (imperative) N'___ pas peur du chien!   h. avait

Expressions with *faire*

Faire is frequently used in time and weather expressions. Table 10.4 lists the most common expressions with this irregular verb.

Table 10.4   Expressions with *faire*

Expression	Meaning
faire attention (à)	to pay attention (to)
faire beau (mauvais)	to be nice (bad) weather
faire de la peine (à)	to grieve, trouble, distress
faire de son mieux	to do one's best

continues

Table 10.4   Expressions with *faire*   (continued)

Expression	Meaning
faire des achats	to go shopping
faire des emplettes	to go shopping
faire des progrès	to make progress
faire du vent (soleil)	to be windy (sunny)
faire exprès	to do on purpose
faire froid (chaud)	to be cold (hot) weather
faire la connaissance de	to meet someone
faire les courses	to go shopping
faire mal à	to hurt someone
faire peur (à)	to frighten someone
faire plaisir à	to please, give pleasure to
faire savoir (à quelqu'un)	to let (someone) know
faire semblant de	to pretend to
faire ses adieux	to say good-bye
faire un voyage	to take a trip
faire une partie de	to play a game of
faire une promenade	to go for a walk
faire venir	to send for
se faire mal	to hurt (oneself)
se faire tard	to grow late

Quel temps fait-il? Il fait froid (chaud).
What's the weather like? It's cold (hot).

N'y fais pas attention.
Don't pay attention to it.

Nous ferons les courses plus tard.
We'll go shopping later.

Je voudrais faire un voyage.
I would like to take a trip.

Il se fait tard.
It's getting late.

Fais de ton mieux!
Do your best!

Il fait plaisir à ses enfants.
He pleases his children.

Ne te fais pas mal!
Don't hurt yourself!

Exercice 4

Select the form of the verb that best completes the sentence:

1. (present) Cette histoire me _____ peur.

   a. a fait   b. fit   c. fera   d. fait

2. (conditional) Si j'avais de l'argent je _____ des achats aujourd'hui.

   a. ferai   b. ferais   c. fasse   d. fait

3. (future) Elles _____ la connaissance de mon cousin ce soir.

   a. feront   b. feraient   c. fassent   d. font

4. (passé simple) Il _____ semblant de tomber.

   a. a fait   b. fasse   c. fit   d. fut

5. (passé composé) Vous _____ une promenade.

   a. fassiez   b. faites   c. avez fait   d. ferez

6. (imperfect) Nous _____ une partie de football quand il a commencé à pleuvoir.

   a. fassions   b. faisions   c. ferions   d. faisons

7. (imperative) _____-moi savoir ton numéro de téléphone.

   a. faites   b. fasses   c. fit   d. fais

8. (subjunctive) Je veux que tu _____ tes adieux à tes amis maintenant.

   a. fasses   b. faisais   c. as fait   d. feras

Other Verbal Expressions

A small number of other verbs express ideas that may come in handy. Table 10.5 lists some regular, reflexive, spelling- and stem-changing verbs, and irregular verbs that are found in only a few phrases.

Table 10.5   Other Common Expressions

Expression	Meaning
adresser la parole à	to address, speak to
aller	to feel (health)
aller à	to suit, fit
aller à la rencontre de	to go to meet
apprendre par coeur	to memorize
donner sur	to face, look out on
éclater de rire	to burst out laughing
entendre dire que	to hear that
entendre parler de	to hear of
en vouloir à	to have a grudge against
envoyer chercher	to send for
être à	to belong to
être d'accord (avec)	to agree (with)
être de retour	to be back
être en train de	to be busy, to be in the act of
être sur le point de	to be on the verge of
poser une question	to ask a question
prendre garde de	to be careful not to
rire de	to laugh at
tenir à	to insist on, be anxious to, value
venir de	to have just
vouloir bien	to be willing
vouloir dire	to mean
y être	to understand, see the point

Cette robe te va.
That dress suits you.

Il va à la rencontre de sa petite amie.
He's going to meet his girlfriend.

J'ai entendu dire qu'ils démissioneront.
I heard that they will resign.

Il a éclaté de rire.
He burst out laughing.

Elle en voulait à sa soeur.
She had a grudge against her sister.

Quand seront-ils de retour?
When will they be back?

J'ai une question à vous poser.
I have a question to ask you.

Ils venaient de rentrer.
They just returned.

Exercice 5

Give the French for the words in parenthesis:

1. (I sent for) _____ le docteur hier soir.

2. (He valued) _____ ses souvenirs.

3. (mean) Qu'est-ce que cela _____?

4. (belongs to) Il est possible que ce portefeuille _____ M. Dupont.

5. (wouldn't laugh at) Ils ne _____ pas de nous.

6. (will memorize) Nous _____ ce poème.

The Passive Voice

The active voice is generally used in speaking or in writing. In this voice, the subject noun or pronoun performs the action. In the passive voice, something or someone else acts upon the subject. It is usually considered preferable to avoid the passive whenever possible.

Active:
The boy bought a car.
Le garçon a acheté une voiture.

Passive:
The car was bought by the boy.
La voiture a été achetée par le garçon.

The passive construction in French mirrors the English construction:

subject + *être* + past participle + *par* + agent (doer if mentioned)

The cake is bought by the child.
Le gâteau est acheté par l'enfant.

The cake was baked by the pastry chef.
Le gâteau a été fait par le pâtissier.

It will be eaten by the whole family.
Il sera mangé par toute la famille.

Regarde! _____

The agent does not have to appear in a passive sentence:

La banque a été volée (par deux hommes).
The bank was robbed (by two men).

Substitute Constructions for the Passive

Because the passive is used less frequently in French than in English, the following constructions may be substituted for the passive:

◆ An active construction with the pronoun *on* followed by the third person singular of the verb:

Ici on parle français.
French is spoken here.

Est-ce qu'on a tout vu?
Has everything been seen?

Peut-on l'aider?
Can he be helped?

◆ In some instances, a reflexive verb may replace a passive construction:

Elle s'appelle Anne.
She is called (Her name is) Anne.

La porte s'est fermée.
The door was shut.

Les billets se vendaient là-bas.
Tickets were (being) sold there.

Attention! _____

In the passive, because the past participle is used like an adjective, it agrees in number and gender with the subject:

L'église a été construite au dix-neuvième siècle.
The church was built in the nineteenth century.

Exercice 6

Express what each famous person did by changing the verb from the active voice to the passive:

Exemple:
Georges Bizet a composé l'opéra *Carmen*.
L'opéra *Carmen* a été composé par Georges Bizet.

1. Antoine de Saint-Exupéry a écrit le roman *Le Petit Prince*. _____

2. Samuel de Champlain a fondé la ville de Québec. _____

3. Napoléon Bonaparte a crée la Légion d'Honneur. _____

4. Edgar Degas a peint les danseuses de l'Opéra. _____

5. Auguste Rodin a sculpté *Le Baiser*. _____

6. Pierre et Marie Curie ont découvert le radium. _____

Exercice 7

Write the sentences expressing what was accomplished around the house by changing the sentence from the passive voice to the active voice:

Exemple:
La vaisselle a été faite.
On a fait la vaisselle.

1. L'aspirateur a été passé.

   _____

2. La table a été mise.

   _____

3. Les lits ont été faits.

   _____

4. Le repas a été préparé.

   _____

5. Les vêtements ont été repassés.

   _____

6. Les fleurs ont été arrosées.

   _____

Récapitulation

1. An idiom is a word or expression whose meaning cannot be readily understood by analyzing its component words.

2. An idiom is considered an acceptable part of the standard vocabulary of the language.

3. Slang refers to colorful, popular, informal words or phrases that are not part of the standard vocabulary of a language.

4. Slang has evolved to describe particular items or situations in street language and is composed of coinages, arbitrarily changed words, and extravagant, forced, or facetious figures of speech.

5. Idioms are acceptable in oral and written phrases, whereas slang is considered substandard in formal writing and speaking.

6. Some idiomatic expressions are formed with regular verbs, reflexive verbs, or verbs with stem or spelling changes.

7. Many idiomatic expressions are formed with irregular verbs.

8. It is important to learn the irregular verbs *avoir* (to have) and *faire* (to make, do), because they are used in common expressions.

9. The active voice is most commonly used in speaking and writing.

10. The passive voice is generally avoided, where possible.

11. In the passive, the past participle is used like an adjective and agrees in number and gender with the subject.

12. An active construction with *on* or a reflexive construction may be substituted for the passive.

The Least You Need to Know

- ◆ Every language has its own peculiar idioms that can't be translated word for word because there is no logic or understandable grammar that explains them.

- ◆ Many idioms are introduced by irregular verbs, which must be memorized in all forms.

- ◆ Many useful French expressions are introduced by *avoir* (to have) and *faire* (to make, do).

- ◆ In French the passive voice is expressed by subject + *être* + past participle (which agrees with the subject) + *par* + agent (doer if mentioned).

- ◆ The passive voice may be avoided by using *on* + an active construction or by using a reflexive construction.

Appendix **A**

Answer Key

Chapter 1

Exercice 1

1. travaillé	2. regardé	3. choisi
4. agi	5. répondu	6. vendu
7. compris	8. décrit	9. découvert
10. souri		

Exercice 2

1. sommes	2. a	3. avez
4. suis	5. as	6. sont
7. est	8. est	

Exercice 3

1. avons chanté (We sang in chorus.)

2. avais fini (You had finished your work early.)

3. eut défendu (The soldier had defended his country.)

4. serai parti(e) (I will have left before his return.)

5. auriez aidées (The girls? You would have helped them, wouldn't you?)

6. soient devenus (It is possible that the boys became chefs.)

7. eusse fait (It was good that he had done that work.)

Exercice 4

1. cherchant	2. réfléchissant	3. attendant
4. voyageant	5. avançant	6. appelant
7. achetant	8. célébrant	

Exercice 5

1. jouant	2. prononçant	3. mangeant
4. applaudissant	5. tondant	6. promenant

Exercice 6

1. Étant rentrée	2. Ayant eu
3. Ayant fait	4. Étant arrivées
5. Ayant voulu	6. Étant tombée

Chapter 2

Exercice 1

1. to adore	2. to accomplish	3. to correspond
4. to applaud	5. to invite	6. to defend
7. to finish	8. to descend	9. to organize
10. to guarantee	11. to respond	12. to telephone

Exercice 2

A.

1. renonce	2. renoncent	3. renonçons
4. renonces	5. renonce	6. renoncez

B.

1. commençais	2. commenciez	3. commençait
4. commencions	5. commençais	6. commençaient

C.

1. lanças	2. menacèrent	3. renonçai
4. anonça	5. avançâmes	6. influençâtes

Exercice 3

A.

1. mangez	2. mange	3. mangent
4. mangeons	5. mange	6. manges

B.

1. rangeait	2. rangeais	3. rangeaient
4. rangions	5. rangeais	6. rangiez

C.

1. déménagèrent	2. nageas	3. corrigeâtes
4. dirigea	5. changea	6. arrangeâmes

Exercice 4

A.

1. emploies	2. employons	3. emploie
4. employez	5. emploie	6. emploient

B.

1. paierons	2. paierez	3. paieront
4. paiera	5. paierai	6. paieras

C.

1. emploierait	2. emploierions	3. emploieraient
4. emploierais	5. emploierais	6. emploieriez

D.

1. essuyions	2. paie	3. envoie
4. essaies	5. nettoierions	6. emploient

Exercice 5

1. achète	2. amènerai	3. promeniez
4. achèveraient	5. pèses	6. enlevons
7. élèveront	8. emmenèneriez	

Exercice 6

1. appelleront	2. jette	3. rappelle
4. feuilletterez	5. rejettez	6. époussetions
7. renouvellerait	8. épelleront	

Exercice 7

A.

1. préfères	2. préférons	3. préfèrent
4. préfère	5. préfère	6. préférez

B.

1. tolères	2. coopère	3. révériez
4. révèle	5. complétions	6. délibèrent

Chapter 3

Exercice 1

1. marchent	2. donne	3. expliquons
4. criez	5. regardes	6. traversez
7. dîne	8. demande	9. dessine
10. remercient		

Exercice 2

1. maigrissons	2. grossissent	3. nourrissez
4. trahis	5. saisit	6. accomplissez
7. obéit	8. garantit	9. remplis
10. réfléchissent		

Exercice 3

1. descendent	2. dépendez	3. répandons
4. prétend	5. mordent	6. prétends
7. répond	8. revendez	9. suspends
10. tond		

Exercice 4

Verb	Je	Nous	Ils
envoyer	envoie	envoyons	envoient
ranger	range	rangeons	rangent
acheter	achète	achetons	achètent
effacer	efface	effaçons	effacent
célébrer	célèbre	célébrons	célèbrent
rappeler	rappelle	rappelons	rappellent
partager	partage	partageons	partagent
employer	emploie	employons	emploient
achever	achève	achevons	achèvent
rejeter	rejette	rejetons	rejettent
protéger	protège	protégeons	protègent
prononcer	prononce	prononçons	prononcent

Exercice 5

1. reçois	2. reçoit	3. reçois
4. recevons	5. reçoivent	6. recevez

Exercice 6

1. se rase
2. se disputent
3. m'inquiète
4. vous exprimez
5. se peignent
6. nous spécialisons
7. t'appelles
8. se lève

Exercice 7

1. va
2. sommes
3. peux
4. avons
5. vient
6. prends
7. écrivent
8. faites

Exercice 8

1. grossissent
2. fumes
3. conduit
4. vis
5. mangeons
6. vont

Exercice 9

1. aie/ne sois pas
2. ne consomme pas/bois
3. suis/ne mange pas
4. ne t'inquiète pas/habitue-toi
5. choisis/ne prends pas

Exercice 10

1. s'est maquillée
2. avez lu
3. sont allées
4. ont passé
5. sont arrivés
6. me suis arrêté(e)
7. es sorti(e)
8. avons eu
9. sont devenus
10. s'est habillée
11. as peint
12. s'est bronzée

Chapter 4

Exercice 1

1. s'amusaient	2. était	3. mangeaient
4. jouait	5. dansais	6. commençait
7. garnissait	8. perdait	9. buvions
10. vérifiez	11. se plaignait	12. paraissait

Exercice 2

1. était	2. faisait	3. n'avais
4. étais	5. ai entendu	6. ai couru
7. ai vu	8. était	9. s'ennuyaient
10. sont venus	11. voulais	12. ai trouvé
13. avais	14. ai éteint	15. ai mis
16. ai écrit	17. allais	18. sommes partis

Exercice 3

1. était	2. avais	3. étais
4. a interdit	5. lisais	6. ai entendu
7. ai ouvert	8. se passait	9. voulaient
10. étaient	11. se sont mis	12. était
13. essayait	14. courait	15. brillait
16. ne pouvait pas	17. s'est cogné	18. est tombé
19. était	20. ne s'est pas levé	21. a commencé
22. est arrivé	23. s'est cassé	24. pouvait
25. a crié	26. ai téléphoné	27. est arrivée
28. n'allait plus		

Exercice 4

1. Nous sommes tombés parce que nous ne faisions pas attention.

2. Tu as appelé Lise parce que tu voulais aller au cinéma.

3. Elle est allée chez le docteur parce qu'elle avait mal à la gorge.

4. J'ai sorti mon parapluie parce qu'il commençait à pleuvoir.

5. Elles se sont réveillées parce que c'était dimanche.

6. Vous êtes devenu(e)(s) nerveux parce que vous changiez de résidence.

Exercice 5

1. conduisait/a eu

2. se promenait/a piquée

3. est tombée/courait

4. avez pris/voyageaient

5. buvais/ai vu

6. sont restées/pouvaient

7. avez pris/êtes allé

8. étions/s'est éteinte

Exercice 6

1. Combien de temps y avait-il qu'Hélène allait à l'université?

   Il y avait un an qu'Hélène allait à l'université.

2. Combien de temps y avait-il que François et Jacques étaient amis?

   Il y avait dix ans qu'ils étaient amis.

3. Combien de temps y avait-il que nous jouions de la guitare?

   Il y avait deux mois que nous jouions (vous jouiez) de la guitare.

4. Combien de temps y avait-il que Patrick avait sa propre voiture?

   Il y avait une semaine qu'il avait sa propre voiture.

5. Combien de temps y avait-il que tu habitais aux États-Unis?

   Il y avait cinq ans que j'habitais aux États-Unis.

6. Combien de temps y avait-il que vous suiviez un régime?

   Il y avait six jours que je suivais un régime.

Exercice 7

1. Nous avions reçu de mauvaises notes.

2. Elle s'était endormie tard hier soir.

3. Tu étais devenu médecin.

4. Elles avaient eu la mauvaise chance.

5. Tu étais resté à la maison.

6. Vous vous êtes cassé le bras.

Chapter 5

Exercice 1

1. The Roman conquest gave Gaul peace and security.

2. Clovis, the king of the Franks, converted to Christianity, the official religion of the country.

3. They betrayed Joan of Arc and burned her alive at Rouen.

4. François I encouraged exploration.

5. Cardinal Richelieu improved the economic life of France and reformed finances and legislation.

6. During the reign of Louis XV, France lost Canada.

7. Napoleon Bonaparte exerted a great influence on his time. He tried to conquer Europe. When enemies invaded the country, he retired to Elba.

8. The Great War between France and Germany broke out in 1914.

Exercice 2

1. Louis David painted scenes of Greek history with precision.

2. Dominique Ingres, a student of David's, became the champion of academic painting.

3. Edouard Manet was one of the founders of the Impressionist school.

4. Paul Gauguin left for Tahiti to continue his painting career.

5. Henri de Toulouse-Lautrec made posters of music hall scenes.

6. Jean-Baptiste Lully wrote music for many of Molière's comedies.

7. Under the reign of Louis XIV, opera was born.

8. Jean de la Fontaine, French fable writer, was born in 1621 and died in 1695.

9. Sully Prudhomme, a poet, received the first Nobel prize in literature in 1901.

10. Jean-Paul Sartre had a great influence on other existentialists.

Exercice 3

1. When we had opened the door, the salesman greeted us.

2. As soon as the boy had told the lie, he regretted it.

3. After I had written him a letter, I destroyed it.

4. As soon as you had awakened, you called your friend.

5. When you had arrived home, you ate.

6. After her parents had come home, she went out

Chapter 6

Exercice 1

1. Je vais écouter des CD.

2. Nous allons regarder la télévision.

3. Elles vont lire.

4. Vous allez aller en ville.

5. Tu vas surfer l'Internet.

6. Ils vont jouer à des jeux vidéo.

Exercice 2

1. jetterons	2. sortira	3. nettoierai
4. rangeront	5. promèneras	6. paierez (payerez)
7. tondra	8. nourriront	

Exercice 3

dirai, irai, voudrez, pourrai, sera, devrai, ferai, viendrai, saurez, vaudra, aura, enverrai

Exercice 4

1. seras, me promènerai

2. viendrai, pourrai

3. irons, achèterai

4. arriverai, enverrai

5. pleuvra, nous ennuierons

6. recevras, ferai

Exercice 5

1. nous serons couchés

2. auront dîné

3. serai rentré

4. Christine se serait déshabillée

5. seras monté

6. aurez fait

Chapter 7

Exercice 1

1. nous occuperions   2. renouvellerais   3. finirais

4. correspondraient   5. nettoierait   6. emmèneriez

7. rangeraient   8. s'achèterait

Exercice 2

1. Les employés ne viendraient pas au bureau.

2. Il vaudrait mieux rester à la maison.

3. Nous aurions peur.

4. Vous n'iriez pas à l'école.

5. Je devrais aider mes parents.

6. Carine ne pourrait pas envoyer son courrier électronique.

7. Tout le monde saurait rester calme.

8. Tu t'inquièterais.

Exercice 3

1. ferais	2. t'achèterais	3. voyagerions
4. iriez	5. dormirait	6. s'amuserait

Exercice 4

1. auraient fait	2. me serais acheté	3. aurions pris
4. serait allée	5. vous seriez retiré(s)	6. serais devenu(e)

Exercice 5

1. recevras/as	2. suis/obtiendrai
3. comprendrez/étudiez	4. travaillent/gagneront
5. faisons/réussirons	6. deviendra/s'applique

Exercice 6

1. avais oublié	2. étais	3. avaient
4. serions allés	5. ferais	6. se serait mariée

Chapter 8

Exercice 1

1. Il est nécessaire que cette fille finisse ses devoirs chaque soir.

2. Il est nécessaire que je réponde à beaucoup de questions en classe.

3. Il est nécessaire que tous les élèves participent consciencieusement.

4. Il est nécessaire que tu réfléchisses avant de parler.

5. Il est nécessaire que nous nous occupions seulement de nos affaires.

6. Il est nécessaire que vous défendiez vos opinions.

Exercice 2

1. Il est important que nous mangions bien.

2. Il est important que elles reçoivent de bonnes notes.

3. Il est important que tu emploies un ordinateur pour faire tes devoirs.

4. Il est important qu'il achève son travail.

5. Il est important que vous buviez beaucoup d'eau.

6. Il est important qu'elle épelle bien les verbes.

7. Il est important qu'ils répètent les mots de vocabulaire.

8. Il est important que je prenne le temps de bien faire mes devoirs.

Exercice 3

1. Il est douteux que Janine et Lise soient en retard.

2. Il est douteux que tu veuilles travailler dimanche.

3. Il est douteux que vous puissiez nous accompagner au musée.

4. Il est douteux qu'ils sachent jouer du piano.

5. Il est douteux qu'elle devienne ingénieur.

6. Il est douteux que j'aie tort.

7. Il est douteux que Jacques se plaigne de son problème.

8. Il est douteux que nous fassions un voyage cet été.

Exercice 4

| 1. vienne | 2. fasse | 3. achetons (achèterons) |
| 4. se réunisse | 5. conduisent | 6. attendez |

Exercice 5

1. s'aperçoivent	2. prenne	3. finissions
4. lisiez	5. résolves	6. sois
7. répondrez	8. mette	

Exercice 6

1. sorte	2. reçoive	3. sachiez
4. suivent	5. coure	6. fassent

Exercice 7

1. Papa donne de l'argent à Mireille pour qu'elle s'achète de nouveaux vêtements.

2. Rose fait tant de bruit parce qu'elle apprend à jouer de la guitare.

3. Je prépare le dîner avant que ma mère puisse me le demander.

4. Thomas regarde la télévision malgré qu'il ait beaucoup de devoirs à faire.

5. Lucien écoute des CD pendant que nous jouons aux échecs.

6. Je lis le journal en attendant que vous m'aidiez.

Exercice 8

1. a	2. soient	3. connaisse
4. puisse	5. sache	6. parte

Exercice 9

1. se soit égarée	2. ait appris
3. soit devenu	4. ait découvert
5. vous soyez arrêté(e)(s)	6. soit née

Exercice 10

1. Il doit faire un voyage en Italie.

2. Je dois écrire une lettre à ma correspondante.

3. Nous devons lire un recueil de poèmes.

4. Claire et Madeleine doivent prendre le métro.

5. Vous devez rester à la maison pendant le week-end.

6. Tu dois te réveiller tôt demain matin.

Exercice 11

1. traduisions	2. vienne	3. choisissent
4. écrivez	5. ait	6. perdes
7. dormons	8. réussissions	9. soit
10. attende	11. agisse	12. connaisse
13. se sert	14. sachions	15. aillent
16. fassent	17. suive	18. répète
19. appelions	20. puissions	

Chapter 9

Exercice 1

1. doit	2. faut	3. me suis fait	4. ne pouvaient
5. Sais	6. voudrions	7. fait	8. devez
9. pourrait	10. Veuillez		

Exercice 2

1. endort, s'endort	2. se conduit, conduit
3. se sert d', sert	4. lève, se lève
5. se demande, demande	6. s'attend à, attend
7. agit, s'agit	8. s'aperçoit, aperçoit

Exercice 3

1. joue du, jouent aux	2. pense à, pensez de
3. vis, habite	4. peux, sais
5. sort, quitte	6. rends, rentre
7. passe, dépense	8. savons, connais
9. laisse, part	10. apporte, amène

Chapter 10

Exercice 1

1. saute aux yeux

2. s'occupe de ses oignons

3. s'entendent comme chien et chat

4. retourne sa veste

5. pique un fard

6. poussent comme un champignon

7. reste bouche bée

8. pleure un bon coup

9. coûte les yeux de la tête

10. donne un coup de main

11. passe devant la glace

12. porte le chapeau

13. regarde voler les mouches

14. se creuse la tête

15. saute du coq à l'âne

16. tomber dans le panneau

Exercice 2

1. f	2. l	3. k	4. i	5. g	6. j
7. b	8. e	9. d	10. a	11. h	12. c

Exercice 3

1. g	2. e	3. h	4. a
5. f	6. d	7. c	8. b

Exercice 4

1. d	2. b	3. a	4. c
5. c	6. b	7. d	8. a

Exercice 5

1. ai envoyé chercher

2. tenait à

3. veut dire

4. soit à

5. riraient

6. apprendrons par coeur

Exercice 6

1. Le roman *Le Petit Prince* a été écrit par Antoine de Saint-Exupéry.

2. La ville de Québec a été fondée par Samuel de Champlain.

3. La Légion d'Honneur a été crée par Napoléon Bonaparte.

4. Les danseuses de l'Opéra ont été peintes par Edgar Degas.

5. *Le Baiser* a été sculpté par Auguste Rodin.

6. Le radium a été découvert par Pierre et Marie Curie.

Exercice 7

1. On a passé l'aspirateur.

2. On a mis la table.

3. On a fait les lits.

4. On a préparé les repas.

5. On a repassé les vêtements.

6. On a arrosé les fleurs.

Verb Charts

This appendix contains high-frequency irregular French verbs. While some verbs are irregular in all of their tenses and all of their forms, others are irregular only in some tenses and/or forms. All irregularities are highlighted in boldface. Compound forms of certain irregular verbs, which follow the same rules for conjugation as the verbs they contain, are listed in Appendix C. Verbs preceded by an asterisk use *être* as their helping verb. Bear in mind that, depending upon the subject, these verbs may require a feminine or plural past participle in all compound tenses.

Regular Verbs

-er Verbs

PARLER   to speak
Present participle: parlant
Past participle: parlé
Commands: Parle! Parlons! Parlez!

Simple Tenses

Present	Imperfect	Passé Simple	Future	Conditional	Subjunctive	Imperfect Subjunctive
parle	parlais	parlai	parlerai	parlerais	parle	parlasse
parles	parlais	parlas	parleras	parlerais	parles	parlasses
parle	parlait	parla	parlera	parlerait	parle	parlât
parlons	parlions	parlâmes	parlerons	parlerions	parlions	parlassions
parlez	parliez	parlâtes	parlerez	parleriez	parliez	parlassiez
parlent	parlaient	parlèrent	parleront	parleraient	parlent	parlassent

Compound Tenses

Passé Composé	Pluperfect	Passé Antérieur	Future Perfect	Conditional Perfect	Past Subjunctive	Pluperfect Subjunctive
ai parlé	avais parlé	eus parlé	aurai parlé	aurais parlé	aie parlé	eusse parlé
as parlé	avais parlé	eus parlé	auras parlé	aurais parlé	aies parlé	eusses parlé
a parlé	avait parlé	eut parlé	aura parlé	aurait parlé	ait parlé	eût parlé
avons parlé	avions parlé	eûmes parlé	aurons parlé	aurions parlé	ayons parlé	eussions parlé
avez parlé	aviez parlé	eûtes parlé	aurez parlé	auriez parlé	ayez parlé	eussiez parlé
ont parlé	avont parlé	eûrent parlé	auront parlé	auraient parlé	aient parlé	eussent parlé

continues

-ir Verbs

CHOISIR to choose

Present participle: choisissant
Past participle: choisi
Commands: Choisis! Choisissons! Choisissez!

Simple Tenses

Present	Imperfect	Passé Simple	Future	Conditional	Subjunctive	Imperfect Subjunctive
choisis	choisissais	choisis	choisirai	choisirais	choisisse	choisisse
choisis	choisissais	choisis	choisiras	choisirais	choisisses	choisisses
choisit	choisissait	choisit	choisira	choisirait	choisisse	choisît
choisissons	choisissions	choisîmes	choisirons	choisirions	choisissions	choisissions
choisissez	choisissiez	choisîtes	choisirez	choisiriez	choisissiez	choisissiez
choisissent	choisissaient	choisirent	choisiront	choisiraient	choisissent	choisissent

Compound Tenses

Passé Composé	Pluperfect	Passé Antérieur	Future Perfect	Conditional Perfect	Past Subjunctive	Pluperfect Subjunctive
ai choisi	avais choisi	eus choisi	aurai choisi	aurais choisi	aie choisi	eusse choisi
as choisi	avais choisi	eus choisi	auras choisi	aurais choisi	aies choisi	eusses choisi
a choisi	avait choisi	eut choisi	aura choisi	aurait choisi	ait choisi	eût choisi
avons choisi	avions choisi	eûmes choisi	aurons choisi	aurions choisi	ayons choisi	eussions choisi

continued

Passé Composé	Pluperfect	Passé Antérieur	Future Perfect	Conditional Perfect	Past Subjunctive	Pluperfect Subjunctive
avez choisi	aviez choisi	eûtes choisi	aurez choisi	auriez choisi	ayez choisi	eussiez choisi
ont choisi	avaiennt choisi	eûrent choisi	auront choisi	auraient choisi	aient choisi	eussent choisi

-re Verbs

VENDRE   to sell
Present participle: vendant
Past participle: vendu
Commands: Vends! Vendons! Vendez!

Simple Tenses

Present	Imperfect	Passé Simple	Future	Conditional	Subjunctive	Imperfect Subjunctive
vends	vendais	vendis	vendrai	vendrais	vende	vendisse
vends	vendais	vendis	vendras	vendrais	vendes	vendisses
vend	vendait	vendit	vendra	vendrait	vende	vendît
vendons	vendions	vendîmes	vendrons	vendrions	vendions	vendissions
vendez	vendiez	vendîtes	vendrez	vendriez	vendiez	vendissiez
vendent	vendaient	vendirent	vendront	vendraient	vendent	vendissent

Compound Tenses

Passé Composé	Pluperfect	Passé Antérieur	Future Perfect	Conditional Perfect	Past Subjunctive	Pluperfect Subjunctive
ai vendu	avais vendu	eus vendu	aurai vendu	aurais vendu	aie vendu	eusse vendu
as vendu	avais vendu	eus vendu	auras vendu	aurais vendu	aies vendu	eusses vendu
a vendu	avait vendu	eut vendu	aura vendu	aurait vendu	ait vendu	eût vendu
avons vendu	avions vendu	eûmes vendu	aurons vendu	aurions vendu	ayons vendu	eussions vendu
avez vendu	aviez vendu	eûtes vendu	aurez vendu	auriez vendu	ayez vendu	eussiez vendu
ont vendu	avaient vendu	eûrent vendu	auront vendu	auraient vendu	aient vendu	eussent vendu

-er Verbs with Spelling Changes

-cer Verbs

LANCER   to throw
Present participle: lançant
Past participle: lance
Commands: Lance! Lançons! Lancez!

Simple Tenses

Present	Imperfect	Passé Simple	Future	Conditional	Subjunctive	Imperfect Subjunctive
lance	lançais	lançai	lancerai	lancerais	lance	lançasse
lances	lançais	lanças	lanceras	lancerais	lances	lançasses
lance	lançait	lança	lancera	lancerait	lance	lançât
lançons	lancions	lançâmes	lancerons	lancerions	lancions	lançassions
lancez	lanciez	lançâtes	lancerez	lanceriez	lanciez	lançassiez
lancent	lançaient	lancèrent	lanceront	lanceraient	lancent	lançassent

Compound Tenses

Passé Composé	Pluperfect	Passé Antérieur	Future Perfect	Conditional Perfect	Past Subjunctive	Pluperfect Subjunctive
ai lancé	avais lancé	eus lancé	aurai lancé	aurais lancé	aie lancé	eusse lancé
as lancé	avais lancé	eus lancé	auras lancé	aurais lancé	aies lancé	eusses lancé
a lancé	avait lancé	eut lancé	aura lancé	aurait lancé	ait lancé	eût lancé
avons lancé	avions lancé	eûmes lancé	aurons lancé	aurions lancé	ayons lancé	eussions lancé
avez lancé	aviez lancé	eûtes lancé	aurez lancé	auriez lancé	ayez lancé	eussiez lancé
ont lancé	avaient lancé	eûrent lancé	auront lancé	auraient lancé	aient lancé	eussent lancé

-ger **Verbs**

MANGER   to eat
Present participle: mangeant
Past participle: mangé
Commands: *Mange! Mangeons! Mangez!*

Simple Tenses

Present	Imperfect	Passé Simple	Future	Conditional	Subjunctive	Imperfect Subjunctive
mange	mangeais	mangeai	mangerai	mangerais	mange	mangeasse
manges	mangeais	mangeas	mangeras	mangerais	manges	mangeasses
mange	mangeait	mangea	mangera	mangerait	mange	mangeât
mangeons	mangions	mangeâmes	mangerons	mangerions	mangions	mangeassions
mangez	mangiez	mangeâtes	mangerez	mangeriez	mangiez	mangeassiez
mangent	mangeaient	mangèrent	mangeront	mangeraient	mangent	mangeassent

Compound Tenses

Passé Composé	Pluperfect	Passé Antérieur	Future Perfect	Conditional Perfect	Past Subjunctive	Pluperfect Subjunctive
ai mangé	avais mangé	eus mangé	aurai mangé	aurais mangé	aie mangé	eusse mangé
as mangé	avais mangé	eus mangé	auras mangé	aurais mangé	aies mangé	eusses mangé
a mangé	avait mangé	eut mangé	aura mangé	aurait mangé	ait mangé	eût mangé
avons mangé	avions mangé	eûmes mangé	aurons mangé	aurions mangé	ayons mangé	eussions mangé
avez mangé	aviez mangé	eûtes mangé	aurez mangé	auriez mangé	ayez mangé	eussiez mangé
ont mangé	avaient mangé	eûrent mangé	auront mangé	auraient mangé	aient mangé	eussent mangé

-yer Verbs

NETTOYER   to clean

Present participle: nettoyant
Past participle: nettoyé
Commands: Nettoie! Nettoyons! Nettoyez!

Simple Tenses

Present	Imperfect	Passé Simple	Future	Conditional	Subjunctive	Imperfect Subjunctive
nettoie	nettoyais	nettoyai	nettoierai	nettoierais	nettoie	nettoyasse
nettoies	nettoyais	nettoyas	nettoieras	nettoierais	nettoies	nettoyasses
nettoie	nettoyait	nettoya	nettoiera	nettoierait	nettoie	nettoyât
nettoyons	nettoyions	nettoyâmes	nettoierons	nettoierions	nettoyions	nettoyassions
nettoyez	nettoyiez	nettoyâtes	nettoierez	nettoieriez	nettoyiez	nettoyassiez
nettoient	nettoyaient	nettoyèrent	nettoieront	nettoieraient	nettoient	nettoyassent

Compound Tenses

Passé Composé	Pluperfect	Passé Antérieur	Future Perfect	Conditional Perfect	Past Subjunctive	Pluperfect Subjunctive
ai nettoyé	avais nettoyé	eus nettoyé	aurai nettoyé	aurais nettoyé	aie nettoyé	eusse nettoyé
as nettoyé	avais nettoyé	eus nettoyé	auras nettoyé	aurais nettoyé	aies nettoyé	eusses nettoyé
a nettoyé	avait nettoyé	eut nettoyé	aura nettoyé	aurait nettoyé	ait nettoyé	eût nettoyé
avons nettoyé	avions nettoyé	eûmes nettoyé	aurons nettoyé	aurions nettoyé	ayons nettoyé	eussions nettoyé

Passé Composé	Pluperfect	Passé Antérieur	Future Perfect	Conditional Perfect	Past Subjunctive	Pluperfect Subjunctive
avez nettoyé	aviez nettoyé	eûtes nettoyé	aurez nettoyé	auriez nettoyé	ayez nettoyé	eussiez nettoyé
ont nettoyé	avaient nettoyé	eûrent nettoyé	auront nettoyé	auraient nettoyé	aient nettoyé	eussent nettoyé

-*e* + Consonant + *er* Verbs

MENER to lead
Present participle: menant
Past participle: mené
Commands: *Mène! Menons! Menez!*

Simple Tenses

Present	Imperfect	Passé Simple	Future	Conditional	Subjunctive	Imperfect Subjunctive
mène	menais	menai	mènerai	mènerais	mène	menasse
mènes	menais	menas	mèneras	mènerais	mènes	menasses
mène	menait	mena	mènera	mènerait	mène	menât
menons	menions	menâmes	mènerons	mènerions	menions	menassions
menez	meniez	menâtes	mènerez	mèneriez	meniez	menassiez
mènent	menaient	menèrent	mèneront	mèneraient	mènent	menassent

Compound Tenses

Passé Composé	Pluperfect	Passé Antérieur	Future Perfect	Conditional Perfect	Past Subjunctive	Pluperfect Subjunctive
ai mené	avais mené	eus mené	aurai mené	aurais mené	aie mené	eusse mené
as mené	avais mené	eus mené	auras mené	aurais mené	aies mené	eusses mené
a mené	avait mené	eut mené	aura mené	aurait mené	ait mené	eût mené
avons mené	avions mené	eûmes mené	aurons mené	aurions mené	ayons mené	eussions mené
avez mené	aviez mené	eûtes mené	aurez mené	auriez mené	ayez mené	eussiez mené
ont mené	avaient mené	eûrent mené	auront mené	auraient mené	aient mené	eussent mené

continues

-er Verbs with Double Consonants

APPELER   to speak
Present participle: appelant
Past participle: appelé
Commands: Appelle! Appelons! Appelez!

Simple Tenses

Present	Imperfect	Passé Simple	Future	Conditional	Subjunctive	Imperfect Subjunctive
appelle	appelais	appelai	appellerai	appellerais	appelle	appelasse
appelles	appelais	appelas	appelleras	appellerais	appelles	appelasses
appelle	appelait	appela	appellera	appellerait	appelle	appelât
appelons	appelions	appelâmes	appellerons	appellerions	appelions	appelassions
appelez	appeliez	appelâtes	appellerez	appelleriez	appeliez	appelassiez
appellent	appelaient	appelèrent	appelleront	appelleraient	appellent	appelassent

Compound Tenses

Passé Composé	Pluperfect	Passé Antérieur	Future Perfect	Conditional Perfect	Past Subjunctive	Pluperfect Subjunctive
ai appelé	avais appelé	eus appelé	aurai appelé	aurais appelé	aie appelé	eusse appelé
as appelé	avais appelé	eus appelé	auras appelé	aurais appelé	aies appelé	eusses appelé
a appelé	avait appelé	eut appelé	aura appelé	aurait appelé	ait appelé	eût appelé
avons appelé	avions appelé	eûmes appelé	aurons appelé	aurions appelé	ayons appelé	eussions appelé

continued

Passé Composé	Pluperfect	Passé Antérieur	Future Perfect	Conditional Perfect	Past Subjunctive	Pluperfect Subjunctive
avez appelé	aviez appelé	eûtes appelé	aurez appelé	auriez appelé	ayez appelé	eussiez appelé
ont appelé	avaient appelé	eurent appelé	auront appelé	auraient appelé	aient appelé	eussent appelé

JETER   to throw
Present participle: jetant
Past participle: jeté
Commands: Jette! Jetons! Jetez!

Simple Tenses

Present	Imperfect	Passé Simple	Future	Conditional	Subjunctive	Imperfect Subjunctive
jette	jetais	jetai	jetterai	jetterais	jette	jetasse
jettes	jetais	jetas	jetteras	jetterais	jettes	jetasses
jette	jetait	jeta	jettera	jetterait	jette	jetât
jetons	jetions	jetâmes	jetterons	jetterions	jetions	jetassions
jetez	jetiez	jetâtes	jetterez	jetteriez	jetiez	jetassiez
jettent	jetaient	jetèrent	jetteront	jetteraient	jettent	jetassent

Compound Tenses

Passé Composé	Pluperfect	Passé Antérieur	Future Perfect	Conditional Perfect	Past Subjunctive	Pluperfect Subjunctive
ai jeté	avais jeté	eus jeté	aurai jeté	aurais jeté	aie jeté	eusse jeté
as jeté	avais jeté	eus jeté	auras jeté	aurais jeté	aies jeté	eusses jeté
a jeté	avait jeté	eut jeté	aura jeté	aurait jeté	ait jeté	eût jeté
avons jeté	avions jeté	eûmes jeté	aurons jeté	aurions jeté	ayons jeté	eussions jeté
avez jeté	aviez jeté	eûtes jeté	aurez jeté	auriez jeté	ayez jeté	eussiez jeté
ont jeté	avaient jeté	eurent jeté	auront jeté	auraient jeté	aient jeté	eussent jeté

-é + Consonant + er Verbs

ESPÉRER to hope
Present participle: esperant
Past participle: espéré
Commands: Espère! Espérons! Espérez!

Simple Tenses

Present	Imperfect	Passé Simple	Future	Conditional	Subjunctive	Imperfect Subjunctive
espère	espérais	espérai	espérerai	espérerais	espère	espérasse
espères	espérais	espéras	espéreras	espérerais	espères	espérasses
espère	espérait	espéra	espérera	espérerait	espère	espérât
espérons	espérions	espérâmes	espérerons	espérerions	espérions	espérassions
espérez	espériez	espérâtes	espérerez	espéreriez	espériez	espérassiez
espèrent	espéraient	espérèrent	espéreront	espéreraient	espèrent	espérassent

Passé Composé	Pluperfect	Passé Antérieur	Future Perfect	Conditional Perfect	Past Subjunctive	Pluperfect Subjunctive
ai espéré	avais espéré	eus espéré	aurai espéré	aurais espéré	aie espéré	eusse espéré
as espéré	avais espéré	eus espéré	auras espéré	aurais espéré	aies espéré	eusses espéré
a espéré	avait espéré	eut espéré	aura espéré	aurait espéré	ait espéré	eût espéré
avons espéré	avions espéré	eûmes espéré	aurons espéré	aurions espéré	ayons espéré	eussions espéré
avez espéré	aviez espéré	eûtes espéré	aurez espéré	auriez espéré	ayez espéré	eussiez espéré
ont espéré	avaient espéré	eûrent espéré	auront espéré	auraient espéré	aient espéré	eussent espéré

Irregular Verbs

ABSOUDRE to absolve
Present participle: **absolvant**
Past participle: **absous**
Commands: **Absous! Absolvons! Absolvez!**

Simple Tenses

Present	Imperfect	Passé Simple	Future	Conditional	Subjunctive	Imperfect Subjunctive
absous	absolvais	—	absoudrai	absoudrais	absolve	
absous	absolvais	—	absoudras	absoudrais	absolves	
absout	absolvait	—	absoudra	absoudrait	absolve	absolut
absolvons	absolvions	—	absoudrons	absoudrions	absolvions	
absolvez	absolviez	—	absoudrez	absoudriez	absolviez	
absolvent	absolvaient	—	absoudront	absoudraient	absolvent	

Compound Tenses

Passé Composé	Pluperfect	Passé Antérieur	Future Perfect	Conditional Perfect	Past Subjunctive	Pluperfect Subjunctive
ai absous	avais absous	eus absous	aurai absous	aurais absous	aie absous	eusse absous
as absous	avais absous	eus absous	auras absous	aurais absous	aies absous	eusses absous
a absous	avait absous	eut absous	aura absous	aurait absous	ait absous	eût absous

continues

continued

Passé Composé	Pluperfect	Passé Antérieur	Future Perfect	Conditional Perfect	Past Subjunctive	Pluperfect Subjunctive
avons absous	avions absous	eûmes absous	aurons absous	aurions absous	ayons absous	eussions absous
avez absous	aviez absous	eûtes absous	aurez absous	auriez absous	ayez absous	eussiez absous
ont absous	avoaiet absous	eûrent absous	auront absous	auraient absous	aient absous	eussent absous

ACQUÉRIR to acquire
Present participle: **aquérant**
Past participle: **acquis**
Commands: **Acquiers! Acquérons! Acquérez!**

Simple Tenses

Present	Imperfect	Passé Simple	Future	Conditional	Subjunctive	Imperfect Subjunctive
acquiers	acquérais	acquis	acquerrai	acquerrais	acquière	acquisse
acquiers	acquérais	acquis	acquerras	acquerrais	acquières	acquisses
acquiert	acquérait	acquit	acquerra	acquerrait	acquière	acquit
acquérons	acquérions	acquîmes	acquerrons	acquerrions	acquérions	acquissions
acquérez	acquériez	acquîtes	acquerrez	acquerriez	acquériez	acquissiez
acquièrent	acquéraient	acquirent	acquerront	acquerraient	acquièrent	acquissent

Compound Tenses

Passé Composé	Pluperfect	Passé Antérieur	Future Perfect	Conditional Perfect	Past Subjunctive	Pluperfect Subjunctive
ai acquis	avais acquis	eus acquis	aurai acquis	aurais acquis	aie acquis	eusse acquis
as acquis	avais acquis	eus acquis	auras acquis	aurais acquis	aies acquis	eusses acquis
a acquis	avait acquis	eut acquis	aura acquis	aurait acquis	ait acquis	eût acquis
avons acquis	avions acquis	eûmes acquis	aurons acquis	aurions acquis	ayons acquis	eussions acquis
avez acquis	aviez acquis	eûtes acquis	aurez acquis	auriez acquis	ayez acquis	eussiez acquis
ont acquis	avaient acquis	eûrent acquis	auront acquis	auraient acquis	aient acquis	eussent acquis

*ALLER   to go

Present participle: allant
Past participle: allé
Commands: **Va! Allons! Allez!**

Simple Tenses

Present	Imperfect	Passé Simple	Future	Conditional	Subjunctive	Imperfect Subjunctive
vais	allais	allai	irai	irais	**aille**	allasse
vas	allais	allas	iras	irais	**ailles**	allasses
va	allait	alla	ira	irait	**aille**	allât
allons	allions	allâmes	irons	irions	allions	allassions
allez	alliez	allâtes	irez	iriez	alliez	allassiez
vont	allaient	allèrent	iront	iraient	**aillent**	allassent

Compound Tenses

Passé Composé	Pluperfect	Passé Antérieur	Future Perfect	Conditional Perfect	Past Subjunctive	Pluperfect Subjunctive
suis allé	étais allé	fus allé	serai allé	serais allé	sois allé	fusse allé
es allé	étais allé	fus allé	seras allé	serais allé	sois allé	fusses allé
est allé	était allé	fut allé	sera allé	serait allé	soit allé	fût allé
sommes allé	étions allé	fûmes allé	serons allé	serions allé	soyons allé	fussions allé
êtes allé	étiez allé	fûtes allé	serez allé	seriez allé	soyez allé	fussiez allé
sont allé	étaient allé	furent allé	seront allé	seraient allé	soient allé	fussent allé

ASSAILLIR to assault
Present participle: **assaillant**
Past participle: assailli
Commands: **Assaille! Assaillons! Assaillez!**

Simple Tenses

Present	Imperfect	Passé Simple	Future	Conditional	Subjunctive	Imperfect Subjunctive
assaille	**assaillais**	assaillis	assaillirai	assaillirais	**assaille**	assaillisse
assailles	**assaillais**	assaillis	assailliras	assaillirais	**assailles**	assaillisses
assaille	**assaillait**	assaillit	assaillira	assaillirait	**assaille**	assaillît
assaillons	**assaillions**	assaillîmes	assaillirons	assaillirions	**assaillions**	assaillissions
assaillez	**assailliez**	assaillîtes	assaillirez	assailliriez	**assailliez**	assaillissiez
assaillent	**assaillaient**	assaillirent	assailliront	assailliraient	**assaillent**	assaillissent

Compound Tenses

Passé Composé	Pluperfect	Passé Antérieur	Future Perfect	Conditional Perfect	Past Subjunctive	Pluperfect Subjunctive
ai assailli	avais assailli	eus assailli	aurai assailli	aurais assailli	aie assailli	eusse assailli
as assailli	avais assailli	eus assailli	auras assailli	aurais assailli	aies assailli	eusses assailli
a assailli	avait assailli	eut assailli	aura assailli	aurait assailli	ait assailli	eût assailli
avons assailli	avions assailli	eûmes assailli	aurons assailli	aurions assailli	ayons assailli	eussions assailli
avez assailli	aviez assailli	eûtes assailli	aurez assailli	auriez assailli	ayez assailli	eussiez assailli
ont assailli	avaient assailli	eûrent assailli	auront assailli	auraient assailli	aient assailli	eussent assailli

Pauline

ASSEOIR to seat

Present participle: asseyant (assoyant)
Past participle: assis
Commands: Assieds! (Assois!) Asseyons! (Assoyons!) Asseyez! (Assoyez!)

Simple Tenses

Present	Imperfect	Passé Simple	Future	Conditional	Subjunctive	Imperfect Subjunctive
assieds (assois)	asseyais (assoyais)	assis	assiérai (assoirai)	assiérais (assoirais)	asseye (assoie)	assisse
assieds (assois)	asseyais (assoyais)	assis	assiéras (assoiras)	assiérais (assoirais)	asseyes (assoies)	assisses
assied (assoit)	asseyait (assoyait)	assit	assiéra (assoira)	assiérait (assoirait)	asseye (assoie)	assît
asseyons (assoyons)	asseyions (assoyions)	assîmes	assiérons (assoirons)	assiérions (assoirions)	asseyions (assoyions)	assissions
asseyez (assoyez)	asseyiez (assoyiez)	assîtes	assiérez (assoirez)	assiériez (assoiriez)	asseyiez (assoyiez)	assissiez
asseyent (assoyaient)	asseyaient (assoyaient)	assirent	assiéront (assoiront)	assiéraient (assoiraient)	asseyent (assoient)	assissent

Compound Tenses

Passé Composé	Pluperfect	Passé Antérieur	Future Perfect	Conditional Perfect	Past Subjunctive	Pluperfect Subjunctive
ai assis	avais assis	eus assis	aurai assis	aurais assis	aie assis	eusse assis
as assis	avais assis	eus assis	auras assis	aurais assis	aies assis	eusses assis
a assis	avait assis	eut assis	aura assis	aurait assis	ait assis	eût assis
avons assis	avions assis	eûmes assis	aurons assis	aurions assis	ayons assis	eussions assis
avez assis	aviez assis	eûtes assis	aurez assis	auriez assis	ayez assis	eussiez assis
ont assis	avaient assis	eûrent assis	auront assis	auraient assis	aient assis	eussent assis

AVOIR to have
Present participle: **ayant**
Past participle: **eu**
Commands: **Aie! Ayons! Ayez!**

Simple Tenses

Present	Imperfect	Passé Simple	Future	Conditional	Subjunctive	Imperfect Subjunctive
ai	avais	eus	aurai	aurais	aie	eusse
as	avais	eus	auras	aurais	aies	eusses
a	avait	eut	aura	aurait	ait	eût
avons	avions	eûmes	aurons	aurions	ayons	eussions
avez	aviez	eûtes	aurez	auriez	ayiez	eussiez
ont	avaient	eurent	auront	auraient	aient	eussent

Compound Tenses

Passé Composé	Pluperfect	Passé Antérieur	Future Perfect	Conditional Perfect	Past Subjunctive	Pluperfect Subjunctive
ai eu	avais eu	eus eu	aurai eu	aurais eu	aie eu	eusse eu
as eu	avais eu	eus eu	auras eu	aurais eu	aies eu	eusses eu
a eu	avait eu	eut eu	aura eu	aurait eu	ait eu	eût eu
avons eu	avions eu	eûmes eu	aurons eu	aurions eu	ayons eu	eussions eu
avez eu	aviez eu	eûtes eu	aurez eu	auriez eu	ayez eu	eussiez eu
ont eu	avaient eu	eûrent eu	auront eu	auraient eu	aient eu	eussent eu

BATTRE   to beat
Present participle: battant
Past participle: battu
Commands: **Bats!** Battons! Battez!

Simple Tenses

Present	Imperfect	Passé Simple	Future	Conditional	Subjunctive	Imperfect Subjunctive
bats	battais	battis	battrai	battrais	batte	battisse
bats	battais	battis	battras	battrais	battes	battisses
bat	battait	battit	battra	battrait	batte	battît
battons	battions	battîmes	battrons	battrions	battions	battissions
battez	battiez	battîtes	battrez	battriez	battiez	battissiez
battent	battaient	battirent	battront	battraient	battent	battissent

Compound Tenses

Passé Composé	Pluperfect	Passé Antérieur	Future Perfect	Conditional Perfect	Past Subjunctive	Pluperfect Subjunctive
ai battu	avais battu	eus battu	aurai battu	aurais battu	aie battu	eusse battu
as battu	avais battu	eus battu	auras battu	aurais battu	aies battu	eusses battu
a battu	avait battu	eut battu	aura battu	aurait battu	ait battu	eût battu
avons battu	avions battu	eûmes battu	aurons battu	aurions battu	ayons battu	eussions battu
avez battu	aviez battu	eûtes battu	aurez battu	auriez battu	ayez battu	eussiez battu
ont battu	avaient battu	eûrent battu	auront battu	auraient battu	aient battu	eussent battu

BOIRE to drink
Present participle: **buvant**
Past participle: **bu**
Commands: Bois! **Buvons! Buvez!**

Simple Tenses

Present	Imperfect	Passé Simple	Future	Conditional	Subjunctive	Imperfect Subjunctive
bois	**buvais**	**bus**	boirai	boirais	**boive**	**busse**
bois	**buvais**	**bus**	boiras	boirais	**boives**	**busses**
boit	**buvait**	**but**	boira	boirait	**boive**	**bût**
buvons	**buvions**	**bûmes**	boirons	boirions	**buvions**	**bussions**
buvez	**buviez**	**bûtes**	boirez	boiriez	**buviez**	**bussiez**
boivent	**buvaient**	**burent**	boiront	boiraient	**boivent**	**bussent**

Compound Tenses

Passé Composé	Pluperfect	Passé Antérieur	Future Perfect	Conditional Perfect	Past Subjunctive	Pluperfect Subjunctive
ai bu	avais bu	eus bu	aurai bu	aurais bu	aie bu	eusse bu
as bu	avais bu	eus bu	auras bu	aurais bu	aies bu	eusses bu
a bu	avait bu	eut bu	aura bu	aurait bu	ait bu	eût bu
avons bu	avions bu	eûmes bu	aurons bu	aurions bu	ayons bu	eussions bu
avez bu	aviez bu	eûtes bu	aurez bu	auriez bu	ayez bu	eussiez bu
ont bu	avaient bu	eûrent bu	auront bu	auraient bu	aient bu	eussent bu

BOUILLIR   to boil
Present participle: **bouillant**
Past participle: bouilli
Commands: **Bous! Bouillons! Bouillez!**

Simple Tenses

Present	Imperfect	Passé Simple	Future	Conditional	Subjunctive	Imperfect Subjunctive
bous	bouillais	bouillis	bouillirai	bouillirais	bouille	bouillisse
bous	bouillais	bouillis	bouilliras	bouillirais	bouilles	bouillisses
bout	bouillait	bouillit	bouillira	bouillirait	bouille	bouillît
bouillons	bouillions	bouillîmes	bouillirons	bouillirions	bouillions	bouillissions
bouillez	bouilliez	bouillîtes	bouillirez	bouilliriez	bouilliez	bouillissiez
bouillent	bouillaient	bouillirent	bouilliront	bouilliraient	bouillent	bouillissent

Compound Tenses

Passé Composé	Pluperfect	Passé Antérieur	Future Perfect	Conditional Perfect	Past Subjunctive	Pluperfect Subjunctive
ai bouilli	avais bouilli	eus bouilli	aurai bouilli	aurais bouilli	aie bouilli	eusse bouilli
as bouilli	avais bouilli	eus bouilli	auras bouilli	aurais bouilli	aies bouilli	eusses bouilli
a bouilli	avait bouilli	eut bouilli	aura bouilli	aurait bouilli	ait bouilli	eût bouilli
avons bouilli	avions bouilli	eûmes bouilli	aurons bouilli	aurions bouilli	ayons bouilli	eussions bouilli
avez bouilli	aviez bouilli	eûtes bouilli	aurez bouilli	auriez bouilli	ayez bouilli	eussiez bouilli
ont bouilli	avaient bouilli	eûrent bouilli	auront bouilli	auraient bouilli	aient bouilli	eussent bouilli

CONCLURE   to conclude
Present participle: concluant
Past participle: **conclu**
Commands: Conclus! Concluons! Concluez!

Simple Tenses

Present	Imperfect	Passé Simple	Future	Conditional	Subjunctive	Imperfect Subjunctive
conclus	concluais	**conclus**	conclurai	conclurais	conclue	**conclusse**
conclus	concluais	**conclus**	concluras	conclurais	conclues	**conclusses**
conclut	concluait	**conclut**	conclura	conclurait	conclue	**conclût**
concluons	concluions	**conclûmes**	conclurons	conclurions	concluions	**conclussions**
concluez	concluiez	**conclûtes**	conclurez	concluriez	concluiez	**conclussiez**
concluent	concluaient	**conclurent**	concluront	concluraient	concluent	**conclussent**

Compound Tenses

Passé Composé	Pluperfect	Passé Antérieur	Future Perfect	Conditional Perfect	Past Subjunctive	Pluperfect Subjunctive
ai **conclu**	avais **conclu**	eus **conclu**	aurai **conclu**	aurais **conclu**	aie **conclu**	eusse **conclu**
as **conclu**	avais **conclu**	eus **conclu**	auras **conclu**	aurais **conclu**	aies **conclu**	eusses **conclu**
a **conclu**	avait **conclu**	eut **conclu**	aura **conclu**	aurait **conclu**	ait **conclu**	eût **conclu**
avons **conclu**	avions **conclu**	eûmes **conclu**	aurons **conclu**	aurions **conclu**	ayons **conclu**	eussions **conclu**
avez **conclu**	aviez **conclu**	eûtes **conclu**	aurez **conclu**	auriez **conclu**	ayez **conclu**	eussiez **conclu**
ont **conclu**	avaient **conclu**	eûrent **conclu**	auront **conclu**	auraient **conclu**	aient **conclu**	eussent **conclu**

CONDUIRE to conduct, drive
Present participle: **conduisant**
Past participle: **conduit**
Commands: Conduis! **Conduisons! Conduisez!**

Simple Tenses

Present	Imperfect	Passé Simple	Future	Conditional	Subjunctive	Imperfect Subjunctive
conduis	conduisais	conduisis	conduirai	conduirais	conduise	conduisisse
conduis	conduisais	conduisis	conduiras	conduirais	conduises	conduisisses
conduit	conduisait	conduisit	conduira	conduirait	conduise	conduisît
conduisons	conduisions	conduisîmes	conduirons	conduirions	conduisions	conduisissions
conduisez	conduisiez	conduisîtes	conduirez	conduiriez	conduisiez	conduisissiez
conduisent	conduisaient	conduisirent	conduiront	conduiraient	conduisent	conduisissent

Compound Tenses

Passé Composé	Pluperfect	Passé Antérieur	Future Perfect	Conditional Perfect	Past Subjunctive	Pluperfect Subjunctive
ai conduit	avais conduit	eus conduit	aurai conduit	aurais conduit	aie conduit	eusse conduit
as conduit	avais conduit	eus conduit	auras conduit	aurais conduit	aies conduit	eusses conduit
a conduit	avait conduit	eut conduit	aura conduit	aurait conduit	ait conduit	eût conduit
avons conduit	avions conduit	eûmes conduit	aurons conduit	aurions conduit	ayons conduit	eussions conduit
avez conduit	aviez conduit	eûtes conduit	aurez conduit	auriez conduit	ayez conduit	eussiez conduit
ont conduit	avaient conduit	eûrent conduit	auront conduit	auraient conduit	aient conduit	eussent conduit

CONNAÎTRE   to know
Present participle: **connaissant**
Past participle: **connu**
Commands: **Connais! Connaissons! Connaissez!**

Simple Tenses

Present	Imperfect	Passé Simple	Future	Conditional	Subjunctive	Imperfect Subjunctive
connais	connaissais	connus	connaîtrai	connaîtrais	connaisse	connusse
connais	connaissais	connus	connaîtras	connaîtrais	connaisses	connusses
connaît	connaissait	connut	connaîtra	connaîtrait	connaisse	connût
connaissons	connaissions	connûmes	connaîtrons	connaîtrions	connaissions	connussions
connaissez	connaissiez	connûtes	connaîtrez	connaîtriez	connaissiez	connussiez
connaissent	connaissaient	connurent	connaîtront	connaîtraient	connaissent	connussent

Compound Tenses

Passé Composé	Pluperfect	Passé Antérieur	Future Perfect	Conditional Perfect	Past Subjunctive	Pluperfect Subjunctive
ai connu	avais connu	eus connu	aurai connu	aurais connu	aie connu	eusse connu
as connu	avais connu	eus connu	auras connu	aurais connu	aies connu	eusses connu
a connu	avait connu	eut connu	aura connu	aurait connu	ait connu	eût connu
avons connu	avions connu	eûmes connu	aurons connu	aurions connu	ayons connu	eussions connu
avez connu	aviez connu	eûtes connu	aurez connu	auriez connu	ayez connu	eussiez connu
ont connu	avaient connu	eûrent connu	auront connu	auraient connu	aient connu	eussent connu

CONSTRUIRE   **to build**
Present participle: **construisant**
Past participle: **construit**
Commands: Construis! **Construisons! Construisez!**

Simple Tenses

Present	Imperfect	Passé Simple	Future	Conditional	Subjunctive	Imperfect Subjunctive
construis	**construisais**	**construisis**	construirai	construirais	**construise**	**construisisse**
construis	**construisais**	**construisis**	construiras	construirais	**construises**	**construisisses**
construit	**construisait**	**construisit**	construira	construirait	**construise**	**construisît**
construisons	construisions	construisîmes	construirons	construirions	construisions	construisissions
construisez	**construisiez**	**construisîtes**	construirez	construiriez	**construisiez**	**construisissiez**
construisent	construisaient	construisirent	construiront	construiraient	construisent	construisissent

Compound Tenses

Passé Composé	Pluperfect	Passé Antérieur	Future Perfect	Conditional Perfect	Past Subjunctive	Pluperfect Subjunctive
ai construit	avais construit	eus construit	aurai construit	aurais construit	aie construit	eusse construit
as construit	avais construit	eus construit	auras construit	aurais construit	aies construit	eusses construit
a construit	avait construit	eut construit	aura construit	aurait construit	ait construit	eût construit
avons construit	avions construit	eûmes construit	aurons construit	aurions construit	ayons construit	eussions construit
avez construit	aviez construit	eûtes construit	aurez construit	auriez construit	ayez construit	eussiez construit
ont construit	avient construit	eûrent construit	auront construit	auraient construit	aient construit	eussent construit

COUDRE   to sew
Present participle: **cousant**
Past participle: **cousu**
Commands: Couds! Cousons! Cousez!

Simple Tenses

Present	Imperfect	Passé Simple	Future	Conditional	Subjunctive	Imperfect Subjunctive
couds	cousais	cousis	coudrai	coudrais	couse	cousisse
couds	cousais	cousis	coudras	coudrais	couses	cousisses
coud	cousait	cousit	coudra	coudrait	couse	cousît
cousons	cousions	cousîmes	coudrons	coudrions	cousions	cousissions
cousez	cousiez	cousîtes	coudrez	coudriez	cousiez	cousissiez
cousent	cousaient	cousirent	coudront	coudraient	cousent	cousissent

Compound Tenses

Passé Composé	Pluperfect	Passé Antérieur	Future Perfect	Conditional Perfect	Past Subjunctive	Pluperfect Subjunctive
ai cousu	avais cousu	eus cousu	aurai cousu	aurais cousu	aie cousu	eusse cousu
as cousu	avais cousu	eus cousu	auras cousu	aurais cousu	aies cousu	eusses cousu
a cousu	avait cousu	eut cousu	aura cousu	aurait cousu	ait cousu	eût cousu
avons cousu	avions cousu	eûmes cousu	aurons cousu	aurions cousu	ayons cousu	eussions cousu
avez cousu	aviez cousu	eûtes cousu	aurez cousu	auriez cousu	ayez cousu	eussiez cousu
ont cousu	avaient cousu	eûrent cousu	auront cousu	auraient cousu	aient cousu	eussent cousu

COURIR to run
Present participle: **courant**
Past participle: **couru**
Commands: **Cours! Courons! Courez!**

Simple Tenses

Present	Imperfect	Passé Simple	Future	Conditional	Subjunctive	Imperfect Subjunctive
cours	courais	courus	courrai	courrais	coure	courusse
cours	courais	courus	courras	courrais	coures	courusses
court	courait	courut	courra	courrait	coure	courût
courons	courions	courûmes	courrons	courrions	courions	courussions
courez	couriez	courûtes	courrez	courriez	couriez	courussiez
courent	couraient	coururent	courront	courraient	courent	courussent

Compound Tenses

Passé Composé	Pluperfect	Passé Antérieur	Future Perfect	Conditional Perfect	Past Subjunctive	Pluperfect Subjunctive
ai couru	avais couru	eus couru	aurai couru	aurais couru	aie couru	eusse couru
as couru	avais couru	eus couru	auras couru	aurais couru	aies couru	eusses couru
a couru	avait couru	eut couru	aura couru	aurait couru	ait couru	eût couru
avons couru	avions couru	eûmes couru	aurons couru	aurions couru	ayons couru	eussions couru
avez couru	aviez couru	eûtes couru	aurez couru	auriez couru	ayez couru	eussiez couru
ont couru	avaient couru	eûrent couru	auront couru	auraient couru	aient couru	eussent couru

CRAINDRE to fear
Present participle: **craignant**
Past participle: **craint**
Commands: **Crains! Craignons! Craignez!**

Simple Tenses

Present	Imperfect	Passé Simple	Future	Conditional	Subjunctive	Imperfect Subjunctive
crains	craignais	craignis	craindrai	craindrais	craigne	craignisse
crains	craignais	craignis	craindras	craindrais	craignes	craignisses
craint	craignait	craignit	craindra	craindrait	craigne	craignît
craignons	craignions	craignîmes	craindrons	craindrions	craignions	craignissions
craignez	craigniez	craignîtes	craindrez	craindriez	craigniez	craignissiez
craignent	craignaient	craignirent	craindront	craindraient	craignent	craignissent

Compound Tenses

Passé Composé	Pluperfect	Passé Antérieur	Future Perfect	Conditional Perfect	Past Subjunctive	Pluperfect Subjunctive
ai craint	avais craint	eus craint	aurai craint	aurais craint	aie craint	eusse craint
as craint	avais craint	eus craint	auras craint	aurais craint	aies craint	eusses craint
a craint	avait craint	eut craint	aura craint	aurait craint	ait craint	eût craint
avons craint	avions craint	eûmes craint	aurons craint	aurions craint	ayons craint	eussions craint
avez craint	aviez craint	eûtes craint	aurez craint	auriez craint	ayez craint	eussiez craint
ont craint	avaient craint	eûrent craint	auront craint	auraient craint	aient craint	eussent craint

CROIRE to believe
Present participle: **croyant**
Past participle: **cru**
Commands: Crois! **Croyons! Croyez!**

Simple Tenses

Present	Imperfect	Passé Simple	Future	Conditional	Subjunctive	Imperfect Subjunctive
crois	**croyais**	**crus**	croirai	croirais	croie	**crusse**
crois	**croyais**	**crus**	croiras	croirais	croies	**crusses**
croit	**croyait**	**crut**	croira	croirait	croie	**crût**
croyons	**croyions**	**crûmes**	croirions	croirions	croyions	**crussions**
croyez	**croyiez**	**crûtes**	croirez	croiriez	croyiez	**crussiez**
croient	**croyaient**	**crurent**	croiront	croiraient	croient	**crussent**

Compound Tenses

Passé Composé	Pluperfect	Passé Antérieur	Future Perfect	Conditional Perfect	Past Subjunctive	Pluperfect Subjunctive
ai cru	avais cru	eus cru	aurai cru	aurais cru	aie cru	eusse cru
as cru	avais cru	eus cru	auras cru	aurais cru	aies cru	eusses cru
a cru	avait cru	eut cru	aura cru	aurait cru	ait cru	eût cru
avons cru	avions cru	eûmes cru	aurons cru	aurions cru	ayons cru	eussions cru
avez cru	aviez cru	eûtes cru	aurez cru	auriez cru	ayez cru	eussiez cru
ont cru	avaient cru	eûrent cru	auront cru	auraient cru	aient cru	eussent cru

CROÎTRE to grow
Present participle: **croissant**
Past participle: **crû**
Commands: **Croîs! Croissons! Croissez!**

Simple Tenses

Present	Imperfect	Passé Simple	Future	Conditional	Subjunctive	Imperfect Subjunctive
croîs	croissais	crûs	croîtrai	croîtrais	croisse	crûsse
croîs	croissais	crûs	croîtras	croîtrais	croisses	crûsses
croît	croissait	crût	croîtra	croîtrait	croisse	crût
croissons	croissions	crûmes	croîtrons	croîtrions	croissions	crûssions
croissez	croissiez	crûtes	croîtrez	croîtriez	croissiez	crûssiez
croissent	croissaient	crûrent	croîtront	croîtraient	croissent	crûssent

Compound Tenses

Passé Composé	Pluperfect	Passé Antérieur	Future Perfect	Conditional Perfect	Past Subjunctive	Pluperfect Subjunctive
ai crû	avais crû	eus crû	aurai crû	aurais crû	aie crû	eusse crû
as crû	avais crû	eus crû	auras crû	aurais crû	aies crû	eusses crû
a crû	avait crû	eut crû	aura crû	aurait crû	ait crû	eût crû
avons crû	avions crû	eûmes crû	aurons crû	aurions crû	ayons crû	eussions crû
avez crû	aviez crû	eûtes crû	aurez crû	auriez crû	ayez crû	eussiez crû
ont crû	avaient crû	eurent crû	auront crû	auraient crû	aient crû	eussent crû

CUEILLIR   to gather
Present participle: **cueillant**
Past participle: cueilli
Commands: **Cueille! Cueillons! Cueillez!**

Simple Tenses

Present	Imperfect	Passé Simple	Future	Conditional	Subjunctive	Imperfect Subjunctive
cueille	**cueillais**	cueillis	**cueillerai**	**cueillerais**	**cueille**	cueillisse
cueilles	**cueillais**	cueillis	**cueilleras**	**cueillerais**	**cueilles**	cueillisses
cueille	**cueillait**	cueillit	**cueillera**	**cueillerait**	**cueille**	cueillît
cueillons	**cueillions**	cueillîmes	**cueillerons**	**cueillerions**	**cueillions**	cueillissions
cueillez	**cueilliez**	cueillîtes	**cueillerez**	**cueilleriez**	**cueilliez**	cueillissiez
cueillent	**cueillaient**	cueillirent	**cueilleront**	**cueilleraient**	**cueillent**	cueillissent

Compound Tenses

Passé Composé	Pluperfect	Passé Antérieur	Future Perfect	Conditional Perfect	Past Subjunctive	Pluperfect Subjunctive
ai cueilli	avais cueilli	eus cueilli	aurai cueilli	aurais cueilli	aie cueilli	eusse cueilli
as cueilli	avais cueilli	eus cueilli	auras cueilli	aurais cueilli	aies cueilli	eusses cueilli
a cueilli	avait cueilli	eut cueilli	aura cueilli	aurait cueilli	ait cueilli	eût cueilli
avons cueilli	avions cueilli	eûmes cueilli	aurons cueilli	aurions cueilli	ayons cueilli	eussions cueilli
avez cueilli	aviez cueilli	eûtes cueilli	aurez cueilli	auriez cueilli	ayez cueilli	eussiez cueilli
ont cueilli	avaient cueilli	eûrent cueilli	auront cueilli	auraient cueilli	aient cueilli	eussent cueilli

CUIRE to cook
Present participle: **cuisant**
Past participle: **cuit**
Commands: **Cuis! Cuisons! Cuisez!**

Simple Tenses

Present	Imperfect	Passé Simple	Future	Conditional	Subjunctive	Imperfect Subjunctive
cuis	cuisais	cuisis	cuirai	cuirais	cuise	cuisisse
cuis	cuisais	cuisis	cuiras	cuirais	cuises	cuisisses
cuit	cuisait	cuisit	cuira	cuirait	cuise	cuisît
cuisons	cuisions	cuisîmes	cuirons	cuirions	cuisions	cuisissions
cuisez	cuisiez	cuisîtes	cuirez	cuiriez	cuisiez	cuisissiez
cuisent	cuisaient	cuisirent	cuiront	cuiraient	cuisent	cuisissent

Compound Tenses

Passé Composé	Pluperfect	Passé Antérieur	Future Perfect	Conditional Perfect	Past Subjunctive	Pluperfect Subjunctive
ai cuit	avais cuit	eus cuit	aurai cuit	aurais cuit	aie cuit	eusse cuit
as cuit	avais cuit	eus cuit	auras cuit	aurais cuit	aies cuit	eusses cuit
a cuit	avait cuit	eut cuit	aura cuit	aurait cuit	ait cuit	eût cuit
avons cuit	avions cuit	eûmes cuit	aurons cuit	aurions cuit	ayons cuit	eussions cuit
avez cuit	aviez cuit	eûtes cuit	aurez cuit	auriez cuit	ayez cuit	eussiez cuit
ont cuit	avaient cuit	eûrent cuit	auront cuit	auraient cuit	aient cuit	eussent cuit

DÉFAILLIR to faint, fail, grow weak
Present participle: —
Past participle: défailli
Commands: —

Simple Tenses

Present	Imperfect	Passé Simple	Future	Conditional	Subjunctive	Imperfect Subjunctive
—	défaillais	défaillis	—	—	—	—
—	défaillais	défaillis	—	—	—	—
—	défaillait	défaillit	—	—	—	—
défaillons	défaillions	défaillîmes	—	—	—	—
défaillez	défailliez	défaillîtes	—	—	—	—
défaillent	défaillaient	défaillirent	—	—	—	—

Compound Tenses

Passé Composé	Pluperfect	Passé Antérieur	Future Perfect	Conditional Perfect	Past Subjunctive	Pluperfect Subjunctive
—	avais défailli	eus défailli	—	—	—	—
—	avais défailli	eus défailli	—	—	—	—
—	avait défailli	eut défailli	—	—	—	—
avons défailli	avions défailli	eûmes défailli	—	—	—	—
avez défailli	aviez défailli	eûtes défailli	—	—	—	—
ont défailli	avaient défailli	eûrent défailli	—	—	—	—

DEVOIR to have to
Present participle: **devant**
Past participle: **dû**
Commands: **Dois! Devons! Devez!**

Simple Tenses

Present	Imperfect	Passé Simple	Future	Conditional	Subjunctive	Imperfect Subjunctive
dois	devais	dus	devrai	devrais	doive	dusse
dois	devais	dus	devras	devrais	doives	dusses
doit	devait	dut	devra	devrait	doive	dût
devons	devions	dûmes	devrons	devrions	devions	dussions
devez	deviez	dûtes	devrez	devriez	deviez	dussiez
doivent	devaient	durent	devront	devraient	doivent	dussent

Compound Tenses

Passé Composé	Pluperfect	Passé Antérieur	Future Perfect	Conditional Perfect	Past Subjunctive	Pluperfect Subjunctive
ai dû	avais dû	eus dû	aurai dû	aurais dû	aie dû	eusse dû
as dû	avais dû	eus dû	auras dû	aurais dû	aies dû	eusses dû
a dû	avait dû	eut dû	aura dû	aurait dû	ait dû	eût dû
avons dû	avions dû	eûmes dû	aurons dû	aurions dû	ayons dû	eussions dû
avez dû	aviez dû	eûtes dû	aurez dû	auriez dû	ayez dû	eussiez dû
ont dû	avaient dû	eûrent dû	auront dû	auraient dû	aient dû	eussent dû

DIRE to say, tell
Present participle: disant
Past participle: **dit**
Commands: Dis! **Disons! Dites!**

Simple Tenses

Present	Imperfect	Passé Simple	Future	Conditional	Subjunctive	Imperfect Subjunctive
dis	**disais**	**dis**	dirai	dirais	**dise**	**disse**
dis	**disais**	**dis**	diras	dirais	**dises**	**disses**
dit	**disait**	**dit**	dira	dirait	**dise**	**dît**
disons	**disions**	**dîmes**	dirons	dirions	**disions**	**dissions**
dites	**disiez**	**dîtes**	direz	diriez	**disiez**	**dissiez**
disent	**disaient**	**dirent**	diront	diraient	**dissent**	**dissent**

Compound Tenses

Passé Composé	Pluperfect	Passé Antérieur	Future Perfect	Conditional Perfect	Past Subjunctive	Pluperfect Subjunctive
ai **dit**	avais **dit**	eus **dit**	aurai **dit**	aurais **dit**	aie **dit**	eusse **dit**
as **dit**	avais **dit**	eus **dit**	auras **dit**	aurais **dit**	aies **dit**	eusses **dit**
a **dit**	avait **dit**	eut **dit**	aura **dit**	aurait **dit**	ait **dit**	eût **dit**
avons **dit**	avions **dit**	eûmes **dit**	aurons **dit**	aurions **dit**	ayons **dit**	eussions **dit**
avez **dit**	aviez **dit**	eûtes **dit**	aurez **dit**	auriez **dit**	ayez **dit**	eussiez **dit**
ont **dit**	avaient **dit**	eûrent **dit**	auront **dit**	auraient **dit**	aient **dit**	eussent **dit**

DISTRAIRE   to distract
Present participle: **distrayant**
Past participle: **distrait**
Commands: Distrais! **Distrayons! Distrayez!**

Simple Tenses

Present	Imperfect	Passé Simple	Future	Conditional	Subjunctive	Imperfect Subjunctive
distrais	**distrayais**	—	distrairai	distrairais	distraie	—
distrais	**distrayais**	—	distrairas	distrairais	distraies	—
distrait	**distrayait**	—	distraira	distrairait	distraie	—
distrayons	distrayions	—	distrairons	distrairions	**distrayions**	—
distrayez	**distrayez**	—	distrairez	distrairiez	**distrayiez**	—
distraient	**distrayaient**	—	distrairont	distrairaient	distraient	—

Compound Tenses

Passé Composé	Pluperfect	Passé Antérieur	Future Perfect	Conditional Perfect	Past Subjunctive	Pluperfect Subjunctive
ai **distrait**	avais **distrait**	eus **distrait**	aurai **distrait**	aurais **distrait**	aie **distrait**	eusse **distrait**
as **distrait**	avais **distrait**	eus **distrait**	auras **distrait**	aurais **distrait**	aies **distrait**	eusses **distrait**
a **distrait**	avait **distrait**	eut **distrait**	aura **distrait**	aurait **distrait**	ait **distrait**	eût **distrait**
avons **distrait**	avions **distrait**	eûmes **distrait**	aurons **distrait**	aurions **distrait**	ayons **distrait**	eussions **distrait**
avez **distrait**	aviez **distrait**	eûtes **distrait**	aurez **distrait**	auriez **distrait**	ayez **distrait**	eussiez **distrait**
ont **distrait**	avaient **distrait**	eûrent **distrait**	auront **distrait**	auraient **distrait**	aient **distrait**	eussent **distrait**

DORMIR to sleep
Present participle: **dormant**
Past participle: dormi
Commands: **Dors! Dormons! Dormez!**

Simple Tenses

Present	Imperfect	Passé Simple	Future	Conditional	Subjunctive	Imperfect Subjunctive
dors	**dormais**	dormis	dormirai	dormirais	**dorme**	dormisse
dors	**dormais**	dormis	dormiras	dormirais	**dormes**	dormisses
dort	**dormait**	dormit	dormira	dormirait	**dorme**	dormît
dormons	**dormions**	dormîmes	dormirons	dormirions	**dormions**	dormissions
dormez	**dormiez**	dormîtes	dormirez	dormiriez	**dormiez**	dormissiez
dorment	**dormaient**	dormirent	dormiront	dormiraient	**dormant**	dormissent

Compound Tenses

Passé Composé	Pluperfect	Passé Antérieur	Future Perfect	Conditional Perfect	Past Subjunctive	Pluperfect Subjunctive
ai dormi	avais dormi	eus dormi	aurai dormi	aurais dormi	aie dormi	eusse dormi
as dormi	avais dormi	eus dormi	auras dormi	aurais dormi	aies dormi	eusses dormi
a dormi	avait dormi	eut dormi	aura dormi	aurait dormi	ait dormi	eût dormi
avons dormi	avions dormi	eûmes dormi	aurons dormi	aurions dormi	ayons dormi	eussions dormi
avez dormi	aviez dormi	eûtes dormi	aurez dormi	auriez dormi	ayez dormi	eussiez dormi
ont dormi	avaient dormi	eûrent dormi	auront dormi	auraient dormi	aient dormi	eussent dormi

ÉCRIRE to write
Present participle: **écrivant**
Past participle: **écrit**
Commands: Écris! Écrivons! Écrivez!

Simple Tenses

Present	Imperfect	Passé Simple	Future	Conditional	Subjunctive	Imperfect Subjunctive
écris	écrivais	écrivis	écrirai	écrirais	écrive	écrivisse
écris	écrivais	écrivis	écriras	écrirais	écrives	écrivisses
écrit	écrivait	écrivit	écrira	écrirait	écrive	écrivît
écrivons	écrivions	écrivîmes	écrirons	écririons	écrivions	écrivissions
écrivez	écriviez	écrivîtes	écrirez	écririez	écriviez	écrivissiez
écrivent	écrivaient	écrivirent	écriront	écriraient	écrivent	écrivissent

Compound Tenses

Passé Composé	Pluperfect	Passé Antérieur	Future Perfect	Conditional Perfect	Past Subjunctive	Pluperfect Subjunctive
ai écrit	avais écrit	eus écrit	aurai écrit	aurais écrit	aie écrit	eusse écrit
as écrit	avais écrit	eus écrit	auras écrit	aurais écrit	aies écrit	eusses écrit
a écrit	avait écrit	eut écrit	aura écrit	aurait écrit	ait écrit	eût écrit
avons écrit	avions écrit	eûmes écrit	aurons écrit	aurions écrit	ayons écrit	eussions écrit
avez écrit	aviez écrit	eûtes écrit	aurez écrit	auriez écrit	ayez écrit	eussiez écrit
ont écrit	avaient écrit	eûrent écrit	auront écrit	auraient écrit	aient écrit	eussent écrit

ÊTRE   to be
Present participle: étant
Past participle: été
Commands: **Sois! Soyons! Soyez!**

Simple Tenses

Present	Imperfect	Passé Simple	Future	Conditional	Subjunctive	Imperfect Subjunctive
suis	étais	fus	serai	serais	sois	fusse
es	étais	fus	seras	serais	sois	fusses
est	était	fut	sera	serait	soit	fût
sommes	étions	fûmes	serons	serions	soyons	fussions
êtes	étiez	fûtes	serez	seriez	soyez	fussiez
sont	étaient	furent	seront	seraient	soient	fussent

Compound Tenses

Passé Composé	Pluperfect	Passé Antérieur	Future Perfect	Conditional Perfect	Past Subjunctive	Pluperfect Subjunctive
ai été	avais été	eus été	aurai été	aurais été	aie été	eusse été
as été	avais été	eus été	auras été	aurais été	aies été	eusses été
a été	avait été	eut été	aura été	aurait été	ait été	eût été
avons été	avions été	eûmes été	aurons été	aurions été	ayons été	eussions été
avez été	aviez été	eûtes été	aurez été	auriez été	ayez été	eussiez été
ont été	avaient été	eûrent été	auront été	auraient été	aient été	eussent été

FAILLIR **to fail, err, come short**
Present participle: faillant
Past participle: failli
Commands: —

Simple Tenses

Present	Imperfect	Passé Simple	Future	Conditional	Subjunctive	Imperfect Subjunctive
—	—	faillis	faudrai	faudrais	—	—
—	—	faillis	faudras	faudrais	—	—
—	—	faillit	faudra (obsolete)	faudrait	—	—
—	—	faillîmes	faudrons	faudrions	—	—
—	—	faillîtes	faudrez	faudriez	—	—
—	—	faillirent	faudront	faudraient	—	—

Compound Tenses

Passé Composé	Pluperfect	Passé Antérieur	Future Perfect	Conditional Perfect	Past Subjunctive	Pluperfect Subjunctive
ai failli	—	—	—	—	—	—
as failli	—	—	—	—	—	—
a failli	—	—	—	—	—	—
avons failli	—	—	—	—	—	—
avez failli	—	—	—	—	—	—
ont failli	—	—	—	—	—	—

FAIRE to make, do
Present participle: **faisant**
Past participle: **fait**
Commands: **Fais! Faisons! Faites!**

Simple Tenses

Present	Imperfect	Passé Simple	Future	Conditional	Subjunctive	Imperfect Subjunctive
fais	faisais	fis	ferai	ferais	fasse	fisse
fais	faisais	fis	feras	ferais	fasses	fisses
fait	faisait	fit	fera	ferait	fasse	fît
faisons	faisions	fîmes	ferons	ferions	fassions	fissions
faites	faisiez	fîtes	ferez	feriez	fassiez	fissiez
font	faisaient	firent	feront	feraient	fassent	fissent

Compound Tenses

Passé Composé	Pluperfect	Passé Antérieur	Future Perfect	Conditional Perfect	Past Subjunctive	Pluperfect Subjunctive
ai fait	avais fait	eus fait	aurai fait	aurais fait	aie fait	eusse fait
as fait	avais fait	eus fait	auras fait	aurais fait	aies fait	eusses fait
a fait	avait fait	eut fait	aura fait	aurait fait	ait fait	eût fait
avons fait	avions fait	eûmes fait	aurons fait	aurions fait	ayons fait	eussions fait
avez fait	aviez fait	eûtes fait	aurez fait	auriez fait	ayez fait	eussiez fait
ont fait	avaient fait	eûrent fait	auront fait	auraient fait	aient fait	eussent fait

FALLOIR   **to be necessary**

Present participle: —

Past participle: fallu

Commands: —

Only used in the third person

Simple Tenses

Present	Imperfect	Passé Simple	Future	Conditional	Subjunctive	Imperfect Subjunctive
il faut	il fallait	il fallut	il faudra	il faudrait	il faille	il fallût

Compound Tenses

Passé Composé	Pluperfect	Passé Antérieur	Future Perfect	Conditional Perfect	Past Subjunctive	Pluperfect Subjunctive
il a fallu	il avait fallu	il eut fallu	il aura fallu	il aurait fallu	il ait fallu	il eût fallu

FUIRI to flee
Present participle: **fuyant**
Past participle: **fui**
Commands: **Fuis! Fuyons! Fuyez!**

Simple Tenses

Present	Imperfect	Passé Simple	Future	Conditional	Subjunctive	Imperfect Subjunctive
fuis	**fuyais**	fuis	fuirai	fuirais	**fuie**	fuisse
fuis	**fuyais**	fuis	fuiras	fuirais	**fuies**	fuisses
fuit	**fuyait**	fuit	fuira	fuirait	**fuie**	fuît
fuyons	**fuyions**	fuîmes	fuirons	fuirions	**fuyions**	fuissions
fuyez	**fuyiez**	fuîtes	fuirez	fuiriez	**fuyiez**	fuissiez
fuient	**fuyaient**	fuirent	fuiront	fuiraient	**fuient**	fuissent

Compound Tenses

Passé Composé	Pluperfect	Passé Antérieur	Future Perfect	Conditional Perfect	Past Subjunctive	Pluperfect Subjunctive
ai **fui**	avais **fui**	eus **fui**	aurai **fui**	aurais **fui**	aie **fui**	eusse **fui**
as **fui**	avais **fui**	eus **fui**	auras **fui**	aurais **fui**	aies **fui**	eusses **fui**
a **fui**	avait **fui**	eut **fui**	aura **fui**	aurait **fui**	ait **fui**	eût **fui**
avons **fui**	avions **fui**	eûmes **fui**	aurons **fui**	aurions **fui**	ayons **fui**	eussions **fui**
avez **fui**	aviez **fui**	eûtes **fui**	aurez **fui**	auriez **fui**	ayez **fui**	eussiez **fui**
ont **fui**	avaient **fui**	eûrent **fui**	auront **fui**	auraient **fui**	aient **fui**	eussent **fui**

HAÏR   to hate
Present participle: haïssant
Past participle: haï
Commands: **Hais!** Haïssons! Haïssez!

Simple Tenses

Present	Imperfect	Passé Simple	Future	Conditional	Subjunctive	Imperfect Subjunctive
hais	haïssais	haïs	haïrai	haïrais	haïsse	haïsse
hais	haïssais	haïs	haïras	haïrais	haïsses	haïsses
haït	haïssait	haït	haïra	haïrait	haïsse	**haït**
haïssons	haïssions	**haïmes**	haïrons	haïrions	haïssions	haïssions
haïssez	haïssiez	**haïtes**	haïrez	haïriez	haïssiez	haïssiez
haïssent	haïssaient	haïrent	haïront	haïraient	haïssent	haïssent

Compound Tenses

Passé Composé	Pluperfect	Passé Antérieur	Future Perfect	Conditional Perfect	Past Subjunctive	Pluperfect Subjunctive
ai haï	avais haï	eus haï	aurai haï	aurais haï	aie haï	eusse haï
as haï	avais haï	eus haï	auras haï	aurais haï	aies haï	eusses haï
a haï	avait haï	eut haï	aura haï	aurait haï	ait haï	eût haï
avons haï	avions haï	eûmes haï	aurons haï	aurions haï	ayons haï	eussions haï
avez haï	aviez haï	eûtes haï	aurez haï	auriez haï	ayez haï	eussiez haï
ont haï	avaient haï	eûrent haï	auront haï	auraient haï	aient haï	eussent haï

JOINDRE to join
Present participle: **joignant**
Past participle: **joint**
Commands: **Joins! Joignons! Joignez!**

Simple Tenses

Present	Imperfect	Passé Simple	Future	Conditional	Subjunctive	Imperfect Subjunctive
joins	joignais	joignis	joindrai	joindrais	joigne	joignisse
joins	joignais	joignis	joindras	joindrais	joignes	joignisses
joint	joignait	joignit	joindra	joindrait	joigne	joignît
joignons	joignions	joignîmes	joindrons	joindrions	joignions	joignissions
joignez	joigniez	joignîtes	joindrez	joindriez	joigniez	joignissiez
joignent	joignaient	joignirent	joindront	joindraient	joignent	joignissent

Compound Tenses

Passé Composé	Pluperfect	Passé Antérieur	Future Perfect	Conditional Perfect	Past Subjunctive	Pluperfect Subjunctive
ai joint	avais joint	eus joint	aurai joint	aurais joint	aie joint	eusse joint
as joint	avais joint	eus joint	auras joint	aurais joint	aies joint	eusses joint
a joint	avait joint	eut joint	aura joint	aurait joint	ait joint	eût joint
avons joint	avions joint	eûmes joint	aurons joint	aurions joint	ayons joint	eussions joint
avez joint	aviez joint	eûtes joint	aurez joint	auriez joint	ayez joint	eussiez joint
ont joint	avaient joint	eûrent joint	auront joint	auraient joint	aient joint	eussent joint

LIRE to read
Present participle: **lisant**
Past participle: **lu**
Commands: Lis! **Lisons! Lisez!**

Simple Tenses

Present	Imperfect	Passé Simple	Future	Conditional	Subjunctive	Imperfect Subjunctive
lis	lisais	lus	lirai	lirais	lise	lusse
lis	lisais	lus	liras	lirais	lises	lusses
lit	lisait	lut	lira	lirait	lise	lût
lisons	lisions	lûmes	lirons	lirions	lisions	lussions
lisez	lisiez	lûtes	lirez	liriez	lisiez	lussiez
lisent	lisaient	lurent	liront	liraient	lisent	lussent

Compound Tenses

Passé Composé	Pluperfect	Passé Antérieur	Future Perfect	Conditional Perfect	Past Subjunctive	Pluperfect Subjunctive
ai lu	avais lu	eus lu	aurai lu	aurais lu	aie lu	eusse lu
as lu	avais lu	eus lu	auras lu	aurais lu	aies lu	eusses lu
a lu	avait lu	eut lu	aura lu	aurait lu	ait lu	eût lu
avons lu	avions lu	eûmes lu	aurons lu	aurions lu	ayons lu	eussions lu
avez lu	aviez lu	eûtes lu	aurez lu	auriez lu	ayez lu	eussiez lu
ont lu	avaient lu	eûrent lu	auront lu	auraient lu	aient lu	eussent lu

MAUDIRE   to curse
Present participle: **maudissant**
Past participle: **maudit**
Commands: *Maudis!* **Maudissons! Maudissez!**

Simple Tenses

Present	Imperfect	Passé Simple	Future	Conditional	Subjunctive	Imperfect Subjunctive
maudis	**maudissais**	**maudis**	maudirai	maudirais	**maudisse**	maudissse
maudis	**maudissais**	**maudis**	maudiras	maudirais	**maudisses**	maudissses
maudit	**maudissait**	**maudit**	maudira	maudirait	**maudisse**	maudît
maudissons	**maudissions**	**maudîmes**	maudirons	maudirions	**maudissions**	maudisssions
maudissez	**maudissiez**	**maudîtes**	maudirez	maudiriez	**maudissiez**	maudisssiez
maudissent	**maudissaient**	maudirent	maudiront	maudiraient	**maudissent**	maudisssent

Compound Tenses

Passé Composé	Pluperfect	Passé Antérieur	Future Perfect	Conditional Perfect	Past Subjunctive	Pluperfect Subjunctive
ai **maudit**	avais **maudit**	eus **maudit**	aurai **maudit**	aurais **maudit**	aie **maudit**	eusse **maudit**
as **maudit**	avais **maudit**	eus **maudit**	auras **maudit**	aurais **maudit**	aies **maudit**	eusses **maudit**
a **maudit**	avait **maudit**	eut **maudit**	aura **maudit**	aurait **maudit**	ait **maudit**	eût **maudit**
avons **maudit**	avions **maudit**	eûmes **maudit**	aurons **maudit**	aurions **maudit**	ayons **maudit**	eussions **maudit**
avez **maudit**	aviez **maudit**	eûtes **maudit**	aurez **maudit**	auriez **maudit**	ayez **maudit**	eussiez **maudit**
ont **maudit**	avaient **maudit**	eûrent **maudit**	auront **maudit**	auraient **maudit**	aient **maudit**	eussent **maudit**

METTRE to put
Present participle: mettant
Past participle: **mis**
Commands: **Mets! Mettons! Mettez!**

Simple Tenses

Present	Imperfect	Passé Simple	Future	Conditional	Subjunctive	Imperfect Subjunctive
mets	mettais	**mis**	mettrai	mettrais	mette	**misse**
mets	mettais	**mis**	mettras	mettrais	mettes	**misses**
met	mettait	**mit**	mettra	mettrait	mette	**mît**
mettons	mettions	**mîmes**	mettrons	mettrions	mettions	**missions**
mettez	mettiez	**mîtes**	mettrez	mettriez	mettiez	**missiez**
mettent	mettaient	**mirent**	mettront	mettraient	mettent	**missent**

Compound Tenses

Passé Composé	Pluperfect	Passé Antérieur	Future Perfect	Conditional Perfect	Past Subjunctive	Pluperfect Subjunctive
ai **mis**	avais **mis**	eus **mis**	aurai **mis**	aurais **mis**	aie **mis**	eusse **mis**
as **mis**	avais **mis**	eus **mis**	auras **mis**	aurais **mis**	aies **mis**	eusses **mis**
a **mis**	avait **mis**	eut **mis**	aura **mis**	aurait **mis**	ait **mis**	eût **mis**
avons **mis**	avions **mis**	eûmes **mis**	aurons **mis**	aurions **mis**	ayons **mis**	eussions **mis**
avez **mis**	aviez **mis**	eûtes **mis**	aurez **mis**	auriez **mis**	ayez **mis**	eussiez **mis**
ont **mis**	avaient **mis**	eûrent **mis**	auront **mis**	auraient **mis**	aient **mis**	eussent **mis**

*MOURIR   to die
Present participle: **mourant**
Past participle: **mort**
Commands: **Meurs! Mourons! Mourez!**

Simple Tenses

Present	Imperfect	Passé Simple	Future	Conditional	Subjunctive	Imperfect Subjunctive
meurs	mourais	mourus	mourrai	mourrais	meure	mourusse
meurs	mourais	mourus	mourras	mourrais	meures	mourusses
meurt	mourait	mourut	mourra	mourrait	meure	mourût
mourons	mourions	mourûmes	mourrons	mourrions	mourions	mourussions
mourez	mouriez	mourûtes	mourrez	mourriez	mouriez	mourussiez
meurent	mouraient	moururent	mourront	mourraient	meurent	mourussent

Compound Tenses

Passé Composé	Pluperfect	Passé Antérieur	Future Perfect	Conditional Perfect	Past Subjunctive	Pluperfect Subjunctive
suis mort	étais mort	fus mort	serai mort	serais mort	sois mort	fusse mort
es mort	étais mort	fus mort	seras mort	serais mort	sois mort	fusses mort
est mort	était mort	fut mort	sera mort	serait mort	soit mort	fût mort
sommes mort	étions mort	fûmes mort	serons mort	serions mort	soyons mort	fussions mort
êtes mort	étiez mort	fûtes mort	serez mort	seriez mort	soyez mort	fussiez mort
sont mort	étaient mort	furent mort	seront mort	seraient mort	soient mort	fussent mort

MOUVOIR to move
Present participle: mouvant
Past participle: **mû**
Commands: **Meus!** *Mouvons! Mouvez!*

Simple Tenses

Present	Imperfect	Passé Simple	Future	Conditional	Subjunctive	Imperfect Subjunctive
meus	mouvais	mus	mouvrai	mouvrais	meuve	musse
meus	mouvais	mus	mouvras	mouvrais	meuves	musses
meut	mouvait	mut	mouvra	mouvrait	meuve	mût
mouvons	mouvions	mûmes	mouvrons	mouvrions	mouvions	mussions
mouvez	mouviez	mûtes	mouvrez	mouvriez	mouviez	mussiez
meuvent	mouvaient	murent	mouvront	mouvraient	meuvent	mussent

Compound Tenses

Passé Composé	Pluperfect	Passé Antérieur	Future Perfect	Conditional Perfect	Past Subjunctive	Pluperfect Subjunctive
ai mû	avais mû	eus mû	aurai mû	aurais mû	aie mû	eusse mû
as mû	avais mû	eus mû	auras mû	aurais mû	aies mû	eusses mû
a mû	avait mû	eut mû	aura mû	aurait mû	ait mû	eût mû
avons mû	avions mû	eûmes mû	aurons mû	aurions mû	ayons mû	eussions mû
avez mû	aviez mû	eûtes mû	aurez mû	auriez mû	ayez mû	eussiez mû
ont mû	avaient mû	eurent mû	auront mû	auraient mû	aient mû	eussent mû

***NAÎTRE** **to be born, to spring**
Present participle: **naissant**
Past participle: **né**
Commands: **Nais! Naissons! Naissez!**

Simple Tenses

Present	Imperfect	Passé Simple	Future	Conditional	Subjunctive	Imperfect Subjunctive
nais	**naissais**	**naiqus**	naîtrai	naîtrais	**naisse**	**naquisse**
nais	**naissais**	**naiqus**	naîtras	naîtrais	**naisses**	**naquisses**
naît	**naissait**	**naiqut**	naîtra	naîtrait	**naisse**	**naquît**
naissons	**naissions**	**naquîmes**	naîtrons	naîtrions	**naissions**	**naquissions**
naissez	**naissiez**	**naquîtes**	naîtrez	naîtriez	**naissiez**	**naquissiez**
naissent	**naissaient**	**naiqurent**	naîtront	naîtraient	**naissent**	**naquissent**

Compound Tenses

Passé Composé	Pluperfect	Passé Antérieur	Future Perfect	Conditional Perfect	Past Subjunctive	Pluperfect Subjunctive
suis **né**	étais **né**	fus **né**	serai **né**	serais **né**	sois **né**	fusse **né**
es **né**	étais **né**	fus **né**	seras **né**	serais **né**	sois **né**	fusses **né**
est **né**	était **né**	fut **né**	sera **né**	serait **né**	soit **né**	fût **né**
sommes **né**	étions **né**	fûmes **né**	serons **né**	serions **né**	soyons **né**	fussions **né**
êtes **né**	étiez **né**	fûtes **né**	serez **né**	seriez **né**	soyez **né**	fussiez **né**
sont **né**	étaient **né**	furent **né**	seront **né**	seraient **né**	soient **né**	fussent **né**

OFFRIR to offer
Present participle: **offrant**
Past participle: **offert**
Commands: **Offre! Offrons! Offrez!**

Simple Tenses

Present	Imperfect	Passé Simple	Future	Conditional	Subjunctive	Imperfect Subjunctive
offre	offrais	offris	offrirai	offrirais	offre	offrisse
offres	offrais	offris	offriras	offrirais	offres	offrisses
offre	offrait	offrit	offrira	offrirait	offre	offrît
offrons	offrions	offrîmes	offrirons	offririons	offrions	offrissions
offrez	offriez	offrîtes	offrirez	offririez	offriez	offrissiez
offrent	offraient	offrirent	offriront	offriraient	offrent	offrissent

Compound Tenses

Passé Composé	Pluperfect	Passé Antérieur	Future Perfect	Conditional Perfect	Past Subjunctive	Pluperfect Subjunctive
ai offert	avais offert	eus offert	aurai offert	aurais offert	aie offert	eusse offert
as offert	avais offert	eus offert	auras offert	aurais offert	aies offert	eusses offert
a offert	avait offert	eut offert	aura offert	aurait offert	ait offert	eût offert
avons offert	avions offert	eûmes offert	aurons offert	aurions offert	ayons offert	eussions offert
avez offert	aviez offert	eûtes offert	aurez offert	auriez offert	ayez offert	eussiez offert
ont offert	avaient offert	eûrent offert	auront offert	auraient offert	aient offert	eussent offert

OUVRIR to open
Present participle: **ouvrant**
Past participle: **ouvert**
Commands: **Ouvre! Ouvrons! Ouvrez!**

Simple Tenses

Present	Imperfect	Passé Simple	Future	Conditional	Subjunctive	Imperfect Subjunctive
ouvre	ouvrais	ouvris	ouvrirai	ouvrirais	ouvre	ouvrisse
ouvres	ouvrais	ouvris	ouvriras	ouvrirais	ouvres	ouvrisses
ouvre	ouvrait	ouvrit	ouvrira	ouvrirait	ouvre	ouvrît
ouvrons	ouvrions	ouvrîmes	ouvrirons	ouvririons	ouvrions	ouvrissions
ouvrez	ouvriez	ouvrîtes	ouvrirez	ouvririez	ouvriez	ouvrissiez
ouvrent	ouvraient	ouvrirent	ouvriront	ouvriraient	ouvrent	ouvrissent

Compound Tenses

Passé Composé	Pluperfect	Passé Antérieur	Future Perfect	Conditional Perfect	Past Subjunctive	Pluperfect Subjunctive
ai ouvert	avais ouvert	eus ouvert	aurai ouvert	aurais ouvert	aie ouvert	eusse ouvert
as ouvert	avais ouvert	eus ouvert	auras ouvert	aurais ouvert	aies ouvert	eusses ouvert
a ouvert	avait ouvert	eut ouvert	aura ouvert	aurait ouvert	ait ouvert	eût ouvert
avons ouvert	avions ouvert	eûmes ouvert	aurons ouvert	aurions ouvert	ayons ouvert	eussions ouvert
avez ouvert	aviez ouvert	eûtes ouvert	aurez ouvert	auriez ouvert	ayez ouvert	eussiez ouvert
ont ouvert	avaient ouvert	eurent ouvert	auront ouvert	auraient ouvert	aient ouvert	eussent ouvert

PARAÎTRE to seem
Present participle: **paraissant**
Past participle: **paru**
Commands: **Parais! Paraissons! Paraissez!**

Simple Tenses

Present	Imperfect	Passé Simple	Future	Conditional	Subjunctive	Imperfect Subjunctive
parais	paraissais	parus	paraîtrai	paraîtrais	paraisse	parusse
parais	paraissais	parus	paraîtras	paraîtrais	paraisses	parusses
paraît	paraissait	parut	paraîtra	paraîtrait	paraisse	parût
paraissons	paraissions	parûmes	paraîtrons	paraîtrions	paraissions	parussions
paraissez	paraissiez	parûtes	paraîtrez	paraîtriez	paraissiez	parussiez
paraissent	paraissaient	parurent	paraîtront	paraîtraient	paraissent	parussent

Compound Tenses

Passé Composé	Pluperfect	Passé Antérieur	Future Perfect	Conditional Perfect	Past Subjunctive	Pluperfect Subjunctive
ai paru	avais paru	eus paru	aurai paru	aurais paru	aie paru	eusse paru
as paru	avais paru	eus paru	auras paru	aurais paru	aies paru	eusses paru
a paru	avait paru	eut paru	aura paru	aurait paru	ait paru	eût paru
avons paru	avions paru	eûmes paru	aurons paru	aurions paru	ayons paru	eussions paru
avez paru	aviez paru	eûtes paru	aurez paru	auriez paru	ayez paru	eussiez paru
ont paru	avaient paru	eûrent paru	auront paru	auraient paru	aient paru	eussent paru

*PARTIR   to leave
Present participle: **partant**
Past participle: parti
Commands: **Pars! Partons! Partez!**

Simple Tenses

Present	Imperfect	Passé Simple	Future	Conditional	Subjunctive	Imperfect Subjunctive
pars	**partais**	partis	partirai	partirais	**parte**	partisse
pars	**partais**	partis	partiras	partirais	**partes**	partisses
part	**partait**	partit	partira	partirait	**parte**	partît
partons	**partions**	partîmes	partirons	partirions	**partions**	partissions
partez	**partiez**	partîtes	partirez	partiriez	**parties**	partissiez
partent	**partaient**	partirent	partiront	partiraient	**partent**	partissent

Compound Tenses

Passé Composé	Pluperfect	Passé Antérieur	Future Perfect	Conditional Perfect	Past Subjunctive	Pluperfect Subjunctive
suis parti	étais parti	fus parti	serai parti	serais parti	sois parti	fusse parti
es parti	étais parti	fus parti	seras parti	serais parti	sois parti	fusses parti
est parti	était parti	fut parti	sera parti	serait parti	soit parti	fût parti
sommes parti	étions parti	fûmes parti	serons parti	serions parti	soyons parti	fussions parti
êtes parti	étiez parti	fûtes parti	serez parti	seriez parti	soyez parti	fussiez parti
sont parti	étaient parti	furent parti	seront parti	seraient parti	soient parti	fussent parti

PEINDRE to paint
Present participle: **peignant**
Past participle: **peint**
Commands: **Peins! Peignons! Peignez!**

Simple Tenses

Present	Imperfect	Passé Simple	Future	Conditional	Subjunctive	Imperfect Subjunctive
peins	peignais	peignis	peindrai	peindrais	peigne	peignisse
peins	peignais	peignis	peindras	peindrais	peignes	peignisses
peint	peignait	peignit	peindra	peindrait	peigne	peignît
peignons	peignions	peignîmes	peindrons	peindrions	peignions	peignissions
peignez	peigniez	peignîtes	peindrez	peindriez	peigniez	peignissiez
peignent	peignaient	peignirent	peindront	peindraient	peignent	peignissent

Compound Tenses

Passé Composé	Pluperfect	Passé Antérieur	Future Perfect	Conditional Perfect	Past Subjunctive	Pluperfect Subjunctive
ai peint	avais peint	eus peint	aurai peint	aurais peint	aie peint	eusse peint
as peint	avais peint	eus peint	auras peint	aurais peint	aies peint	eusses peint
a peint	avait peint	eut peint	aura peint	aurait peint	ait peint	eût peint
avons peint	avions peint	eûmes peint	aurons peint	aurions peint	ayons peint	eussions peint
avez peint	aviez peint	eûtes peint	aurez peint	auriez peint	ayez peint	eussiez peint
ont peint	avont peint	eûrent peint	auront peint	auraient peint	aient peint	eussent peint

PLAIRE   to please
Present participle: **plaisant**
Past participle: **plu**
Commands: **Plais! Plaisons! Plaisez!**

Simple Tenses

Present	Imperfect	Passé Simple	Future	Conditional	Subjunctive	Imperfect Subjunctive
plais	plaisais	plus	plairai	plairais	plaise	plusse
plais	plaisais	plus	plairas	plairais	plaises	plusses
plaît	plaisait	plut	plaira	plairait	plaise	plût
plaisons	plaisions	plûmes	plairons	plairions	plaisions	plussions
plaisons	plaisiez	plûtes	plairez	plairiez	plaisiez	plussiez
plaisent	plaisaient	plurent	plairont	plairaient	plaisent	plussent

Compound Tenses

Passé Composé	Pluperfect	Passé Antérieur	Future Perfect	Conditional Perfect	Past Subjunctive	Pluperfect Subjunctive
ai plu	avais plu	eus plu	aurai plu	aurais plu	aie plu	eusse plu
as plu	avais plu	eus plu	auras plu	aurais plu	aies plu	eusses plu
a plu	avait plu	eut plu	aura plu	aurait plu	ait plu	eût plu
avons plu	avions plu	eûmes plu	aurons plu	aurions plu	ayons plu	eussions plu
avez plu	aviez plu	eûtes plu	aurez plu	auriez plu	ayez plu	eussiez plu
ont plu	avaient plu	eûrent plu	auront plu	auraient plu	aient plu	eussent plu

PLEUVOIR   to rain
Present participle: **pleuvant**
Past participle: **plu**
Commands: —
(Impersonal)

Simple Tenses

Present	Imperfect	Passé Simple	Future	Conditional	Subjunctive	Imperfect Subjunctive
il pleut	il pleuvait	il plut	il pleuvra	il pleuvrait	il pleuve	il plût

Compound Tenses

Passé Composé	Pluperfect	Passé Antérieur	Future Perfect	Conditional Perfect	Past Subjunctive	Pluperfect Subjunctive
il a plu	il avait plu	il eut plu	il aura plu	il aurait plu	il ait plu	il eût plu

POURVOIR to provide
Present participle: **pourvoyant**
Past participle: **pourvu**
Commands: Pourvois! **Pourvoyons! Pourvoyez!**

Simple Tenses

Present	Imperfect	Passé Simple	Future	Conditional	Subjunctive	Imperfect Subjunctive
pourvois	pourvoyais	pourvus	pourvoirai	pourvoirais	pourvoie	pourvusse
pourvois	pourvoyais	pourvus	pourvoiras	pourvoirais	pourvoies	pourvusses
pourvoit	pourvoyait	pourvut	pourvoira	pourvoirait	pourvoie	pourvût
pourvoyons	pourvoyions	pourvûmes	pourvoirons	pourvoirions	pourvoyions	pourvussions
pourvoyez	pourvoyiez	pourvûtes	pourvoirez	pourvoiriez	pourvoyiez	pourvussiez
pourvoient	pourvoyaient	pourvurent	pourvoiront	pourvoiraient	pourvoient	pourvussent

Compound Tenses

Passé Composé	Pluperfect	Passé Antérieur	Future Perfect	Conditional Perfect	Past Subjunctive	Pluperfect Subjunctive
ai pourvu	avais pourvu	eus pourvu	aurai pourvu	aurais pourvu	aie pourvu	eusse pourvu
as pourvu	avais pourvu	eus pourvu	auras pourvu	aurais pourvu	aies pourvu	eusses pourvu
a pourvu	avait pourvu	eut pourvu	aura pourvu	aurait pourvu	ait pourvu	eût pourvu
avons pourvu	avions pourvu	eûmes pourvu	aurons pourvu	aurions pourvu	ayons pourvu	eussions pourvu
avez pourvu	aviez pourvu	eûtes pourvu	aurez pourvu	auriez pourvu	ayez pourvu	eussiez pourvu
ont pourvu	avaient pourvu	eûrent pourvu	auront pourvu	auraient pourvu	aient pourvu	eussent pourvu

POUVOIR to be able to, can
Present participle: pouvant
Past participle: **pu**
Commands: —

Simple Tenses

Present	Imperfect	Passé Simple	Future	Conditional	Subjunctive	Imperfect Subjunctive
peux (puis)	pouvais	pus	pourrai	pourrais	puisse	pusse
peux	pouvais	pus	pourras	pourrais	puisses	pusses
peut	pouvait	put	pourra	pourrait	puisse	pût
pouvons	pouvions	pûmes	pourrons	pourrions	puissions	pussions
pouvez	pouviez	pûtes	pourrez	pourriez	puissiez	pussiez
peuvent	pouvaient	purent	pourront	pourraient	puissant	pussent

Compound Tenses

Passé Composé	Pluperfect	Passé Antérieur	Future Perfect	Conditional Perfect	Past Subjunctive	Pluperfect Subjunctive
ai **pu**	avais **pu**	eus **pu**	aurai **pu**	aurais **pu**	aie **pu**	eusse **pu**
as **pu**	avais **pu**	eus **pu**	auras **pu**	aurais **pu**	aies **pu**	eusses **pu**
a **pu**	avait **pu**	eut **pu**	aura **pu**	aurait **pu**	ait **pu**	eût **pu**
avons **pu**	avions **pu**	eûmes **pu**	aurons **pu**	aurions **pu**	ayons **pu**	eussions **pu**
avez **pu**	aviez **pu**	eûtes **pu**	aurez **pu**	auriez **pu**	ayez **pu**	eussiez **pu**
ont **pu**	avoaiet **pu**	eûrent **pu**	auront **pu**	auraient **pu**	aient **pu**	eussent **pu**

PRENDRE to take
Present participle: **prenant**
Past participle: **pris**
Commands: Prends! **Prenons! Prenez!**

Simple Tenses

Present	Imperfect	Passé Simple	Future	Conditional	Subjunctive	Imperfect Subjunctive
prends	prenais	pris	prendrai	prendrais	prenne	prisse
prends	prenais	pris	prendras	prendrais	prennes	prisses
prend	prenait	prit	prendra	prendrait	prenne	prît
prenons	prenions	prîmes	prendrons	prendrions	prenions	prissions
prenez	preniez	prîtes	prendrez	prendriez	preniez	prissiez
prennent	prenaient	prirent	prendront	prendraient	prennent	prissent

Compound Tenses

Passé Composé	Pluperfect	Passé Antérieur	Future Perfect	Conditional Perfect	Past Subjunctive	Pluperfect Subjunctive
ai pris	avais pris	eus pris	aurai pris	aurais pris	aie pris	eusse pris
as pris	avais pris	eus pris	auras pris	aurais pris	aies pris	eusses pris
a pris	avait pris	eut pris	aura pris	aurait pris	ait pris	eût pris
avons pris	avions pris	eûmes pris	aurons pris	aurions pris	ayons pris	eussions pris
avez pris	aviez pris	eûtes pris	aurez pris	auriez pris	ayez pris	eussiez pris
ont pris	avaient pris	eûrent pris	auront pris	auraient pris	aient pris	eussent pris

RECEVOIR to receive
Present participle: **recevant**
Past participle: **reçu**
Commands: **Reçois! Recevons! Recevez!**

Simple Tenses

Present	Imperfect	Passé Simple	Future	Conditional	Subjunctive	Imperfect Subjunctive
reçois	recevais	reçus	recevrai	recevrais	reçoive	reçusse
reçois	recevais	reçus	recevras	recevrais	reçoives	reçusses
reçoit	recevait	reçut	recevra	recevrait	reçoive	reçût
recevons	recevions	reçûmes	recevrons	recevrions	recevions	reçussions
recevez	receviez	reçûtes	recevrez	recevriez	receviez	reçussiez
reçoivent	recevaient	reçurent	recevront	recevraient	reçoivent	reçussent

Compound Tenses

Passé Composé	Pluperfect	Passé Antérieur	Future Perfect	Conditional Perfect	Past Subjunctive	Pluperfect Subjunctive
ai reçu	avais reçu	eus reçu	aurai reçu	aurais reçu	aie reçu	eusse reçu
as reçu	avais reçu	eus reçu	auras reçu	aurais reçu	aies reçu	eusses reçu
a reçu	avait reçu	eut reçu	aura reçu	aurait reçu	ait reçu	eût reçu
avons reçu	avions reçu	eûmes reçu	aurons reçu	aurions reçu	ayons reçu	eussions reçu
avez reçu	aviez reçu	eûtes reçu	aurez reçu	auriez reçu	ayez reçu	eussiez reçu
ont reçu	avaient reçu	eûrent reçu	auront reçu	auraient reçu	aient reçu	eussent reçu

RÉSOUDRE   to resolve
Present participle: **résolvant**
Past participle: **résolu** (to determine, to decide)
          résous (to change one thing into another)
Commands: **Résous! Résolvons! Résolvez!**

Simple Tenses

Present	Imperfect	Passé Simple	Future	Conditional	Subjunctive	Imperfect Subjunctive
résous	résolvais	résolus	résoudrai	résoudrais	résolve	résolusse
résous	résolvais	résolus	résoudras	résoudrais	résolves	résolusses
résout	résolvait	résolut	résoudra	résoudrait	résolve	résolut
résolvons	résolvions	résolûmes	résoudrons	résoudrions	résolvions	résolussions
résolvez	résolviez	résolûtes	résoudrez	résoudriez	résolviez	résolussiez
résolvent	résolvaient	résolurent	résoudront	résoudraient	résolvent	résolussent

Compound Tenses

Passé Composé	Pluperfect	Passé Antérieur	Future Perfect	Conditional Perfect	Past Subjunctive	Pluperfect Subjunctive
ai résolu (résous)	avais résolu (résous)	eus résolu (résous)	aurai résolu (résous)	aurais résolu (résous)	aie résolu (résous)	eusse résolu (résous)
as résolu (résous)	avais résolu (résous)	eus résolu (résous)	auras résolu (résous)	aurais résolu (résous)	aies résolu (résous)	eusses résolu (résous)
a résolu (résous)	avait résolu (résous)	eut résolu (résous)	aura résolu (résous)	aurait résolu (résous)	ait résolu (résous)	eût résolu (résous)
avons résolu (résous)	avions résolu (résous)	eûmes résolu (résous)	aurons résolu (résous)	aurions résolu (résous)	ayons résolu (résous)	eussions résolu (résous)
avez résolu (résous)	aviez résolu (résous)	eûtes résolu (résous)	aurez résolu (résous)	auriez résolu (résous)	ayez résolu (résous)	eussiez résolu (résous)
ont résolu (résous)	avaient résolu (résous)	eûrent résolu (résous)	auront résolu (résous)	auraient résolu (résous)	aient résolu (résous)	eussent résolu (résous)

RIRE   to laugh
Present participle: riant
Past participle: **ri**
Commands: Ris! Rions! Riez!

Simple Tenses

Present	Imperfect	Passé Simple	Future	Conditional	Subjunctive	Imperfect Subjunctive
ris	riais	**ris**	rirai	rirais	rie	**risse**
ris	riais	**ris**	riras	rirais	ries	**risses**
rit	riait	**rit**	rira	rirait	rie	**rît**
rions	riions	**rîmes**	rirons	ririons	riions	**rissions**
riez	riiez	**rîtes**	rirez	ririez	riiez	**rissiez**
rient	riaient	**rirent**	riront	riraient	rient	**rissent**

Compound Tenses

Passé Composé	Pluperfect	Passé Antérieur	Future Perfect	Conditional Perfect	Past Subjunctive	Pluperfect Subjunctive
ai **ri**	avais **ri**	eus **ri**	aurai **ri**	aurais **ri**	aie **ri**	eusse **ri**
as **ri**	avais **ri**	eus **ri**	auras **ri**	aurais **ri**	aies **ri**	eusses **ri**
a **ri**	avait **ri**	eut **ri**	aura **ri**	aurait **ri**	ait **ri**	eût **ri**
avons **ri**	avions **ri**	eûmes **ri**	aurons **ri**	aurions **ri**	ayons **ri**	eussions **ri**
avez **ri**	aviez **ri**	eûtes **ri**	aurez **ri**	auriez **ri**	ayez **ri**	eussiez **ri**
ont **ri**	avaient **ri**	eurent **ri**	auront **ri**	auraient **ri**	aient **ri**	eussent **ri**

SAVOIR to know
Present participle: **sachant**
Past participle: **su**
Commands: **Sache! Sachons! Sachez!**

Simple Tenses

Present	Imperfect	Passé Simple	Future	Conditional	Subjunctive	Imperfect Subjunctive
sais	savais	sus	saurai	saurais	sache	susse
sais	savais	sus	sauras	saurais	saches	susses
sait	savait	sut	saura	saurait	sache	sût
savons	savions	sûmes	saurons	saurions	sachions	sussions
savez	saviez	sûtes	saurez	sauriez	sachiez	sussiez
savent	savaient	surent	sauront	sauraient	sachent	sussent

Compound Tenses

Passé Composé	Pluperfect	Passé Antérieur	Future Perfect	Conditional Perfect	Past Subjunctive	Pluperfect Subjunctive
ai su	avais su	eus su	aurai su	aurais su	aie su	eusse su
as su	avais su	eus su	auras su	aurais su	aies su	eusses su
a su	avait su	eut su	aura su	aurait su	ait su	eût su
avons su	avions su	eûmes su	aurons su	aurions su	ayons su	eussions su
avez su	aviez su	eûtes su	aurez su	auriez su	ayez su	eussiez su
ont su	avaient su	eûrent su	auront su	auraient su	aient su	eussent su

SENTIR to feel, smell
Present participle: **sentant**
Past participle: senti
Commands: **Sens! Sentons! Sentez!**

Simple Tenses

Present	Imperfect	Passé Simple	Future	Conditional	Subjunctive	Imperfect Subjunctive
sens	**sentais**	sentis	sentirai	sentirais	**sente**	sentisse
sens	**sentais**	sentis	sentiras	sentirais	**sentes**	sentisses
sent	**sentait**	sentit	sentira	sentirait	**sente**	sentît
sentons	**sentions**	sentîmes	sentirons	sentirions	**sentions**	sentissions
sentez	**sentiez**	sentîtes	sentirez	sentiriez	**sentiez**	sentissiez
sentent	**sentaient**	sentirent	sentiront	sentiraient	**sentient**	sentissent

Compound Tenses

Passé Composé	Pluperfect	Passé Antérieur	Future Perfect	Conditional Perfect	Past Subjunctive	Pluperfect Subjunctive
ai senti	avais senti	eus senti	aurai senti	aurais senti	aie senti	eusse senti
as senti	avais senti	eus senti	auras senti	aurais senti	aies senti	eusses senti
a senti	avait senti	eut senti	aura senti	aurait senti	ait senti	eût senti
avons senti	avions senti	eûmes senti	aurons senti	aurions senti	ayons senti	eussions senti
avez senti	aviez senti	eûtes senti	aurez senti	auriez senti	ayez senti	eussiez senti
ont senti	avaient senti	eûrent senti	auront senti	auraient senti	aient senti	eussent senti

SERVIR to serve
Present participle: **servant**
Past participle: servi
Commands: **Sers! Servons! Servez!**

Simple Tenses

Present	Imperfect	Passé Simple	Future	Conditional	Subjunctive	Imperfect Subjunctive
sers	**servais**	servis	servirai	servirais	**serve**	servisse
sers	**servais**	servis	serviras	servirais	**serves**	servisses
sert	**servait**	servit	servira	servirait	**serve**	servît
servons	**servions**	servîmes	servirons	servirions	**servions**	servissions
servez	**serviez**	servîtes	servirez	serviriez	**serviez**	servissiez
servent	**servaient**	servirent	serviront	serviraient	**servent**	servissent

Compound Tenses

Passé Composé	Pluperfect	Passé Antérieur	Future Perfect	Conditional Perfect	Past Subjunctive	Pluperfect Subjunctive
ai servi	avais servi	eus servi	aurai servi	aurais servi	aie servi	eusse servi
as servi	avais servi	eus servi	auras servi	aurais servi	aies servi	eusses servi
a servi	avait servi	eut servi	aura servi	aurait servi	ait servi	eût servi
avons servi	avions servi	eûmes servi	aurons servi	aurions servi	ayons servi	eussions servi
avez servi	aviez servi	eûtes servi	aurez servi	auriez servi	ayez servi	eussiez servi
ont servi	avaient servi	eurent servi	auront servi	auraient servi	aient servi	eussent servi

*SORTIR **to go out**
Present participle: **sortant**
Past participle: sorti
Commands: **Sors! Sortons! Sortez!**

Simple Tenses

Present	Imperfect	Passé Simple	Future	Conditional	Subjunctive	Imperfect Subjunctive
sors	**sortais**	sortis	sortirai	sortirais	**sorte**	sortisse
sors	**sortais**	sortis	sortiras	sortirais	**sortes**	sortisses
sort	**sortait**	sortit	sortira	sortirait	**sorte**	sortît
sortons	**sortions**	sortîmes	sortirons	sortirions	**sortions**	sortissions
sortez	**sortiez**	sortîtes	sortirez	sortiriez	**sortiez**	sortissiez
sortent	**sortaient**	sortirent	sortiront	sortiraient	**sortent**	sortissent

Compound Tenses

Passé Composé	Pluperfect	Passé Antérieur	Future Perfect	Conditional Perfect	Past Subjunctive	Pluperfect Subjunctive
suis sorti	étais sorti	fus sorti	serai sorti	serais sorti	sois sorti	fusse sorti
es sorti	étais sorti	fus sorti	seras sorti	serais sorti	sois sorti	fusses sorti
est sorti	était sorti	fut sorti	sera sorti	serait sorti	soit sorti	fût sorti
sommes sorti	étions sorti	fûmes sorti	serons sorti	serions sorti	soyons sorti	fussions sorti
êtes sorti	étiez sorti	fûtes sorti	serez sorti	seriez sorti	soyez sorti	fussiez sorti
sont sorti	étaient sorti	furent sorti	seront sorti	seraient sorti	soient sorti	fussent sorti

SOUFFRIR to suffer
Present participle: **souffrant**
Past participle: **souffert**
Commands: **Souffre! Souffrons! Souffrez!**

Simple Tenses

Present	Imperfect	Passé Simple	Future	Conditional	Subjunctive	Imperfect Subjunctive
souffre	**souffrais**	souffris	souffrirai	souffrirais	**souffre**	souffrisse
souffres	**souffrais**	souffris	souffriras	souffrirais	**souffres**	souffrisses
souffre	**souffrait**	souffrit	souffrira	souffrirait	**souffre**	souffrît
souffrons	**souffrions**	souffrîmes	souffrirons	souffririons	**souffrions**	souffrissions
souffrez	**souffriez**	souffrîtes	souffrirez	souffririez	**souffriez**	souffrissiez
souffrent	**souffraient**	souffrirent	souffriront	souffriraient	**souffrent**	souffrissent

Compound Tenses

Passé Composé	Pluperfect	Passé Antérieur	Future Perfect	Conditional Perfect	Past Subjunctive	Pluperfect Subjunctive
ai **souffert**	avais **souffert**	eus **souffert**	aurai **souffert**	aurais **souffert**	aie **souffert**	eusse **souffert**
as **souffert**	avais **souffert**	eus **souffert**	auras **souffert**	aurais **souffert**	aies **souffert**	eusses **souffert**
a **souffert**	avait **souffert**	eut **souffert**	aura **souffert**	aurait **souffert**	ait **souffert**	eût **souffert**
avons **souffert**	avions **souffert**	eûmes **souffert**	aurons **souffert**	aurions **souffert**	ayons **souffert**	eussions **souffert**
avez **souffert**	aviez **souffert**	eûtes **souffert**	aurez **souffert**	auriez **souffert**	ayez **souffert**	eussiez **souffert**
ont **souffert**	avaient **souffert**	eûrent **souffert**	auront **souffert**	auraient **souffert**	aient **souffert**	eussent **souffert**

SUFFIRE to suffice, be enough
Present participle: **suffisant**
Past participle: **suffi**
Commands: Suffis! **Suffisons! Suffisez!**

Simple Tenses

Present	Imperfect	Passé Simple	Future	Conditional	Subjunctive	Imperfect Subjunctive
suffis	**suffisais**	suffisis	suffirai	suffirais	**suffise**	suffisse
suffis	**suffisais**	suffisis	suffiras	suffirais	**suffises**	suffisses
suffit	**suffisait**	suffisit	suffira	suffirait	**suffise**	suffît
suffisons	**suffisions**	suffisîmes	suffirons	suffirions	**suffisions**	suffissions
suffisez	**suffisiez**	suffisîtes	suffirez	suffiriez	**suffisiez**	suffissiez
suffisent	**suffisaient**	suffisirent	suffiront	suffiraient	**suffisent**	suffissent

Compound Tenses

Passé Composé	Pluperfect	Passé Antérieur	Future Perfect	Conditional Perfect	Past Subjunctive	Pluperfect Subjunctive
ai **suffi**	avais **suffi**	eus **suffi**	aurai **suffi**	aurais **suffi**	aie **suffi**	eusse **suffi**
as **suffi**	avais **suffi**	eus **suffi**	auras **suffi**	aurais **suffi**	aies **suffi**	eusses **suffi**
a **suffi**	avait **suffi**	eut **suffi**	aura **suffi**	aurait **suffi**	ait **suffi**	eût **suffi**
avons **suffi**	avions **suffi**	eûmes **suffi**	aurons **suffi**	aurions **suffi**	ayons **suffi**	eussions **suffi**
avez **suffi**	aviez **suffi**	eûtes **suffi**	aurez **suffi**	auriez **suffi**	ayez **suffi**	eussiez **suffi**
ont **suffi**	avaient **suffi**	eûrent **suffi**	auront **suffi**	auraient **suffi**	aient **suffi**	eussent **suffi**

SUIVRE **to follow**
Present participle: suivant
Past participle: **suivi**
Commands: **Suis!** Suivons! Suivez!

Simple Tenses

Present	Imperfect	Passé Simple	Future	Conditional	Subjunctive	Imperfect Subjunctive
suis	suivais	suivis	suivrai	suivrais	suive	suivisse
suis	suivais	suivis	suivras	suivrais	suives	suivisses
suit	suivait	suivit	suivra	suivrait	suive	suivît
suivons	suivions	suivîmes	suivrons	suivrions	suivions	suivissions
suivez	suiviez	suivîtes	suivrez	suivriez	suiviez	suivissiez
suivent	suivaient	suivirent	suivront	suivraient	suivent	suivissent

Compound Tenses

Passé Composé	Pluperfect	Passé Antérieur	Future Perfect	Conditional Perfect	Past Subjunctive	Pluperfect Subjunctive
ai **suivi**	avais **suivi**	eus **suivi**	aurai **suivi**	aurais **suivi**	aie **suivi**	eusse **suivi**
as **suivi**	avais **suivi**	eus **suivi**	auras **suivi**	aurais **suivi**	aies **suivi**	eusses **suivi**
a **suivi**	avait **suivi**	eut **suivi**	aura **suivi**	aurait **suivi**	ait **suivi**	eût **suivi**
avons **suivi**	avions **suivi**	eûmes **suivi**	aurons **suivi**	aurions **suivi**	ayons **suivi**	eussions **suivi**
avez **suivi**	aviez **suivi**	eûtes **suivi**	aurez **suivi**	auriez **suivi**	ayez **suivi**	eussiez **suivi**
ont **suivi**	avaient **suivi**	eûrent **suivi**	auront **suivi**	auraient **suivi**	aient **suivi**	eussent **suivi**

TAIRE to conceal, keep secret
Present participle: **taisant**
Past participle: **tu**
Commands: Tais! **Taisons! Taisez!**

Simple Tenses

Present	Imperfect	Passé Simple	Future	Conditional	Subjunctive	Imperfect Subjunctive
tais	taisais	tus	tairai	tairais	taise	tusse
tais	taisais	tus	tairas	tairais	taises	tusses
tait	taisait	tut	taira	tairait	taise	tût
taisons	taisions	tûmes	tairons	tairions	taisions	tussions
taisez	taisiez	tûtes	tairez	tairiez	taisiez	tussiez
taisent	taisaient	turent	tairont	tairaient	taisent	tussent

Compound Tenses

Passé Composé	Pluperfect	Passé Antérieur	Future Perfect	Conditional Perfect	Past Subjunctive	Pluperfect Subjunctive
ai **tu**	avais **tu**	eus **tu**	aurai **tu**	aurais **tu**	aie **tu**	eusse **tu**
as **tu**	avais **tu**	eus **tu**	auras **tu**	aurais **tu**	aies **tu**	eusses **tu**
a **tu**	avait **tu**	eut **tu**	aura **tu**	aurait **tu**	ait **tu**	eût **tu**
avons **tu**	avions **tu**	eûmes **tu**	aurons **tu**	aurions **tu**	ayons **tu**	eussions **tu**
avez **tu**	aviez **tu**	eûtes **tu**	aurez **tu**	auriez **tu**	ayez **tu**	eussiez **tu**
ont **tu**	avaient **tu**	eûrent **tu**	auront **tu**	auraient **tu**	aient **tu**	eussent **tu**

TENIR   to hold
Present participle: **tenant**
Past participle: **tenu**
Commands: **Tiens! Tenez! Tenons!**

Simple Tenses

Present	Imperfect	Passé Simple	Future	Conditional	Subjunctive	Imperfect Subjunctive
tiens	tenais	tins	tiendrai	tiendrais	tienne	tinsse
tiens	tenais	tins	tiendras	tiendrais	tiennes	tinsses
tient	tenait	tint	tiendra	tiendrait	tienne	tînt
tenons	tenions	tînmes	tiendrons	tiendrions	tenions	tinssions
tenez	teniez	tîntes	tiendrez	tiendriez	teniez	tinssiez
tiennent	tenaient	tinrent	tiendront	tiendraient	tiennent	tinssent

Compound Tenses

Passé Composé	Pluperfect	Passé Antérieur	Future Perfect	Conditional Perfect	Past Subjunctive	Pluperfect Subjunctive
ai tenu	avais tenu	eus tenu	aurai tenu	aurais tenu	aie tenu	eusse tenu
as tenu	avais tenu	eus tenu	auras tenu	aurais tenu	aies tenu	eusses tenu
a tenu	avait tenu	eut tenu	aura tenu	aurait tenu	ait tenu	eût tenu
avons tenu	avions tenu	eûmes tenu	aurons tenu	aurions tenu	ayons tenu	eussions tenu
avez tenu	aviez tenu	eûtes tenu	aurez tenu	auriez tenu	ayez tenu	eussiez tenu
ont tenu	avaient tenu	eûrent tenu	auront tenu	auraient tenu	aient tenu	eussent tenu

VAINCRE **to conquer**
Present participle: **vainquant**
Past participle: vaincu
Commands: Vaincs! **Vainquons! Vainquez!**

Simple Tenses

Present	Imperfect	Passé Simple	Future	Conditional	Subjunctive	Imperfect Subjunctive
vaincs	vainquais	**vainquis**	vaincrai	vaincrais	**vainque**	**vainquisse**
vaincs	vainquais	**vainquis**	vaincras	vaincrais	**vainques**	**vainquisses**
vainc	vainquait	**vainquit**	vaincra	vaincrait	**vainques**	**vainquît**
vainquons	vainquions	**vainquîmes**	vaincrons	vaincrions	**vainquions**	**vainquissions**
vainquez	vainquiez	**vainquîtes**	vaincrez	vaincriez	**vainquiez**	**vainquissiez**
vainquent	vainquaient	**vainquirent**	vaincront	vaincraient	**vainquent**	**vainquissent**

Compound Tenses

Passé Composé	Pluperfect	Passé Antérieur	Future Perfect	Conditional Perfect	Past Subjunctive	Pluperfect Subjunctive
ai vaincu	avais vaincu	eus vaincu	aurai vaincu	aurais vaincu	aie vaincu	eusse vaincu
as vaincu	avais vaincu	eus vaincu	auras vaincu	aurais vaincu	aies vaincu	eusses vaincu
a vaincu	avait vaincu	eut vaincu	aura vaincu	aurait vaincu	ait vaincu	eût vaincu
avons vaincu	avions vaincu	eûmes vaincu	aurons vaincu	aurions vaincu	ayons vaincu	eussions vaincu
avez vaincu	aviez vaincu	eûtes vaincu	aurez vaincu	auriez vaincu	ayez vaincu	eussiez vaincu
ont vaincu	avaient vaincu	eûrent vaincu	auront vaincu	auraient vaincu	aient vaincu	eussent vaincu

VALOIR to be worth
Present participle: valant
Past participle: valu
Commands: **Vaux!** Valons! Valez!

Simple Tenses

Present	Imperfect	Passé Simple	Future	Conditional	Subjunctive	Imperfect Subjunctive
vaux	valais	valus	vaudrai	vaudrais	vaille	valusse
vaux	valais	valus	vaudras	vaudrais	vailles	valusses
vaut	valait	valut	vaudra	vaudrait	vaille	valût
valons	valions	valûmes	vaudrons	vaudrions	valions	valussions
valez	valiez	valûtes	vaudrez	vaudriez	valiez	valussiez
valent	valaient	valurent	vaudront	vaudraient	vaillent	valussent

Compound Tenses

Passé Composé	Pluperfect	Passé Antérieur	Future Perfect	Conditional Perfect	Past Subjunctive	Pluperfect Subjunctive
ai valu	avais valu	eus valu	aurai valu	aurais valu	aie valu	eusse valu
as valu	avais valu	eus valu	auras valu	aurais valu	aies valu	eusses valu
a valu	avait valu	eut valu	aura valu	aurait valu	ait valu	eût valu
avons valu	avions valu	eûmes valu	aurons valu	aurions valu	ayons valu	eussions valu
avez valu	aviez valu	eûtes valu	aurez valu	auriez valu	ayez valu	eussiez valu
ont valu	avaient valu	eûrent valu	auront valu	auraient valu	aient valu	eussent valu

*VENIR   to come
Present participle: **venant**
Past participle: **venu**
Commands: **Viens! Venons! Venez!**

Simple Tenses

Present	Imperfect	Passé Simple	Future	Conditional	Subjunctive	Imperfect Subjunctive
viens	venais	vins	viendrai	viendrais	vienne	vinsse
viens	venais	vins	viendras	viendrais	viennes	vinsses
vient	venait	vint	viendra	viendrait	vienne	vînt
venons	venions	vînmes	viendrons	viendrions	venions	vinssions
venez	veniez	vîntes	viendrez	viendriez	veniez	vinssiez
viennent	venaient	vinrent	viendront	viendraient	viennent	vinssent

Compound Tenses

Passé Composé	Pluperfect	Passé Antérieur	Future Perfect	Conditional Perfect	Past Subjunctive	Pluperfect Subjunctive
suis venu	étais venu	fus venu	serai venu	serais venu	sois venu	fusse venu
es venu	étais venu	fus venu	seras venu	serais venu	sois venu	fusses venu
est venu	était venu	fut venu	sera venu	serait venu	soit venu	fût venu
sommes venu	étions venu	fûmes venu	serons venu	serions venu	soyons venu	fussions venu
êtes venu	étiez venu	fûtes venu	serez venu	seriez venu	soyez venu	fussiez venu
sont venu	étaient venu	furent venu	seront venu	seraient venu	soient venu	fussent venu

VÊTIR to clothe
Present participle: **vêtant**
Past participle: **vêtu**
Commands: **Vêts! Vêtons! Vêtez!**

Simple Tenses

Present	Imperfect	Passé Simple	Future	Conditional	Subjunctive	Imperfect Subjunctive
vêts	**vêtais**	vêtis	vêtirai	vêtirais	**vête**	vêtisse
vêts	**vêtais**	vêtis	vêtiras	vêtirais	**vêtes**	vêtisses
vêt	**vêtait**	vêtit	vêtira	vêtirait	**vête**	vêtît
vêtons	**vêtions**	vêtîmes	vêtirons	vêtirions	**vêtions**	vêtissions
vêtez	**vêtiez**	vêtîtes	vêtirez	vêtiriez	**vêtiez**	vêtissiez
vêtent	**vêtaient**	vêtirent	vêtiront	vêtiraient	**vêtent**	vêtissent

Compound Tenses

Passé Composé	Pluperfect	Passé Antérieur	Future Perfect	Conditional Perfect	Past Subjunctive	Pluperfect Subjunctive
ai **vêtu**	avais **vêtu**	eus **vêtu**	aurai **vêtu**	aurais **vêtu**	aie **vêtu**	eusse **vêtu**
as **vêtu**	avais **vêtu**	eus **vêtu**	auras **vêtu**	aurais **vêtu**	aies **vêtu**	eusses **vêtu**
a **vêtu**	avait **vêtu**	eut **vêtu**	aura **vêtu**	aurait **vêtu**	ait **vêtu**	eût **vêtu**
avons **vêtu**	avions **vêtu**	eûmes **vêtu**	aurons **vêtu**	aurions **vêtu**	ayons **vêtu**	eussions **vêtu**
avez **vêtu**	aviez **vêtu**	eûtes **vêtu**	aurez **vêtu**	auriez **vêtu**	ayez **vêtu**	eussiez **vêtu**
ont **vêtu**	avaient **vêtu**	eûrent **vêtu**	auront **vêtu**	auraient **vêtu**	aient **vêtu**	eussent **vêtu**

VIVRE to live
Present participle: vivant
Past participle: **vécu**
Commands: **Vis!** Vivons! Vivez!

Simple Tenses

Present	Imperfect	Passé Simple	Future	Conditional	Subjunctive	Imperfect Subjunctive
vis	vivais	vécus	vivrai	vivrais	vive	vécusse
vis	vivais	vécus	vivras	vivrais	vives	vécusses
vit	vivait	vécut	vivra	vivrait	vive	vécût
vivons	vivions	vécûmes	vivrons	vivrions	vivions	vécussions
vivez	viviez	vécûtes	vivrez	viviez	viviez	vécussiez
vivent	vivaient	vécurent	vivront	vivraient	vivent	vécussent

Compound Tenses

Passé Composé	Pluperfect	Passé Antérieur	Future Perfect	Conditional Perfect	Past Subjunctive	Pluperfect Subjunctive
ai vécu	avais vécu	eus vécu	aurai vécu	aurais vécu	aie vécu	eusse vécu
as vécu	avais vécu	eus vécu	auras vécu	aurais vécu	aies vécu	eusses vécu
a vécu	avait vécu	eut vécu	aura vécu	aurait vécu	ait vécu	eût vécu
avons vécu	avions vécu	eûmes vécu	aurons vécu	aurions vécu	ayons vécu	eussions vécu
avez vécu	aviez vécu	eûtes vécu	aurez vécu	auriez vécu	ayez vécu	eussiez vécu
ont vécu	avaient vécu	eurent vécu	auront vécu	auraient vécu	aient vécu	eussent vécu

272 Appendix B

VOIR **to see**
Present participle: **voyant**
Past participle: **vu**
Commands: Vois! Voyons! Voyez!

Simple Tenses

Present	Imperfect	Passé Simple	Future	Conditional	Subjunctive	Imperfect Subjunctive
vois	voyais	vis	verrai	verrais	voie	visse
vois	voyais	vis	verras	verrais	voies	visses
voit	voyait	vit	verra	verrait	voie	vît
voyons	voyions	vîmes	verrons	verrions	voyions	vissions
voyez	voyiez	vîtes	verrez	verriez	voyiez	vissiez
voient	voyaient	virent	verront	verraient	voient	vissent

Compound Tenses

Passé Composé	Pluperfect	Passé Antérieur	Future Perfect	Conditional Perfect	Past Subjunctive	Pluperfect Subjunctive
ai vu	avais vu	eus vu	aurai vu	aurais vu	aie vu	eusse vu
as vu	avais vu	eus vu	auras vu	aurais vu	aies vu	eusses vu
a vu	avait vu	eut vu	aura vu	aurait vu	ait vu	eût vu
avons vu	avions vu	eûmes vu	aurons vu	aurions vu	ayons vu	eussions vu
avez vu	aviez vu	eûtes vu	aurez vu	auriez vu	ayez vu	eussiez vu
ont vu	avaient vu	eûrent vu	auront vu	auraient vu	aient vu	eussent vu

VOULOIR   to want
Present participle: voulant
Past participle: **voulu**
Commands: **Veuille! Veuillons! Veuillez!**

Simple Tenses

Present	Imperfect	Passé Simple	Future	Conditional	Subjunctive	Imperfect Subjunctive
veux	voulais	voulus	voudrai	voudrais	veuille	voulusse
veux	voulais	voulus	voudras	voudrais	veuilles	voulusses
veut	voulait	voulut	voudra	voudrait	veuille	voulût
voulons	voulions	voulûmes	voudrons	voudrions	voulions	voulussions
voulez	vouliez	voulûtes	voudrez	voudriez	vouliez	voulussiez
veulent	voulaient	voulurent	voudront	voudraient	veuillent	voulussent

Compound Tenses

Passé Composé	Pluperfect	Passé Antérieur	Future Perfect	Conditional Perfect	Past Subjunctive	Pluperfect Subjunctive
ai **voulu**	avais **voulu**	eus **voulu**	aurai **voulu**	aurais **voulu**	aie **voulu**	eusse **voulu**
as **voulu**	avais **voulu**	eus **voulu**	auras **voulu**	aurais **voulu**	aies **voulu**	eusses **voulu**
a **voulu**	avait **voulu**	eut **voulu**	aura **voulu**	aurait **voulu**	ait **voulu**	eût **voulu**
avons **voulu**	avions **voulu**	eûmes **voulu**	aurons **voulu**	aurions **voulu**	ayons **voulu**	eussions **voulu**
avez **voulu**	aviez **voulu**	eûtes **voulu**	aurez **voulu**	auriez **voulu**	ayez **voulu**	eussiez **voulu**
ont **voulu**	avaient **voulu**	eûrent **voulu**	auront **voulu**	auraient **voulu**	aient **voulu**	eussent **voulu**

Appendix C

Compound Verbs

Compound verbs are made up of a prefix and an irregular verb. Compound verbs are conjugated in the same manner as the irregular verb they contain. The following are the most common French compound verbs:

absoudre   to absolve

> dissoudre   to dissolve

asseoir   to seat

> rasseoir   to reseat

battre   to beat

> abbattre   to knock down
>
> combattre   to fight
>
> débattre   to debate
>
> rabattre   to fold back, reduce
>
> rebattre   to beat again

boire   to drink

> emboire   to coat (with oil or wax)
>
> reboire   to drink again

bouillir   to boil

>   rebouillir   to boil again

conduire   to conduct, drive

>   éconduire   to dismiss, reject, turn away

>   déduire   to deduce

>   reconduire   to reconduct, take back, confusing

construire   to construct, build

>   déconstruire   to deconstruct

>   reconstuire   to reconstruct

connaître   to know

>   méconnaître   not to recognize

>   reconnaître   to recognize

coudre   to sew

>   découdre   to unstitch

>   recoudre   to restitch

courir   to run

>   accourir (à)   to run up (to run to)

>   concourir   to converge, combine

>   discourir   to discourse, speak at length

>   encourir   to incur

>   parcourir   to cover, survey

>   recourir (à)   to run again

>   secourir   to help, rescue

croître   to grow

>   accroître   to increase

>   décroître   to decrease

>   recroître   to grow again

cueillir   to pick

>   accueillir   to welcome

>   recueillir   to collect

cuire   to cook

>   recuire   to recook

dire   to say

The compounds of *dire* are conjugated like *dire* except in the *vous* form of the present where the endings are *-disez:*

>   contredire   to contradict

>   dédire   to disavow

>   se dédire   to back out, go back on one's word

>   interdire   to forbid

>   médire (de)   to slander

>   prédire   to predict

>   redire (à)   to repeat

distraire   to distract

>   abstraire   to abstract

>   extraire   to extract

>   soustraire   to subtract

>   traire   to milk

dormir   to sleep

>   endormir   to put to sleep

>   redormir   to sleep again

>   rendormir   to put to sleep again

écrire   to write

    décrire   to describe

faire   to do, make

    contrefaire   to counterfeit, forge

    défaire   to undo

    parfaire   to perfect, complete

    redéfaire   to undo again

    refaire   to redo

    satisfaire   to satisfy

    surfaire   to overcharge

fuir   to flee

    s'enfuir   to run away

joindre   to join

    adjoindre   to adjoin

    conjoindre   to unite, join together, combine

    déjoindre   to disjoin

    disjoindre   to separate

    enjoindre   to enjoin

    oindre   to anoint

    rejoindre   to rejoin

lire   to read

    élire   to elect

    réélire   to re-elect

    relire   to reread

    prélire   to read in advance

mettre   to put

    admettre   to admit

    commettre   to commit

    compromettre   to compromise

    démettre   to put out (of joint)

    émettre   to emit

    s'entremettre   to mediate

    omettre   to omit

    permettre   to permit

    promettre   to promise

    réadmettre   to readmit

    repromettre   to promise again

    soumettre   to submit

    transmettre   to transmit

mouvoir   to move

    émouvoir   to move (touch emotionally), upset

    promouvoir   to promote

naître   to be born

    renaître   to be reborn

ouvrir   to open

    couvrir   to cover

    découvrir   to discover

    entr'ouvrir   to open partly

    recouvrir   to cover again

    rouvrir   to reopen

paraître   to seem

    apparaître   to appear

    comparaître   to appear before

    disparaître   to disappear

    reparaître   to reappear

partir   to leave

    repartir   to go back, return

    répartir   to to share, divide up

peindre   to paint

    dépeindre   to depict, to describe

    repeindre   to repaint

plaire   to please

    complaire   to (try to) please

    déplaire   to displease

prendre   to take

    apprendre   to learn

    comprendre   to understand

    dépendre   to depend

    entreprendre   to undertake

    s'éprendre de   to fall in love with

    se méprendre sur   to be mistaken about

    rapprendre (or réapprendre)   to relearn

    reprendre   to retake

    surprendre   to surprise

rire   to laugh

    sourire   to smile

sentir   to feel

    consentir   to contradict

    démentir   to wrap up

    mentir   to to lie

    pressentir   to foresee

    ressentir   to resent, feel

    se repentir   to repent

servir   to serve

    desservir   to serve, clear the table, do a disservice

suffire   to suffice

The past participle of the following verb differs: confit

    confire   to pickle, preserve

sortir   to go out

    ressortir   to go out again, to stand out

tenir   to hold

    s'abstenir   to refrain

    appartenir   to belong

    contenir   to contain

    détenir   to detain

    entretenir   to maintain, converse

    maintenir   to maintain

    obtenir   to obtain

    retenir   to retain

    soutenir   to support, sustain

valoir   to be worth

    équivaloir à   to be equivalent to

    se prévaloir de   to pride oneself on, to take advantage of

    revaloir   to pay back, repay, get even with

vaincre   to conquer

    convaincre   to convince

venir   to come

Verbs with an asterisk (*) take *avoir* as their helping verb in compound tenses.

    advenir   to happen

    *circonvenir   to circumvent

    *contrevenir   to contravene, transgress

    *convenir (à)   to suit

    convenir (de)   to agree on something

    devenir   to become

    intervenir   to intervene

    parvenir   to reach, attain

    *prévenir   to inform, prevent

    provenir de   to proceed from, arise from

    redevenir   to become again

    revenir   to come back

    se souvenir de   to remember, to recollect

    *subvenir à   to relieve

    survenir   to occur

vêtir   to clothe

    dévêtir   to divest, strip

    revêtir   to clothe, invest

    se revêtir   to dress oneself

vivre   to live

>   revivre   to come back to life

>   survivre   to survive

voir   to see

>   entrevoir   to distinguish, glimpse, make out

>   prévoir   to foresee

>   revoir   to see again

Related Verbs

Related verbs have the same endings or endings similar to those of other verbs. For this reason they are conjugated with the same endings as the verbs to which they are related. Common related verbs include the following:

acquérir   to acquire

>   conquérir   to conquer

>   s'enquérir   to inquire after

>   requérir   to beg, demand

>   reconquérir   to reconquer

assaillir   to assail

>   tressaillir   to start, jump

conclure   to conclude

>   exclure   to exclude

>   inclure   to include

conduire   to drive, conduct

>   enduire   to smear, plaster

>   induire   to lead, induce

>   introduire   to lead (show) in, bring in

>   produire   to produce

>   réduire   to reduce

>   reproduire   to reproduce

>   séduire   to seduce

traduire   to translate

construire   to construct

détruire   to destroy

instruire   to instruct

nuire   to damage, harm

craindre   to fear

contraindre   to compel

plaindre   to pity

écrire   to write

circonscrire   to circumscribe

décrire   to describe

inscrire   to inscribe, write down, register

préscrire   to prescribe, stipulate

proscrire   to prohibit

récrire   to rewrite

souscrire   to subscribe

transcrire   to transcribe

peindre   to paint

astreindre   to subject, compel

atteindre   to attain, reach

déteindre   to take out the color

empreindre   to imprint

enceindre   to encircle, surround

enfreindre   to infringe, break

éteindre   to extinguish, turn off

étreindre   to embrace, seize

feindre   to pretend, feign

geindre   to moan

restreindre   to restrain

reteindre   to dye again

teindre   to dye

Regular -*er* Verbs

Note: An asterisk (*) indicates a shoe verb with two changes (see Chapter 2).

accessoiriser   to accessorize

abaisser   to lower

abandonner   to abandon

abdiquer   to abdicate

abhorrer   to abhor, loathe

abîmer   to damage

abjurer   to renounce, recant

abominer   to abominate, hate

abonder (en)   to abound (in)

abonner (s') (à)   to subscribe (to)

aborder   to reach

abouter   to join end to end

abreuver   to water (animals)

abriter (de/contre)   to shelter (from)

absenter (s') (de)   to absent oneself from

absorber   to absorb

abuser (de)   to abuse

accabler   to overwhelm

accentuer   to accentuate

accepter   to accept

accidenter   to injure

acclamer   to acclaim, cheer

acclimater   to acclimate

accommoder   to accommodate

accompagner   to accompany

accorder   to grant, admit

accorder (s') (pour/avec)   to agree (to/with)

accoster   to accost

accoucher (de)   to give birth (to)

accouder (s')   to lean on one's elbows

accoupler   to couple

accoutumer (s') (à)   to get accustomed (to)

accréditer   to substantiate, accredit, give credence to

accrocher   to hang (up), hook

acculer   to corner someone

accumuler   to accumulate

accuser   to accuse

acharner (s')   to go at fiercely

acheminer   to direct toward; to forward

acquitter (de)   to release from

actionner   to activate, operate

activer   to speed up

actualiser   to bring up to date

adapter (à)   to adapt (to)

additionner   to add up

adjurer   to beg

administrer   to administer

admirer   to admire

adonner (s') (à)   to devote oneself (to)

adopter   to adopt

adorer   to adore

adosser (à) (contre)   to stand against

adresser   to address

aduler   to flatter, admire

affamer   to starve

affecter (de)   to pretend (to)

affectionner   to have a liking for

affermer   to lease, rent

afficher   to post

affilier   to affiliate

affirmer   to affirm

affliger (de)   to afflict (with)

affluer   to rush, flow

affoler   to terrify

affronter   to confront

agacer   to annoy, bother

agenouiller (s')   to kneel

aggraver   to aggravate

agiter   to wave

agrafer   to hook, fasten (up)

agréer   to accept

agrémenter (de)   to embellish (with)

agresser   to attack

agripper   to grab, clutch

aguicher   to entice, tantalize

aider   to help

aiduiller   to direct

aiguiser   to sharpen

aimer   to like, love

ajourner   to adjourn, postpone

ajouter   to add

ajuster   to adjust

alarmer   to alarm

alerter (de)   to warn (about)

aligner   to align

alimenter (de)   to feed (with)

allier   to combine, unite

allouer   to allocate, grant

allumer   to light

alphabétiser   to teach to read
and write

alterner   to alternate

amasser   to amass

ambitionner (de)   to aspire (to)

améliorer   to improve

amender   to amend

américaniser   to Americanize

amidonner   to starch

amplifier (de)   to amplify (with/by)

amputer   to amputate

amuser   to amuse

analyser   to analyze

angoisser   to distress

animer   to animate

annihiler   to annihilate

annualiser   to annualize

annuler   to void

anticiper   to anticipate

apaiser   to calm

appliquer   to apply

apporter   to bring

apprécier   to appreciate, estimate,
evaluate

appréhender   to apprehend

apprêter   to get ready

apprivoiser   to tame

approcher   to approach

approprier   to suit, fit

approuver   to approve of

arbitrer   to arbitrate

arracher   to pull out

arranger   to arranger

arrêter   to stop

arriver   to arrive

arroser   to water

articuler   to articulate

aspirer (à)   to inhale (to aspire to)

assaisonner   to season

assassiner   to assassinate

assembler   to assemble

assigner   to assign

assimiler   to assimilate

assister (à)   to attend

associer   to associate

assumer   to assume

assurer   to assure

attabler (s')   to sit at the table

attacher   to attach

attaquer   to attack

attarder   to make late

atténuer   to ease

attester   to attest, testify

attirer   to attract

attraper   to catch

attribuer (à)   to attribute (to)

augmenter   to increase

autoriser   to authorize

avaler   to swallow

avoisiner   to be close to

aventurer   to venture

aviser   to advise

avouer   to confess

babiller (sur)   to gossip (about)

bachoter   to cram for a test

bâcler   to botch

badiner   to banter, jest

bafouer   to scorn

bafouiller   to stammer

bâfrer   to guzzle

bagarrer   to argue

baigner   to bathe

bâiller   to yawn

baiser   to kiss

baisser   to lower

balader   to take for a walk

balancer   to sway, swing

balayer   to sweep

balbutier   to stammer

banaliser   to make commonplace

bander   to bandage

baptiser   to baptize

baratiner   to sweet talk

barber   to bore

barbouiller (de)   to smear

barrer   to bar, block, cross out

basculer   to topple over

baser   to base

batailler   to battle

bâtonner   to beat with a stick

bavarder   to chat

baver   to dribble

bénéficier (de)   to benefit, enjoy

bercer   to rock

besogner   to toil

beurrer   to butter

bigarrer   to color in many hues

blaguer   to joke

blâmer   to blame

blaser (se) (de)   to become indifferent (to)

blasphémer   to blaspheme

blesser   to hurt, harm

bloquer   to block

bluffer   to bluff

bobiner   to wind

boiter   to limp

bombarder   to bombard

border   to border

borner   to limit

boucher   to block, clog

boucler   to buckle, block

bouder   to sulk

bouffer   to gobble; to be full, have volume

bouger   to move

bougonner   to grumble

bouillonner   to bubble

bouler   to roll

bouleverser   to move deeply, over-whelm, turn upside down

bourdonner   to buzz

bourrer   to stuff

boursoufler   to bloat, puff up

bousculer   to shove, bump

boutonner   to button

boxer   to box

boycotter   to boycott

brancher (sur)   to connect (to), plug (into)

branler   to shake

braver   to brave, defy

bredouiller   to stammer

bricoler   to do odd jobs

briller   to shine

briser   to break

broder   to embroider

bronzer   to tan

brosser   to brush

brouiller   to blur

bruiner   to drizzle

brûler   to burn

brusquer   to rush

brutaliser   to brutalize

cacher   to hide

cajoler   to cajole, flatter, cuddle

calculer   to calculate

calibrer   to calibrate

câliner   to cuddle

calmer   to calm

calomnier   to slander

cambrioler   to burglarize

camoufler   to camouflage

camper   to camp; to portray, depict

canaliser   to channel

canoniser   to canonize

canoter   to go boating

cantonner   to confine

capitaliser   to capitalize

capituler   to surrender

capoter   to overturn (car)

captiver   to captivate

capturer   to capture

caractériser   to characterize

caresser   to caress

caricaturer   to caricature

carrer   to square

cascader   to cascade

casser   to break

cataloguer   to catalogue

causer   to cause, chat

cautionner   to guarantee

censurer   to censure

centraliser   to centralize

cercler (de)   to encircle (with)

cerner   to encircle, surround

certifier   to certify

cesser   to stop

chagriner   to pain, worry, cause chagrin

chahuter   to create an uproar

chaîner   to chain

chanter   to sing

chantonner   to sing to oneself, hum

chaperonner   to chaperon

charger   to charge, load

charmer   to charm

chasser   to chase, hunt

châtier   to punish

chatouiller   to tickle

chauffer   to warm up

chausser   to put shoes on

cheminer   to walk along

chercher   to look for, search

chevaucher   to straddle

chicaner   to quibble

chiffonner   to crumple

chiffrer   to (en)code, decipher, put a price on

chiper   to steal

chiquer   to chew

chômer   to be unemployed

choquer   to shock

chuchoter   to whisper

chuter   to fall

cibler   to target

cingler   to lash

circuler   to circulate

cirer   to wax

citer   to quote

civiliser   to civilize

clapper   to click (one's tongue)

claquer   to bang, hit

clarifier   to clarify

classer   to classify

classifier   to classify

cligner   to blink, wink

clignoter   to blink, flash, twinkle

climatiser   to air condition

cliquer   to click

clouer   to nail

cocher   to check off

coder   to (en)code

codifier   to codify

coexister   to coexist

cogner   to hit, knock

coiffer   to do someone's hair

collaborer   to collaborate

collectionner   to collect

coller (à)   to glue (to)

coloniser   to colonize

colorer   to color

colorier   to colorize

combiner   to combine

combler (de)   to fill (with)

commander   to command, order

commémorer   to commemorate

commercialiser   to commercialize

communier   to receive communion

communiquer   to communicate

comparer   to compare

compenser   to compensate

compiler   to compile

complimenter   to compliment

compliquer   to complicate

comploter   to plot

comporter   to comprise

comporter (se)   to behave

composer   to compose

compter   to count

compulser   to consult (official documents)

concasser   to crush

concentrer   to concentrate

concilier   to reconcile

concorder (avec)   to agree (with)

condamner   to condemn

conditionner   to condition

confectionner   to make

confesser   to confess

confier   to entrust

confiner   to confine

confirmer   to confirm

confisquer   to confiscate

confluer   to join, flow together

conformer   to conform

conforter   to reinforce

confronter   to confront

congédier   to dismiss, fire

congratuler   to congratulate

conjecturer   to guess

conjuguer   to conjugate, combine efforts

conjurer   to avert

consacrer   to devote, dedicate

conseiller   to advise, counsel, recommend

conserver   to conserve

consister   to consist

consoler   to console

consolider   to consolidate

consommer   to consume

conspirer   to conspire

constater   to notice, take note

consterner   to dismay

constituer   to constitute

consulter   to consult

contenter   to content, please

conter   to relate

contester   to contest, dispute

continuer   to continue

contracter   to contract

contrarier   to annoy

contraster   to contrast

contribuer   to contribute

contrôler   to control

converser   to converse

convier (à)   to invite (to)

convoquer   to summon, convene

coordonner   to coordinate

copier   to copy

cotiser   to pay dues, subscribe

coucher   to put to bed

couler   to flow

couper   to cut

courber   to bend

couronner   to crown

coûter   to cost

cracher   to spit

craquer   to crack

créditer (de)   to credit (with)

créer   to create

creuser   to dig

crever (de)   to puncture, burst (with)

crier   to shout

crisper   to tense

critiquer   to criticize

croiser   to cross

croquer   to crunch, bite, sketch

crouler   to collapse, crumble

crucifier   to crucify

cuisiner   to cook

culbuter   to tumble

cultiver   to cultivate

dactylographier   to type

daigner   to deign, condescend

damner   to damn

danser   to dance

dater (de)   to date (from)

déballer   to unpack

débarrasser   to clear off

débarquer (de)   to disembark (from)

débiter   to debit

déboguer   to debug

déborder   to overflow

débrancher   to unplug

débrouiller   to disentangle

débuter   to start out

décerner   to award

déchanter   to become disillusioned

décharger   to unload

déchausser   to take off someone's shoes

déchiffrer   to decipher

déchirer   to rip, tear

décider   to decide

déclarer   to declare

déclencher   to release, set off

décliner   to decline

décoiffer   to mess someone's hair

décoller   to unstick, to take off (plane)

décolorer   to decolorize

décommander   to cancel an order

décomposer   to decompose

déconseiller   to advise against

décorer (de)   to decorate (with)

découcher   to spend the night away from home

découper   to cut up

décourager (de)   to discourage (from)

décrier   to decry

décrocher   to unhook

dédaigner   to disdain

dédier (à)   to dedicate (to)

dédommager   to compensate for damage

défavoriser   penalize

déferler   to break (waves)

défier   to challenge

défoncer   to push the bottom out

déformer   to deform

dégager (de)   to release (from)

dégonfler   to deflate

dégoûter   to disgust

dégoutter   to drip

dégrader   to demote

dégrafer   to unfasten

déguiser   to disguise

déguster   to taste, savor

déjeuner   to have lunch

déjouer   to foil

délabrer   to ruin

délacer   to unlace

délaisser   to abandon, quit

délibrer   to deliberate

délier   to untie

délivrer   to deliver, set free

déloger   to dislodge

demander   to ask (for)

demander (se)   to wonder

démanger   to itch

démarrer   to start out

démasquer   to unmask

démêler   to untangle

déménager   to move (residence)

démériter (de)   to be unworthy (of)

demeurer   to live, remain

démissioner (de)   to resign (from)

démoder   to make obsolete

démonter   to dismantle

démontrer   to demonstrate

dénigrer   to denigrate

dénoncer   to denounce

dénoter   to denote

dénouer   to untie

dépasser   to go beyond, transcend

dépayser   to disorientate, disorient

dépêcher   to dispatch

dépenser   to spend (money)

déplacer   to displace

déplier   to unfold

déplorer   to deplore

déporter   to deport

déposer   to put down, drop off, dump

déprimer   to depress

déraciner   to uproot

dérouler   to unroll

dérouter   to divert, puzzle, mystify

désapprouver   to disapprove of

déserter   to desert

déshabiller   to undress someone

désigner   to designate

désirer   to desire

désister   to desist

désoler   to distress, sadden

dessécher   to dry out

dessiner   to draw

destiner   to intend

détacher   to detach

détecter   to detect

déteriorer   to deteriorate

déterminer   to determine

détester   to hate

détourner   to divert, reroute

détourner (se) (de)   to turn oneself away (from)

détraquer   to put out of order

détromper (de)   to disabuse

dévaster   to devastate

développer   to develop

déverser   to pour

dévider   to unwind

dévier   to deviate

deviner   to guess

dévorer   to devour

dialoguer   to converse with

dicter   to dictate

diffamer   to defame

diffuser   to diffuse

diminuer   to diminish

dîner   to dine, have dinner

discerner   to discern

discipliner   to discipline

discontinuer   to discontinue

discriminer   to distinguish, discriminate

discuter   to discuss, argue, question

dispenser   to exempt

disperser   to disperse, spread out

disposer   to arrange, dispose

disputer   to dispute

disqualifier   to disqualify

disséminer   to disseminate, scatter

dissimuler   to hide

dissiper   to dissipate

dissuader (de)   to dissuade (from)

distinguer   to distinguish

distribuer   to distribute

diversifier   to diversify

diviser   to divide

divulguer   to divulge

documenter   to document

domestiquer   to tame

dominer   to dominate

donner   to give

dorer   to gild

doubler   to double

douer   to endow

douter   to doubt

douter (de)   to doubt

dresser   to draw up a document, to erect, to train an animal

duper   to dupe, trick

dupliquer   to duplicate

durer   to last

ébaucher   to sketch

écarter   to separate, spread apart

échanger   to exchange

échapper   to escape

écharper   to tear to pieces, mutilate

échauffer   to overheat

échelonner   to space (spread) out

échouer   to fail

éclabousser   to splash

éclairer   to light (up), illuminate

éclater (en)   to burst (into)

écoeurer   to make someone feel sick

économiser   to economize

écouter   to listen (to)

écraser   to crush

écumer   to skim

éditer   to edit

éduquer   to educate

effacer   to erase

effarer   to alarm

effectuer   to effectuate

effleurer   to touch lightly

effrayer   to frighten

égaler   to equal

égaliser   to equalize

égayer   to amuse

éliminer   to eliminate

éloigner (de)   to move away (from)

élucider   to elucidate

émaner   to emanate

emballer   to pack

embarquer   to embark

embarrasser   to hinder, clutter

embaucher   to hire

embêter   to bother, worry

embrasser   to kiss, hug

embrouiller   to tangle up

émigrer   to emigrate

emmerder   to bother someone (slang)

empêcher   to prevent

emporter   to carry away

empresser (s')   to hurry

emprunter   to borrow

émuler   to emulate

enchaîner   to put in chains

enchanter   to enchant

encombrer   to clutter

encourager   to encourage

endommager   to damage

endurer   to endure, put up with

énerver   to overexcite, irritate, annoy

enfermer   to shut away; to lock in

engraisser   to fatten

enivrer   to intoxicate

enjamber   to stride over

enregistrer   to record, register

enrhumer   to give someone a cold

enseigner   to teach

entamer   to start

enterrer   to bury

enthousiasmer   to enthuse

entourer   to surround

entraîner   to carry away, train a person

entrecouper (de)   to interrupt (with)

entrer   to enter

envelopper   to envelope, wrap up

envier   to envy

épargner   to save, spare someone something

épier   to spy on

éplucher   to peel

éponger   to sponge

épouser   to marry

épouvanter   to terrify

éprouver   to feel, try, experience

épuiser   to exhaust, use up

équilbrer   to balance

équiper (de)   to equip (with)

ériger   to erect

errer   to wander

escamoter   to evade, dodge

escompter   to anticipate, discount (financial)

espionner   to spy on

esquisser   to sketch

essayer   to try (on)

essouffler   to make breathless

estimer   to esteem, estimate

étaler   to display, spread out

éternuer   to sneeze

étonner   to astonish

étouffer   to suffocate

étrangler   to strangle

étudier   to study

évacuer   to evacuate

évaluer   to evaluate

éveiller   to awaken, arouse

éviter   to avoid

évoquer   to evoke

exacerber   to aggravate

examiner   to examine

exceller   to excel

exciter   to excite

excuser   to excuse

exécuter   to execute

exhiber   to exhibit

exiger   to demand, require

exister   to exist

expédier   to send

expliquer   to explain

exploiter   to exploit

exporter   to export

exposer   to expose

exprimer   to express

expulser   to expel

exterminer   to exterminate

fabriquer   to manufacture

fâcher   to anger

faciliter   to facilitate

façonner   to fashion, shape

falsifier   to falsify

familiariser   to familiarize

fasciner   to fascinate

fatiguer   to tire

fausser   to distort

favoriser   to favor

féliciter   to congratulate

fermer   to close

ficher   to file, open a file on

fier (se) (à)   to trust

figurer   to represent

filer   to run off

filmer   to film

filtrer   to filter

fixer   to fix, decide on

flairer   to smell

flamber   to burn

flâner   to stroll

flanquer   to flank, fling

flatter   to flatter

flirter   to flirt

flotter   to float

folâtrer   to frolic, romp

fonctionner   to function, work

fonder   to found, establish

forcer   to force

former   to form

formuler   to formulate

fortifier   to fortify

fouetter   to whip

fouiller   to dig deep, search

fracasser   to smash, shatter

frapper   to knock, hit

fredonner   to hum

freiner   to slow down, brake

fréquenter   to frequent

friser   to curl

frissonner   to shiver

froisser   to crumple

frôler   to brush against

froncer   to wrinkle

frotter   to rub

fumer   to smoke

fuser   to burst forth, spurt out

fusiller   to shoot

gâcher   to spoil

gagner   to win, earn

garder   to guard, keep

garer   to park

gaspiller   to waste

gâter   to spoil, damage

gêner   to bother, inconvenience

germer   to sprout

gicler   to spurt

gifler   to smack, slap

glisser   to slip, glide

gonfler   to inflate

goûter   to taste

graisser   to grease

gratter   to scratch, scrape

grelotter   to shiver

griffonner   to scribble

griller   to grill

grimper   to climb

grogner   to grumble, moan

gronder   to scold

grouper   to group

guetter   to watch

guider   to guide

habiliter   to authorize

habiller   to dress someone

habiter   to live (in), inhabit

habituer   to accustom

hacher   to chop

hanter   to haunt

harasser   to exhaust

hasarder   to risk, hazard

hâter   to hurry

hausser   to raise

hériter   to inherit

hésiter   to hesitate

heurter   to knock against

hisser   to hoist

hocher   to nod

honorer   to honor

horrifier   to horrify

hospitaliser   to hospitalize

huiler   to oil, lubricate

hurler   to howl

hypnotiser   to hypnotize

idéaliser   to idealize

identifier   to identify

idolâtrer   to idolize

ignorer   to be unaware of, ignore

illuminer   to illuminate

illustrer   to illustrate

imaginer   to imagine

imbiber   to soak

imiter   to imitate

immatriculer   to register

immigrer   to immigrate

immobiliser   to immobilize

immortaliser   to immortalize

impatienter   to irritate, annoy

implanter   to introduce

impliquer   to imply, implicate

implorer   to implore, beg

importer   to import; to matter, be important

imposer   to impose

impressionner   to impress

imprimer   to print

improviser   to improvise

inaugurer   to unveil

incendier   to set on fire

inciter   to incite

incliner   to incline

incommoder   to inconvenience

incorporer   to incorporate

incriminer   to incriminate

indiquer   to indicate

indisposer   to upset

individualiser   to individualize

infecter (de)   to infect (with)

infester (de)   to infest (with)

infiltrer   to infiltrate

informatiser   to computerize

informer   to inform

infuser   to infuse

inhiber   to inhibit

initier (à)   to initiate (into)

injecter   to inject

injurier   to abuse, insult

innover   to innovate

inonder   to flood

insinuer   to insinuate

insister   to insist

inspecter   to inspect

inspirer   to inspire

installer   to install

instituer   to institute

insulter   to insult

intensifier   to intensify

intéresser   to interest

interposer (entre)   to interpose (between)

interviewer   to interview

intimider   to intimidate

intituler   to title

invalider   to invalidate

inventer   to invent

inverser   to reverse the order

inviter   to invite

invoquer   to put forward, call upon

irriter   to irritate

isoler (de)   to isolate (from)

jacasser   to chatter

japper   to yelp

jardiner   to garden

jaser   to chatter

jeûner   to fast

jongler   to juggle

jouer   to play

jurer   to swear

justifier   to justify

juxtaposer   to juxtapose

kidnapper   to kidnap

klaxonner   to sound a horn, honk

labourer   to plow

lâcher   to loosen, let go

laisser   to let, allow, leave

lamenter   to lament

laver   to wash

lier   to tie

liguer   to unite

limiter   to limit

liquider   to liquidate

lisser   to smooth down

livrer (à)   to deliver (to)

localiser   to localize

loger   to lodge

louer   to rent; to praise

lustrer   to shine

lutter   to struggle, fight

mâcher   to chew

machiner   to plot

magasiner   to go shopping

maîtriser   to control

maltraiter   to mistreat

mander   to command

manier   to handle

manifester   to manifest

manipuler   to manipulate

manoeuvrer   to maneuver, manipulate

manquer   to miss, lack

manufacturer   to manufacture

maquiller   to apply make-up to someone

marchander   to bargain

marcher   to walk; to function

marier (à)   to marry someone to someone else

marier (se) (avec)   to marry

marquer (de)   to mark (with)

masquer (à)   to conceal (from)

massacrer   to massacre

mastiquer   to chew

matelasser   to pad

méditer   to meditate

méfier (se) (de)   to distrust

mélanger   to mix

mêler   to mix

mémoriser   to memorize

mendier   to beg

mentionner   to mention

mépriser   to scorn

mériter   to deserve

mesurer   to measure

meubler (de)   to furnish (with)

mijoler   to simmer

moderniser   to modernize

modifier   to modify

moduler   to modulate

monter   to go up; to take up

montrer   to show

mortifier   to mortify

motiver   to motivate

mouiller   to wet

mousser   to bubble

multiplier   to multiply

murmurer   to murmur

mutiler   to mutilate

mystifier   to mystify

napper (de)   to coat (with)

narrer   to narrate

naviguer   to navigate

navrer   to distress, upset

nécessiter   to require

négocier   to negociate

neutraliser   to neutralize

nier   to deny

nommer   to name

noter   to note

notifier   to notify

nouer   to tie

numéroter   to number

objecter   to object

observer   to observe

obstiner (s') (à)   to persist in

occasionner   to cause

occuper   to occupy

offenser   to offend

onduler   to ripple

opposer   to oppose, put up an argument, to match or pit against

oppresser   to weigh down

opprimer   to oppress

opter (pour)   to opt (for)

ordonner   to order, arrange

organiser   to organize

orienter   to orient

orner (de)   to decorate (with)

osciller   to oscillate

oser   to dare

ôter   to remove

oublier   to forget

pacifier   to pacify

palpiter   to palpitate

paniquer   to panic

parachuter   to parachute

paralyser   to paralyze

pardonner   to forgive

parer   to adorn

parfumer   to perfume

parier (sur)   to bet (on)

parler   to speak

parquer   to park a car

participer (à)   to participate (in)

passer   to pass, spend (time)

passionner   to fascinate; to grip

patienter   to wait

patiner   to skate

patronner   to patronize, sponsor

payer   to pay

pêcher   to fish

pédaler   to pedal

peigner   to comb someone's hair

pencher   to tip, tilt, bend

penser   to think

percer   to pierce

percher   to perch

perfectionner   to perfect

perforer   to perforate

perpétuer   to perpetuate

persécuter   to persecute

persister   to persist

personnifier   to personify

persuader   to persuade

perturber   to disrupt

pétiller   to crackle, bubble

pétrifier   to petrify

peupler   to populate

photocopier   to photocopy

photographier   to photograph

piloter   to pilot

piquer   to sting

pivoter   to pivot

plaider   to plead

plaisanter   to joke

planer (sur)   to hover (over)

planter   to plant

pleurer   to cry

pleurnicher   to whine

plier (en)   to fold (into)

plisser   to pleat, crease

polluer (de)   to pollute (with)

pomper   to pump

ponctuer   to punctuate

porter   to wear, carry

poser   to place, pose

poudrer   to powder

pousser   to push, grow

pratiquer   to practice

prêcher   to preach

précipiter   to push, throw

préciser   to specify, make clear

prédisposer   to predispose

prédominer (sur)   to prevail (over)

préméditer   to premeditate

prénommer   to give a first name to

préoccuper   to preoccupy, worry

préparer   to prepare

préposer (à)   to appoint to

présenter   to introduce, present

préserver (de)   to preserve (from)

presser   to press, squeeze

présumer   to presume

présupposer   to presuppose

prêter   to lend

prier   to pray, beg, request

priver   to deprive

proclamer   to proclaim

procurer   to procure

professer   to profess

profiter (de)   to profit (from)

programmer   to program

progresser   to progress

prohiber   to prohibit

proposer   to propose

protester   to protest

prouver   to prove

provoquer   to provoke

publier   to publish

puer   to stink

purifier   to purify

quadrupler   to quadruple

qualifier   to qualify

quantifier   to quantify

quereller   to scold

questionner   to question

quêter   to seek, to collect (money)

quitter   to leave, remove

rabaisser   to disparage

raccommoder   to mend

raccompagner   to take or see back

raccorder (à)   to connect (to)

raccrocher   to hang up

raconter   to relate

raffiner   to refine

rager   to rage

railler   to scoff (jeer) at

raisonner   to reason

rajouter   to add more

rallumer   to light again

ramasser   to pick up, collect

ramer   to row

ranimer   to revive

râper   to grate

rapporter   to bring back

rapprocher (de)   to bring closer (to)

raser   to shave

rassembler   to assembler

rassurer   to reassure

rater   to miss, fail

rattacher   to reattach

rattraper   to catch up

rayer   to rule, line, cross out

rayonner   to shine

réaliser   to fulfill, realize

rebaisser   to reduce, decrease, fall again

réchauffer   to reheat

rechercher   to search, hunt for

réciter   to recite

réclamer   to ask for, claim

recommander   to recommend

récompenser   to compensate

réconcilier   to reconcile

réconforter   to comfort

recoucher   to put back to bed

recouper   to cut again

récréer   to recreate

rectifier   to correct

reculer   to step back

recycler   to recycle

redonner   to give again

redouter (de)   to dread, fear

redresser   to set upright

refuser   to refuse

réfuter   to refute

regagner   to regain

regarder   to look (at), watch

regretter   to regret, miss

relâcher   to loosen, release

remarquer   to notice

rembourser   to reimburse

remercier   to thank

remonter   to go up again

remporter   to take away (again)

remuer   to move, stir

rencontrer   to meet

renfermer   to enclose

renommer   to reappoint

rénover   to renovate

renseigner   to inform

rentrer   to return

renverser   to overturn

répandre   to spill, scatter, spread

réparer   to repair

repasser   to iron; to pass (by) again

répercuter (sur)   to pass on (to)

replier   to fold again

répliquer   to reply

reposer   to put back

repousser   to push away

représenter   to represent

réprimander   to reprimand

réprimer   to repress

reprocher   to reproach

répudier   to repudiate

réserver   to reserve

résister   to resist

respecter   to respect

respirer   to breathe

ressembler (à)   to resemble

rester   to remain, stay

restituer   to restore

résumer   to summarize

retirer   to take off, remove, withdraw

retomber   to fall again

retourner   to return, to turn over

retrouver   to find again

réveiller   to awaken someone

revendiquer   to claim

rêver   to dream

réviser   to revise

ridiculiser   to ridicule

rigoler   to laugh

riposter   to answer back

risquer   to risk

rivaliser   to rival

ronfler   to snore

rouler   to roll

ruiner   to ruin

ruser   to use trickery

sacrifier   to sacrifice

saigner   to bleed

saliver   to salivate

saluer   to greet

sanctionner   to sanction, recognize, to punish

sangloter   to sob

saturer (de)   to saturate (with)

sauter   to jump

sauver   to save

savourer   to savor

scintiller   to sparkle

scolariser   to educate

sculpter   to sculpt

secouer   to shake

séjourner   to live somewhere temporarily

sélectionner   to select

sembler   to seem

séparer   to separate

serrer   to grasp, to press

siffler   to whistle

signaler   to signal, point out

signer   to sign

signifier   to mean

simplifier   to simplify

simuler   to simulate

singulariser   to single out

situer   to situate

skier   to ski

socialiser   to socialize

soigner   to care for

solliciter   to solicit

somnoler   to doze

sonner   to ring

souffler   to blow

souhaiter   to wish

souiller   to dirty

souligner   to underline

soupçonner   to suspect

souper   to have supper

soupirer   to sigh

spécifier   to specify

spéculer   to speculate

stationner   to park

stériliser   to sterilize

stigmatiser   to stigmatize

stimuler   to stimulate

stipuler   to stipulate

stresser   to put under stress

subordonner   to subordinate

subsister (de)   to live (on)

substituer (à)   to substitute

succomber   to succumb

sucrer   to sweeten

suer   to sweat

suffoquer   to suffocate

supplier   to beg, implore

supporter   to support, tolerate

supposer   to suppose

supprimer   to suppress

surexciter   to overexcite

surfer   to surf

surmonter   to surmount, overcome

surpasser   to surpass

sursauter   to jump, give a start

surveiller   to watch

survoler   to fly over

suspecter (de)   to suspect (of)

symboliser   to symbolize

sympathiser (avec)   to get on well with

synchoniser   to synchronize

tâcher   to try

tacher (de)   to stain (with)

tailler   to cut, sharpen, trim

tamiser   to sift

tamponner   to stamp

tanner   to pester

taper   to tap, type

tapoter   to tap

taquiner   to tease

tarder   to delay

tasser   to pack down

tâter   to feel by touching

tâtonner   to grope

tatouer   to tattoo

teinter   to tint

télécopier   to fax

télégraphier   to telegraph

téléphoner   to telephone

téléviser   to televise

témoigner   to testify, witness

tenter   to attempt, tempt

terminer   to terminate, finish

terrifier   to terrify

tester   to test

tinter   to ring

tirer   to pull, shoot

tisser   to weave

tomber   to fall

tonner   to thunder

toquer   to knock

torturer   to torture

totaliser   to total

toucher   to touch, cash

tourmenter   to tourment

tourner   to turn

tousser   to cough

tracasser   to bother, worry

traîner   to drag

traiter   to treat

trancher   to slice, cut

transformer (en)   to transform (into)

transgresser   to transgress

transporter   to transport

travailler   to work

traverser   to cross

trébucher   to stumble

trembler (de)   to tremble (with)

tremper   to soak

tresser   to braid

tricher   to trick, cheat

tricoter   to knit

trier   to sort

triompher   to triumph

tripler   to triple

tripoter   to fiddle with

tromper   to deceive

troquer   to fix, swap

trotter   to trot

trouer   to make a hole in

trouver   to find

truquer   to fake

tuer   to kill

tyranniser   to tyrannize

unifier   to unify

uniformiser   to standardize

urbaniser   to urbanize

user   to wear out, use up

utiliser   to use

vacciner (contre)   to vaccinate (against)

vaciller   to sway

vagabonder   to wander

vaguer   to roam, wander

valider   to validate

valser   to waltz

vanter   to praise

vaporiser   to vaporize

varier   to vary

veiller   to keep watch, stay up

ventiler   to ventilate

verbaliser   to verbalize

vérifier   to verify

verser   to pour

vexer   to vex

vibrer   to vibrate

vider   to empty

violer   to violate

virer   to turn a vehicle; to transfer money

viser (à)   to aim (at)

visiter   to visit

vocaliser   to vocalize

voler   to fly; to steal

voter   to vote

vouer (à)   to dedicate (to), vow

vriller   to spin, whirl

vulgariser   to vulgarize

zébrer (de)   to streak, stripe (with)

zigzaguer   to zigzag

zipper   to zip up

zoomer   to zoom in

-cer Verbs

acquiescer   to approve, agree

agacer   to annoy

agencer   to organize

annoncer   to announce

avancer   to advance

balancer   to balance

bercer   to rock

coincer   to wedge, trap

commencer   to begin

commercer (avec)   to trade (with)

défoncer   to push the bottom out

délacer   to unlace

dénoncer   to denounce

déplacer   to move, displace

devancer   to precede, anticipate

effacer   to erase

enfoncer   to plunge in

enlacer   to embrace

énoncer   to state

entrelacer   to intertwine

exaucer   to grant

foncer   to dash along, make dark

forcer   to force

froncer   to wrinkle

grimacer   to grimace

grincer   to creak, grind

influencer   to influence

lacer   to lace

lancer   to throw

menacer (de)   to threaten (with)

percer   to pierce

pincer   to pinch

placer   to place, put

policer   to civilize

prononcer   to pronounce

recommencer   to begin again

reinforcer   to reinforce

remplacer   to replace

renoncer   to renounce

replacer   to replace

rincer   to rinse

sucer   to suck

tracer   to trace

transpercer   to pierce

-ger Verbs

abréger*   to shorten

abroger   to repeal

adjuger   to auction

afliger   to afflict

allonger   to lengthen

aménager   to fit out, develop

arranger   to arrange

bouger   to move

changer   to change

charger   to charge, load, burden

converger   to converge

corriger   to correct

déloger   to dislodge

démanger   to itch

déménager   to move residence

déranger   to disturb

désengager   to disengage

diriger   to direct

diverger   to diverge

échanger   to exchange

encourager   to encourage

endommager   to damage

engager   to engage, start up

envisager   to envision

éponger   to sponge

ériger   to erect

exiger   to demand, require

figer   to clot

gager   to bet

immerger   to immerse

infliger (à)   to inflict (upon)

interroger   to interrogate

juger   to judge

loger   to lodge

louanger   to praise, extol

manger   to eat

ménager   to handle carefully

nager   to swim

négliger   to neglect

obliger   to oblige

outrager   to outrage

partager   to share, divide

piéger*   to trap

plonger   to dive, plunge

préjuger   to prejudge

présager   to predict, foresee

prolonger   to prolong

protéger*   to protect

rager   to rage

rallonger   to lengthen

ranger   to tidy

ravager   to ravage

réaménager   to redevelop

réarranger   to rearrange

recharger   to reload, refill

rédiger   to edit

siéger*   to be in session

singer   to mimic

songer   to dream, think

soulager   to relieve

submerger   to submerge

surcharger   to overload

venger   to avenge

voltiger   to flit (flutter) about

voyager   to travel

-yer Verbs

aboyer   to bark

apitoyer   to move to pity

appuyer   to lean, press

bégayer   to stammer

broyer   to crush, grind

chatoyer   to glisten, shimmer

côtoyer   to be next to, mix with

déployer   to open (spread) out

employer   to use, employ

ennuyer   to bore

envoyer   to send

essuyer   to wipe

flamboyer   to blaze, flame

foudroyer   to strike

larmoyer   to whimper

nettoyer   to clean

noyer   to drown

ondoyer   to undulate

ployer   to bend

renvoyer   to send back, fire

tournoyer   to whirl

tutoyer   to use the "tu" form

vouvoyer   to use the "vous" form

-e + consonant + er verbs

All verbs take a grave accent except those highlighted in boldface, which double the consonant.

acheter   to buy

achever   to achieve, finish, complete

amener   to bring, lead

amonceler   to pile up

appeler   to call

cacheter   to seal

caqueter   to prattle, cackle

celer   to conceal

chanceler   to stagger

colleter   to grab by the collar

congeler   to deep freeze

crocheter   to pick, crochet

déceler   to detect

décongeler   to defrost

dégeler   to thaw

écheveler   to ruffle, tousle, dishevel

élever   to raise

emmener   to lead away

empaqueter   to pack

enlever   to remove, carry away

épeler   to spell

épousseter   to dust

étinceler   to sparkle

étiqueter   to label

feuilleter   to leaf through

ficeler   to tie

geler   to freeze

haleter   to pant

harceler   to harass

jeter   to throw

lever   to raise, lift

malmener   to mishandle

mener   to lead

modeler   to model

morceler   to parcel out, divide up

niveler   to level

parsemer   to sprinkle (strew) with

peler   to peel

pelleter   to shovel up

peser   to weigh

prélever   to take a sample of

projeter   to project

promener   to take for a walk

racheter   to buy back

ramener   to bring back

rappeler   to call back, remind

regeler   to refreeze

rejeter   to reject

relever   to raise again

renouveler   to renew

ruisseler   to stream

semer   to sow

soulever   to raise

tacheter   to spot

-*é* + consonant + *er* Verbs

accéder   to attain

accélérer   to accelerate

adhérer   to adhere

aérer   to aerate

agglomérer   to pile up

agréger*   to aggregate

aliéner   to alienate

allécher   to make one's mouth water

alléger*   to lighten

alléguer   to allege

altérer   to alter

assécher   to drain, dry

assiéger*   to lay siege to

céder   to yield

célébrer   to celebrate

compléter   to complete

concéder   to concede

conférer   to confer

considérer   to consider

coopérer   to cooperate

décéder   to die

décolérer   to always be in a bad temper

déléguer   to delegate

délibérer   to deliberate

désespérer   to drive to despair

désintégrer   to disintegrate

différer   to differ

digérer   to digest

énumérer   to enumerate

espérer   to hope

exagérer   to exaggerate

gérer   to manage

incinérer   to incinerate

indifférer   to make indifferent

inférer (de)   to infer from

ingérer   to ingest

inquiéter   to worry, upset

insérer   to insert

intégrer   to integrate

intercéder   to intercede

interpréter   to interpret

lacérer   to lacerate

lécher   to lick

léguer   to bequeath

libérer   to liberate

macérer   to soak

modérer   to moderate

oblitérer   to obliterate

obséder   to haunt, obsess

opérer   to operate

pécher   to sin

pénétrer   to penetrate

perpétrer   to perpetrate

persévérer   to persevere

posséder   to possess

précéder   to precede

préférer   to prefer

procéder (de)   to proceed (from)

prospérer   to prosper

recéder   to recede

récupérer   to recuperate

référer   to refer

refléter   to reflect

réfrigérer   to refrigerate

régénérer   to regenerate

régler   to regulate

régner   to rule

réitérer   to reiterate

rémunérer   to remunerate

repérer   to spot

répéter   to repeat

révéler   to reveal

réverbérer   to reverberate

révérer   to revere

sécher   to dry

sécréter   to secrete

succéder (à)   to succeed

suggérer   to suggest

tolérer   to tolerate

transférer   to transfer

ulcérer   to ulcerate

végéter   to vegetate

vénérer   to venerate

Regular *-ir* and *-oir* Verbs

-ir Verbs

abasourdir   to stun

abolir   to abolish

aboutir (à)   to succeed, lead to, result in

abrutir   to exhaust

accomplir   to accomplish

accroupir (s)   to squat, crouch

adoucir   to make milder

affaiblir   to weaken

affermir   to consolidate, strengthen

affranchir   to stamp

agir   to act

agrandir   to widen, enlarge

ahurir   to dumbfound

aigrir   to embitter

alourdir (de)   to weigh down

amaigrir   to make thin

amincer   to thin down

amoindrir   to lessen, weaken

amollir   to soften

anéantir   to annihilate

anoblir   to ennoble

aplatir   to level

appauvrir   to impoverish

appesantir   to weigh down

applaudir   to applaud

approfondir   to deepen

arrondir   to make round, round off

asservir   to enslave

assombrir   to darken

assortir   to match

assoupir   to make drowsy

assouplir   to soften, to relax a rule

assourdir   to deafen

attendrir   to move, soften, tenderize

atterrir   to land (plane)

avertir   to warn

bannir (de)   to banish

bâtir   to build

bénir   to bless

blanchir   to whiten

blêmir   to go pale

bleuir   to become blue

blondir   to become fairer

blottir   to curl up

bondir   to leap

brunir   to become brown

chérir   to cherish

choisir   to choose

compatir   to sympathize

convertir   to convert

croupir   to stagnate

définir   to define

démolir   to demolish

désobéir (à)   to disobey

désunir   to disunite, divide

divertir   to amuse

durcir   to harden

éblouir   to dazzle

éclaircir   to light up

élargir   to enlarge

embellir   to embellish, beautify

endurcir   to harden, toughen

enfouir   to bury

engourdir   to make numb

enhardir   to make bold

enlaidir   to make ugly

enrichir   to enrich

ensevelir   to bury

envahir   to invade

établir   to establish

étourdir   to daze

évanouir (s')   to faint

faiblir   to weaken

farcir   to stuff

finir   to finish

fléchir   to bend

flétrir (se)   to wither, condemn

fleurir   to flourish

fournir   to furnish

fraîchir   to get cooler

franchir   to clear, get over

frémir   to quake, tremble

garantir   to guarantee

garnir (de)   to garnish

gémir   to moan

grandir   to grow

gravir   to climb

grossir   to put on weight

guérir   to cure

honnir   to hold in contempt

invertir   to invert

investir   to invest

jaillir   to well, gush

jaunir   to become yellow

jouir   to enjoy

languir   to languish

maigrir   to become thin

meurtrir   to hurt, bruise

mincir   to get thinner

mollir   to give way, yield

mugir   to bellow, roar

munir (de)   to equip (with)

mûrir   to ripen, mature

noircir   to blacken

nourrir   to nourish

obéir   to obey

obscurcir   to obscure

pâlir   to become pale

périr   to perish

polir   to polish

pourrir   to rot

punir   to punish

raccourcir   to shorten

raidir   to stiffen

radoucir   to soften

rafraîchir   to refresh

rajeunir   to make younger

ralentir   to slow down

ramollir   to soften, weaken

ravir   to delight

réagir   to react

réfléchir   to reflect, think

refroidir   to cool

réjouir   to rejoice

remplir   to fill

resplendir   to shine

rétablir   to reestablish

retentir   to ring

rétrécir   to take in, shrink

réunir (à)   to reunite

réussir   to succeed

rosir   to become pink

rougir   to blush

saisir   to seize

salir   to dirty

subir   to undergo

subvertir   to subvert

surgir   to appear suddenly, shoot up

tiédir   to cool down

trahir   to betray

unir   to unite

vernir   to varnish

vieillir   to get old

vomir   to vomit

vrombir   to buzz, throb

-oir Verbs

apercevoir   to notice

concevoir   to conceive

décevoir   to deceive

devoir   to have to, be obligated to, to owe

percevoir   to perceive

recevoir   to receive

redevoir   to still owe someone

Regular -*re* Verbs

Note: An asterisk (*) indicates that the verb adds a final -*t* to the third person singular form (il, elle, on).

attendre   to wait (for)

confondre   to confuse

correspondre   to correspond

corrompre*   to corrupt

défendre   to defend, prohibit

dépendre (de)   to depend on

descendre   to go down, take down

détendre   to slacken, loosen

entendre   to hear

étendre   to stretch

fendre   to split, crack

fondre   to melt

interrompre*   to interrupt

mordre   to bite

pendre   to hang

perdre   to lose

prétendre   to claim

rendre   to return

répandre   to spread

reperdre   to lose again

répondre   to answer

revendre   to sell again

rompre*   to break

suspendre   to suspend

tendre   to strain, tighten

tondre   to shear, clip, mow

tordre   to twist

vendre   to sell

Appendix G

Common Reflexive Verbs

s'abstenir (de)   to abstain (from)

s'accoutumer (à)   to become
accustomed (to)

s'agenouiller   to kneel

s'acheter   to buy for oneself

s'agir (de)   to be a question (of),
be about

s'améliorer   to improve

s'amuser à   to have fun, enjoy

s'apercevoir de   to realize,
become aware of

s'appeler   to be named

s'apprêter à   to get ready for,
ready to

s'approcher de   to approach,
come near

s'arrêter de   to stop

s'asseoir   to sit

s'attendre à   to expect

se baigner   to bathe

se battre   to fight

se blesser   to hurt oneself

se bronzer   to tan

se brosser   to brush

se brûler   to burn oneself

se cacher   to hide oneself

se casser   to break

se changer de   to change clothes

se coiffer   to do one's hair

se cogner contre   to bump into
something

se conduire   to behave

se contenter de   to be satisfied
with

se coucher   to go to bed

se couper   to cut oneself

se décider à   to decide

se déguiser en   to disguise oneself as

se demander   to wonder

se dépêcher de   to hurry

se déshabiller   to undress oneself

se dire   to tell oneself

se disposer à   to be available to

se disputer   to quarrel

se douter de   to suspect

s'échapper   to escape

s'écrier   to exclaim, cry out

s'écrire   to write to one another

s'écrouler   to collapse

s'effondrer   to collapse

s'efforcer de   to strive to

s'éloiner de   to move away from

s'embrasser   to hug, kiss each other

s'emparer de   to seize, grab

s'empresser de   to hasten to

s'en aller   to leave, go away

s'endormir   to go to sleep

s'enfuir   to flee

s'ennuyer (à/de)   to get bored (with, by)

s'enquérir de   to inquire about

s'entendre   to get along

s'entraider   to help one another

s'envoler   to fly off

s'étonner de   to be surprised at

s'évader   to escape

s'évanouir   to faint

s'exercer à   to practice

s'exprimer   to express oneself

se fâcher contre   to get angry with

se fiancer avec   to get engaged to

se fier à   to trust

se figurer   to imagine

s'habiller   to dress oneself

s'habituer à   to get used to

se heurter (contre)   to collide (with)

s'imaginer   to imagine oneself

s'impatienter   to become impatient

s'installer   to settle down, to set up shop

s'inquiéter (de)   to worry (about)

se lamenter (de)   to lament, grieve (over, about)

se laver   to wash oneself

se lever   to get up

se loger   to lodge, find accommodations

se maquiller   to put on makeup

se marier avec   to get married to

se méfier de   to mistrust

se mettre à   to begin to

se moquer de   to make fun of

s'obstiner à   to persist in

s'occuper de   to take care of

se parler   to talk to each other

se passer   to happen

se passer de   to do without

se peigner   to comb one's hair

se plaindre de   to complain about

se plaire à   to enjoy, be fond of

se préparer à   to get ready to

se présenter   to introduce oneself

se promener   to take a walk

se rappeler de   to remember

se raser   to shave oneself

se réconcilier   to reconcile, make up
with each other

se réfugier   to take refuge

se regarder   to look at oneself/
each other

se rencontrer   to meet each other

se repentir   to repent

se reposer   to rest

se résigner à   to resign oneself to

se respecter   to respect oneself/one
another

se retrouver   to meet again, be back
again

se réunir   to meet each other

se réveiller   to wake up (oneself)

se sauver   to run away

se sentir   to feel

se servir de   to use

se soucier de   to care about, concern
oneself about

se souvenir de   to remember

se spécialiser en   to specialize in

se suicider   to commit suicide

se taire   to be quiet, become silent

se téléphoner   to telephone each other

se tromper   to be mistaken

se trouver   to be, happen to be

se vanter de   to boast of, about

se voir   to see one another

Appendix H

Irregular Past Participles

Note: An asterisk (*) indicates that the verb uses être as its helping verb in compound tenses.

Verb	Meaning	Past Participle
absoudre	to absolve	absous
acquérir	to acquire	acquis
asseoir	to seat	assis
avoir	to have	eu
boire	to drink	bu
conclure	to conclude	conclu
conduire	to drive	conduit
connaître	to know	connu
coudre	to sew	cousu
courir	to run	couru
craindre	to fear	craint
croire	to believe	cru
croître	to grow	crû
devoir	to owe, have to	dû
dire	to say, tell	dit
distraire	to distract	distrait
écrire	to write	écrit
être	to be	été

continues

continued

Verb	Meaning	Past Participle
faire	to make, do	fait
falloir	to be necessary	fallu
joindre	to join	joint
lire	to read	lu
mettre	to put	mis
mourir*	to die	mort
mouvoir	to move	mû
naître*	to be born	né
nuire	to harm	nui
offrir	to offer	offert
ouvrir	to open	ouvert
paraître	to seem	paru
peindre	to paint	peint
plaire	to please	plu
pleuvoir	to rain	plu
pourvoir	to provide	pourvu
pouvoir	to be able to, was able to	pu
prendre	to take	pris
prévoir	to foresee	prévu
recevoir	to receive	reçu
résoudre	to resolve (to result)	résolu (résous)
rire	to laugh	ri
savoir	to know	su
souffrir	to suffer	souffert
suffire	to be enough	suffi
suivre	to follow	suivi
taire	to conceal	tu
tenir	to hold	tenu
valoir	to be worth	valu
venir *	to come	venu
vêtir	to dress	vêtu
vivre	to live	vécu
voir	to see	vu
vouloir	to want, wish	voulu

Index

A–B

active voice versus passive voice, 167
adjectives, using subjunctives with, 119-121
agir (to act), 143
agreement (past participles), 56-59
  avoir conjugates, 16-17
  être conjugates, 16-17
  reflexive verbs, 16-17
aident (they help), 108
aller (to go), 86
apercevoir (to see, notice), 143
asseoir (to seat), 143
attendre (to wait for), 62, 143
avoir (to have), 22
  agreement of past participles, 16-17
  compound tense formation, 11
  exercises, 15
  usage guidelines, 13-15
  verbal expressions with, 161-163

battre (to beat), 143
bâtir (to build), 78

C

cacher (to hide something), 143
-cer verbs
  exercises, 27-28
  imperfect tense, 65

passé simple, 78
present participles, 19
present tense, 44
spelling changes, 27
changer (to replace, alter), 143
chanter (to sing), 40
choisir (to choose), 62
cognates, regular verbs, 26
commands, 124
common verbal expressions, 165-167
compound tense, 6-7, 22
  negatives, 13
  passé antérieur
    exercises, 83
    forming, 82-83
    usage guidelines, 82-83
  pluperfect tense
    exercises, 74
    forming, 73-74
    usage guidelines, 73-74
  using *avoir*, 11
  using *être*, 12-13
conditional mood, 6, 104-105
  exercises, 101
  irregular verbs, 98-100
  reflexive verbs, 96
  regular verbs
    -er verbs, 96
    -ir verbs, 96
    -re verbs, 96
  shoe verbs
    -e + consonant + *er* verbs, 97
    exercises, 97-98
    -yer verbs, 97
  usage guidelines, 100

conditional perfect tense, 105
  exercises, 102
  forming, 101-102
  usage guidelines, 101-102
conditional sentences, 102-105
  contrary-to-fact conditions, 103-104
  real conditions, 103
conduire (to drive, conduct), 143
conjugations
  future tense
    -e + consonant + *er* verbs, 88
    irregular verbs, 89-90
    regular verbs, 87
    -yer verbs, 88
  imperfect tense, 63
  present tense
    -er verbs, 40-41
    -evoir verbs, 45
    impersonal verbs, 46
    irregular verbs, 50-51
    -ir verbs, 41-42
    -oir verbs, 45
    -re verbs, 42
conjunctions, 121-123
connaître (to know), 145-146
connotations
  connaître and *savoir*, 145-146
  dépenser and *passer*, 146
  désirer and *souhaiter*, 146
  exercises, 150-151
  habiter and *demeurer*, 150
  jouer à and *jouer de*, 149
  laisser and *sortir*, 147
  partir and *quitter*, 146-147

penser à and *penser de*, 149
porter and *mener*, 148
pouvoir and *savoir*, 148-149
rendre and *retourner*, 147
revenir and *rentrer*, 147
vivre, 150
contrary-to-fact conditions
(conditional sentences),
103-104
coucher (to put to bed), 143

D

défendre (to defend), 78
demander (to ask), 143
demeurer (to live), 150
dépenser (to spend money),
146
désirer (to wish), 146
devoir, 136-137, 151
doubt (expressions of), indicatives versus subjunctives,
117-119
douter de (to doubt, to question), 143

E

endormir (to put to sleep),
143
ennuyer (to bore [someone]),
143
-*er* verbs
conditional mood, 96
future tense, 87
imperfect tense, 62
passé simple, 78
past participles, 8
present participles, 19
present subjunctives,
108-109
present tense
conjugations, 40-41
exercises, 41

-*evoir* verbs
conjugations, 45
exercises, 46
exercises
conditional moods, 97-101
irregular verbs, 99-100
shoe verbs, 97-98
conditional perfect tense,
102
conditional sentences
contrary-to-fact condi-
tions, 104
real conditions, 103
future perfect, 93-94
future tense, 89-92
helping verbs, 15
idiomatic expressions
irregular and spelling-
change verbs, 161
regular verbs, 157-158
imperatives, 55
imperfect tense
shoe verbs, 65-66
versus *passé composé*,
69-71
passé antérieur tense, 83
passé composé tense, 57
passé simple tense
irregular verbs, 81-82
shoe verbs, 79
passive voice, 169
past participles, 11
past subjunctives, 126
perfect participles, 21
pluperfect tense, 74
present participles, 20-21
present subjunctives
after adjectives express-
ing feelings, 120-121
expressions of doubt,
119
following conjunctions,
123
irregular verbs, 112-113

superlative expressions,
125
verbs with two stems,
110
present tense, 53
-*er* verbs, 41
-*evoir* verbs, 46
irregular verbs, 51
-*ir* verbs, 42
-*oir* verbs, 46
-*re* verbs, 43
shoe verbs, 44-45
regular verbs, 109
shoe verbs
-*cer* verbs, 27-28
-*e* + consonant + *er*
verbs, 31-32
-*é* + consonant + *er*
verbs, 33-34
ger verbs, 28-29
yer verbs, 30
special uses of verbs, 142
different verbs with dif-
ferent connotations,
150-151
verbs with special
reflexive meanings,
144-145
verbal expressions
avoir, 163
common expressions,
167
faire, 165
expressions
idiomatic expressions
irregular and spelling-
change verbs, 158-161
regular verbs, 155-158
verbal expressions
avoir, 161-163
common expressions,
165-167
faire, 163-165

être, 22
   agreement of past partici-
      ples, 16-17
   compound tense forma-
      tion, 12-13
   exercises, 15
   usage guidelines, 13-15

F

faire (to make, do), 137-138,
   151, 163-165
falloir, 138-139, 151
finissent (they finish), 108
future perfect tense
   exercises, 93-94
   forming, 92
   usage guidelines, 92
future tense, 86-94
   aller, 86
   exercises, 89-92
   irregular verbs
      conjugations, 89-90
      exercises, 91
   reflexive verbs, 87
   regular verbs, 87
   shoe verbs
      -e + consonant + er
         verbs, 88
      yer verbs, 88
   usage guidelines, 91
   using present tense to
      express future, 86

G–H

gender, past participle agreement, 16-18
ger verbs
   exercises, 28-29
   imperfect tense, 65
   passé simple, 79
   present participles, 19

present tense, 44
spelling changes, 28

habiter (to live), 150
helping verbs
   avoir, 13-15, 22
   exercises, 15
   être, 13-15, 22

I

idioms
   defining characteristics,
      154
   idiomatic expressions
      irregular and spelling-
         change verbs, 158-161
      regular verbs, 155-158
imperative mood, 6
imperatives, 58
   exercises, 55
   forming, 53-54
   reflexive verbs, 54-55
   usage guidelines, 53-54
imperfect subjunctives, 7,
   129-132
imperfect tense
   irregular verbs, 63
   reflexive verbs, 64
   regular verbs, 62
   shoe verbs
      -cer verbs, 65
      exercises, 65-66
      -ger verbs, 65
   versus *passé composé*, 66-71
      exercises, 69-71
      tips, 68-69
impersonal expressions,
   113-116
impersonal verbs, 46
indicative mood, 6
indicatives versus subjunctives, 117-119

infinitive mood, 6
intransitive verbs, 13
-ir verbs
   conditional mood, 96
   future tense, 87
   imperfect tense, 62
   passé simple, 78
   past participles, 8
   present participles, 19
   present subjunctives,
      108-109
   present tense
      conjugations, 41-42
      exercises, 42
irregular past participles,
   10-11
irregular present participles,
   19
irregular verbs, 4, 22, 136
   common verbs, 34-35
   conditional moods, 98-100
   devoir, 136-137
   exercises, 142
   faire, 137-138
   falloir, 138-139
   future tense
      conjugations, 89-90
      exercises, 91
   idiomatic expressions,
      158-161
   imperfect tense, 63
   -oir verbs, 9
   passé simple tense, 79-82
      exercises, 81-82
      stems, 80-81
   pouvoir, 139-140
   present subjunctives,
      111-113, 130-131
   present tense
      conjugations, 50-51
      exercises, 51
      rules, 49
   savoir, 140-141
   vouloir, 141-142

J–K

jouer à (to play games [sports]), 149, 152
jouer de (to play a musical instrument), 149, 152

L–M

laisser (to leave behind), 147, 151
laver (to wash), 143
lever (to raise, lift), 143

marcher (to walk), 78
mener (leading), 148
moods, 5, 22
    conditional, 6, 104-105
        exercises, 101
        irregular verbs, 98-100
        reflexive verbs, 96
        regular verbs, 96
        shoe verbs, 97-98
        usage guidelines, 100
    imperative, 6
    indicative, 6
    infinitive, 6
    subjunctive, 6

N–O

negatives, compound tense formation, 13

obéir (to obey), 87, 96
occuper (to occupy), 143
-oir verbs
    past participles, 9
    present participles, 19
    present tense
        conjugations, 45
        exercises, 46

P

parler (to speak), 62, 87, 96
participles
    past participles, 22
        agreement, 16-17, 56-59
        usage, 18-19
    perfect participles, 21-22
        exercises, 21
        forming, 21
    present participles, 19-22
        exercises, 20-21
        forming, 19
        irregular present participles, 19
        usage, 20
partir (to go away), 146-147, 151
passé antérieur tense, 82-84
    exercises, 83
    forming, 82-83
    usage guidelines, 82-83
passé composé tense, 58
    exercises, 57
    forming, 55-56
    usage guidelines, 55-56
    versus imperfect tense, 66-71
        exercises, 69-71
        tips, 68-69
passé simple tense, 78-84
    irregular verbs, 79-82
        exercises, 81-82
        stems, 80-81
    reflexive verbs, 78
    regular verbs, 78
    shoe verbs
        -cer verbs, 78
        -ger verbs, 79
        exercises, 79
passer (to spend time), 144-146

passive voice
    construction of, 168
    exercises, 169
    substitute construction for, 168
    versus active voice, 167
past conditional tense
    exercises, 102
    forming, 101-102
    usage guidelines, 101-102
past participles, 22
    agreement, 56-59
        avoir conjugates, 16-17
        être conjugates, 16-17
        reflexive verbs, 16-17
    exercises, 11
    irregular past participles, 10-11
    -oir verbs, 9
    regular verbs
        -er verbs, 8
        -ir verbs, 8
        -re verbs, 8
    usage, 18-19
past subjunctives, 131
    exercises, 126
    forming, 125-126
    usage guidelines, 125-126
penser à (to think about), 149, 152
penser de (to have an opinion of), 149, 152
perfect participles, 21-22
    exercises, 21
    forming, 21
plaindre (to pity), 144
pluperfect subjunctives, 7, 129-132
pluperfect tense
    exercises, 74
    forming, 73-74
    usage guidelines, 73-74
porter (to carry), 148

pouvoir (to be able to have permission to), 139-140, 148-149
present participles, 19-22
  exercises, 21
  forming
    exercises, 20
    irregular present participles, 19
    regular verbs, 19
  usage, 20
present subjunctives
  irregular verbs, 111-113, 130-131
  regular verbs, 130
    -*er* verbs, 108
    exercises, 109
    -*ir* verbs, 108-109
    -*re* verbs, 108-109
  usage guidelines, 131
    adjectives expressing feeling, 119-121
    after certain verbs, 116-117
    expressions of doubt, 117-119
    following conjunctions, 121-123
    impersonal expressions, 113-116
    relative clauses, 124
    superlative expressions, 124-125
    third-person commands, 124
  verbs with two stems, 109-110, 130
  versus indicatives, 117-119
present tense
  exercises, 53
  impersonal verbs, 46
  irregular verbs
    conjugations, 50-51
    exercises, 51
    rules, 49

reflexive verbs, 46-48
regular verbs
  -*er* verbs, 40-41
  -*ir* verbs, 41-42
  -*re* verbs, 42-43
  shoe verbs, 44
    exercises, 44-45
    -*oir* and -*evoir* verbs, 45-46
  usage guidelines, 51
  using to express future, 86
pronouns
  reflexive pronouns, 47-48
  subject pronouns, 4

Q-R

quitter (to leave), 146-147, 151

rappeler (to call again), 144
-*re* verbs
  conditional mood, 96
  future tense, 87
  imperfect tense, 62
  passé simple, 78
  past participles, 8
  present participles, 19
  present subjunctives, 108-109
  present tense
    conjugations, 42
    exercises, 43
real conditions (conditional sentences), 103
réfléchir (to reflect), 149
réfléchir à, 152
reflexive pronouns, 47-48
reflexive verbs, 13, 58
  conditional moods, 96
  future tense, 87
  imperatives, 54-55
  imperfect tense, 64
  passé simple, 78

past participle agreement, 16-17
present tense, 46-48
special reflexive meanings, 142-145
regular verbs, 4, 22, 26
  -*er* verbs
    conditional mood, 96
    future tense, 87
    imperfect tense, 62
    passé simple, 78
    past participles, 8
    present participles, 19
    present subjunctives, 108-109
    present tense, 40-41
  -*ir* verbs
    conditional moods, 96
    future tense, 87
    imperfect tense, 62
    passé simple, 78
    past participles, 8
    present participles, 19
    present subjunctives, 108-109
    present tense, 41-42
  -*re* verbs
    conditional mood, 96
    future tense, 87
    imperfect tense, 62
    passé simple, 78
    past participles, 8
    present participles, 19
    present subjunctives, 108-109
    present tense, 42-43
  cognates, 26
  idiomatic expressions, 155-158
  -*oir* verbs, 19
  past participles, 8
relative clauses, 124
rendre (to return), 147, 152
rentrer (to come back home), 147, 152

retourner (to go back), 147, 152
revenir (to come back), 147, 152

S

savoir (to know), 140-141, 145-146
sentences (conditional), 102-105
  contrary-to-fact conditions, 103-104
  real conditions, 103
servir (to serve), 144
shoe verbs, 26
  -*cer* verbs
    exercises, 27-28
    imperfect tense, 65
    passé simple, 78
    spelling changes, 27
  -*e* + consonant + *er* verbs
    conditional mood, 97
    exercises, 31-32
    future tense, 88
    spelling changes, 31-32
  -*é* + consonant + *er* verbs
    exercises, 33-34
    spelling changes, 33
  -*ger* verbs
    exercises, 28-29
    imperfect tense, 65
    passé simple, 79
    spelling changes, 28
  -*yer* verbs
    conditional mood, 97
    exercises, 30
    future tense, 88
    spelling changes, 29
  present tense, 44
    exercises, 44-45
    -*oir* and -*evoir* verbs, 45-46

simple tenses, 6-7, 22
songer à (to contemplate or consider doing something), 149, 152
sortir (to go out), 147, 151
souhaiter (to make a wish), 146, 151
special uses of verbs
  devoir, 136-137
  exercises, 142
  faire, 137-138
  falloir, 138-139
  pouvoir, 139-140
  savoir, 140-141
  verbs with special reflexive meanings, 142-145
  vouloir, 141-142
spelling-change verbs. *See* shoe verbs
stems (verbs with two stems), present subjunctives, 109-110
subject pronouns, 4
subjunctive mood, 6
subjunctives
  avoiding use of, 126-128
  imperfect subjunctives, 7, 129-132
  past subjunctives, 131
    exercises, 126
    forming, 125-126
    usage guidelines, 125-126
  pluperfect subjunctives, 7, 129-132
  present subjunctives
    irregular verbs, 111-113, 130-131
    regular verbs, 108-109, 130
    usage guidelines, 113-125, 131

verbs with two stems, 109-110, 130
versus indicatives, 117-119
superlative expressions, 124-125

T

tenses
  compound tenses, 6-7, 22
    negatives, 13
    using *avoir*, 11
    using *être*, 12-13
  conditional perfect tense, 105
    exercises, 102
    forming, 101-102
    usage guidelines, 101-102
  future perfect
    exercises, 93-94
    forming, 92
    usage guidelines, 92
  future tense, 87-94
    exercises, 89-92
    irregular verbs, 89-91
    reflexive verbs, 87
    regular verbs, 87
    shoe verbs, 88
    usage guidelines, 91
  imperfect tense
    irregular verbs, 63
    reflexive verbs, 64
    regular verbs, 62
    shoe verbs, 65-66
    versus *passé composé* tense, 66-71
  passé antérieur tense, 82-84
    exercises, 83
    forming, 82-83
    usage guidelines, 82-83

passé simple tense, 78-84
    irregular verbs, 79-82
    reflexive verbs, 78
    regular verbs, 78
    shoe verbs, 78-79
pluperfect tense
    exercises, 74
    forming, 73-74
    usage guidelines, 73-74
present tense
    exercises, 53
    impersonal verbs, 46
    irregular verbs, 49-51
    reflexive verbs, 46-48
    regular verbs, 40-43
    shoe verbs, 44-46
    usage guidelines, 51
simple tense, 6-7, 22
third-person commands, 124
tromper (to deceive), 144

V-W-X

venden (they sell), 108
vendre (to sell), 87, 96
verbal expressions
    avoir, 161-163
    common expressions, 165,
     167
    faire, 163-165
    idiomatic expressions
      irregular and spelling-
       change verbs, 158-161
      regular verbs, 155-158
vivre (to be alive), 150
vouloir, 141-142, 151

Y-Z

-yer verbs
    conditional mood, 97
    exercises, 30
    future tense, 88
    present tense, 44
    spelling changes, 29

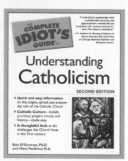

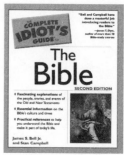

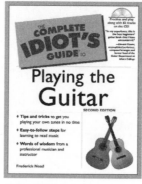

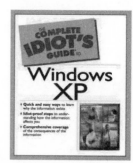